the knot guide to
destination weddings

the knot guide to
destination weddings

CARLEY RONEY
WITH JOANN GREGOLI

Clarkson Potter/Publishers
New York

Library of Congress Cataloging-in-Publication Data
Roney, Carley.
The Knot guide to destination weddings / by Carley Roney with
JoAnn Gregoli — 1st ed.
    p.   cm.
Includes index.
1. Weddings—Planning.   2. Destination weddings—Planning.   I. Gregoli, JoAnn.   II. Title.
HQ745.R64952 2007
395.2´2—dc22

2006015160

ISBN: 978-0-307-34192-1

Printed in the United States of America

Design by Jennifer K. Beal

10   9

First Edition

your destination wedding to-do list

Keep your wedding plans on target by sticking to this schedule. Read it all the way through to get a good sense of how the entire process progresses. Each to-do comes with a page number telling you where to find detailed advice on the topic. The earlier you can handle any of the tasks, the better.

Do Your Research (10+ Months)

○ **THINK ABOUT DESTINATIONS.** Do you want to wed in a castle in Scotland or on a breezy beach in the Caribbean? Envision your wedding and jot down the elements that are most important to you. Page 25

○ **THINK ABOUT YOUR HONEYMOON, TOO.** Will you marry and honeymoon in the same spot? Page 44

○ **FIGURE OUT YOUR BUDGET.** Hosting a DW involves extra expenses. Page 194

○ **CONSIDER WHAT SIZE WEDDING YOU WANT.** Two hundred and fifty guests require a far different level of attention—and budget—than fifty. Page 86

○ **SELECT YOUR DESTINATION AND LOOK AT LOCATIONS.** Make sure you understand the marriage requirements of your locale. Page 151

○ **RESEARCH WEDDING CONSULTANTS.** A planner or travel agent who specializes in your destination may have preferred access to flights, accommodations, or activities. Page 52

○ **CHOOSE YOUR TIMING.** Be sure to check with key family and close friends before finalizing the date— you want to make sure all the important people can be there! Page 12

○ **START GOWN SHOPPING.** First look at photos online. Keep in mind that certain fabrics travel better than others. Page 18

10+ months

Start Making Decisions (8 to 10 Months)

○ **INVITE YOUR ATTENDANTS.** Choose your bridesmaids and groomsmen and introduce them to one another with an e-mail. Be clear about your expectations, but be sensitive to the expense! Page 80

○ **BOOK YOUR WEDDING LOCATION.** But before you sign on the dotted line, visit, if possible, and take a look at our contract pointers on page 42.

○ **RESERVE ROOMS FOR YOUR GUESTS.** You must have this information in hand when you create your save-the-dates. Page 87

○ **CREATE YOUR WEDDING WEBSITE.** Update it with more details as you go along. Page 93

○ **ORGANIZE THE GUEST LIST.** Collect proper names and addresses (both mail and e-mail) for all parties on the list. Page 86

○ **PLAN YOUR SCOUTING TRIPS.** Try to make at least one visit to your location prior to the wedding. Page 31

○ **BEGIN SELECTING YOUR VENDORS.** Determine what services are included with your location: Who will you find locally and who will you fly in from home? Page 49

○ **BOOK YOUR CATERER.** If your caterer is on-site at your location, now's the time to have a tasting. Page 57

○ **BOOK YOUR ENTERTAINMENT.** The ceremony, cocktail hour, reception, and even after-party all need music. Page 68

○ **BOOK YOUR PHOTOGRAPHER.** You'll be dealing with this vendor a lot *after* the wedding, so like many couples, you may choose to fly one in from home. Page 70

○ **BOOK YOUR VIDEOGRAPHER.** A recommendation from your photographer is a good place to start. Page 70

8 to 10 months

Focus on the Fun Stuff (6 to 8 Months)

○ **SEND OUT SAVE-THE-DATES.** Your guests need to start making travel arrangements as early as possible. Page 87

○ **BOOK YOUR WEDDING TRAVEL.** Plan to arrive in your location at least two days prior to the wedding to make final arrangements.

○ **BOOK YOUR FLORIST.** Get the conversation started with photos of the look you want for your ceremony and reception. Page 66

○ **REGISTER FOR GIFTS.** Update your registry list after your engagement party and a week prior to the wedding. Page 95

○ **ORDER YOUR GOWN.** Many dresses are made to order in Europe, so as much lead time as possible is advised.

○ **PICK YOUR BRIDESMAID DRESSES.** Give your girls an aggressive deadline by which to place their orders. Page 85

○ **BOOK YOUR HONEYMOON.** Arrange any additional flights, hotels, and car rentals.

○ **CHOOSE AN OFFICIANT.** With his or her assistance, start planning your ceremony. Page 120

6 to 8 months

Finalize the Details (3 to 6 Months)

○ **FIND YOUR CAKE PROVIDER.** Many hotels have talented pastry chefs on staff. Page 63

○ **PICK OUT INVITATIONS.** Also track down a calligrapher and get the final, formal address list in order. Page 87

○ **PLAN THE GROOM'S ATTIRE.** Let your groomsmen know what they'll be wearing. If you're renting tuxes, it's best to do it from home. Page 83

○ **CONFIRM LOCAL MARRIAGE LICENSE REQUIREMENTS.** They differ from one destination to another. Pages 151–187

○ **GET YOUR PAPERS IN ORDER.** Make sure your passport is current if you're traveling outside the United States. Page 116

○ **SHOP FOR YOUR WEDDING RINGS.** You'll need to order them at least four months in advance if your rings are customized.

3 to 6 months

Invite Everyone! (2 to 4 Months)

○ **MAIL YOUR INVITATIONS.** Send them out about three months before your wedding. Page 93

○ **THINK ABOUT WEDDING DAY HAIRSTYLES.** Be sure to keep the climate of your wedding location in mind. Page 73

○ **BOOK YOUR HAIR STYLIST AND MAKEUP ARTIST.** Some brides bring along their hairstylist. Page 74

○ **MAKE OR BUY YOUR FAVORS.** Incorporate the theme of your wedding—beach, ski, a specific color, etc.—into your favors. Page 143

○ **RECORD YOUR RSVPS.** Come up with a solid system to keep track of who is coming. Page 97

○ **SHOP FOR GIFTS.** Leave time for bridesmaid and groomsmen gifts to get personalized—it makes them more meaningful. Page 85

2 to 4 months

Little Details (3 to 6 weeks)

O **ARRANGE OTHER WEEKEND EVENTS.**
Put the finishing touches on the
rehearsal dinner, wedding party
luncheons, the morning-after
brunch, and so on. Page 102

O **SEND A PRE-WEDDING INFO PACKET TO
GUESTS.** Include final details on all
additional activities. Page 94

O **FINALIZE YOUR CEREMONY.** Finish
writing your vows, choose final
readings and music, and start coordinating your program. Organize
any religious articles you may need
for your ceremony, such as a chalice
from which to drink or a glass to
break. Page 121

O **PLAN WELCOME BAGS FOR YOUR
GUESTS.** Make any online purchases
far enough in advance to avoid rush
shipping. Page 102

O **MAKE A LIST OF LITTLE DETAILS YOU
NEED TO ATTEND TO.** Get prescrip-
tions refilled. Buy attendant gifts.
Shop for your honeymoon attire.

O **SEND OUT INFORMATION PACKETS.** Ask
guests to RSVP for any activities
beyond the wedding, such as group
sailing excursions or golf games,
via a preaddressed postcard or an
e-mail.

O **MAKE HAIR AND BEAUTY APPOINT-
MENTS.** Any hair treatments (cut
and color) should be scheduled no
less than ten days before your
event. But you can wait to wax
until the day before you leave.

3 to 6 weeks

The Countdown Begins (2 Weeks)

○ **GET HITCHED.** If a marriage in your location isn't recognized by the United States, and you want to be legally married before the "ceremony," plan it now. Page 117

○ **CONFIRM ALL TRAVEL RESERVATIONS.** Ask key guests (parents, wedding party) for their final travel plans.

○ **ORGANIZE WEDDING INSURANCE PAPERS.** Make sure your policy is in place and paid up. Page 56

○ **SHIP ANY WEDDING GEAR AHEAD.** Be sure your hotel concierge or wedding planner knows when your boxes are slated to arrive. Page 202

○ **GET YOUR GIFTS READY.** Wrap all gifts for the wedding party and your parents, and write each a nice note. Page 85

○ **FINALIZE THE HEAD COUNT.** If you still haven't received a few RSVPs, it's time to make phone calls to your tardy guests.

○ **PICK UP WEDDING RINGS.** Be sure to check the inscriptions before you leave the store.

○ **ORGANIZE YOUR TEAM.** Determine any wedding day assignments for members of the wedding party, and call or e-mail them with the info.

○ **CALL HOTELS WHERE YOU'VE RESERVED ROOMS.** They can give you a final count on how many guests have booked, and you can release any unreserved rooms.

○ **UPDATE YOUR WEDDING WEBSITE.** Make sure all the final details are up and accurate, as guests will be checking the site in the days before their departure. Page 93

○ **PRINT YOUR PROGRAM.** Don't rely on the resort's business center as a resource; complete this project at home. Page 25

2 weeks

Get Ready to Go (1 Week)

○ **PACK!** You might want to send your suitcase for your honeymoon to your wedding location ahead of time. Page 207

○ **FINALIZE THE PHOTO SCHEDULE.** Type up a schedule for any formal family portraits you want so the photographer doesn't miss a shot. Page 72

○ **CONFIRM FINAL VENDOR MEETINGS.** Contact all vendors you need to meet with once you arrive, and call the location manager to make sure they'll have access to the site when they need it.

○ **UPDATE YOUR TRANSPORTATION PROVIDERS.** Fax a schedule and addresses for both pickups at the airport on the wedding day and other weekend events.

○ **FINALIZE THE SEATING PLAN.** Double-check that you have all the necessary place cards, escort cards, and table cards. Page 142

○ **CONFIRM GUEST RESERVATIONS.** Call the hotel(s) to reconfirm when all the guests will be arriving.

○ **PACK UP GIFTS AND FAVORS.** Ask family and wedding party members to pack some items in their carry-on luggage.

○ **ASSEMBLE A TROUBLESHOOTING KIT.** Include all the basics to divert disaster on your wedding day.

○ **HAVE FINAL BEAUTY TREATMENTS.** Schedule anything that you won't be having done at your destination, including bikini waxing and eyebrow grooming (wait and have your manicure and pedicure closer to the big event).

○ **PICK UP YOUR DRESS.** Make sure you have all the key elements (accessories, undergarments) for your rehearsal dinner and wedding day outfits. Page 18

1 week

The Day Before You Depart (3 to 4 Days Prewedding)

○ **TOUCH BASE WITH YOUR POINT PERSON.** Call your coordinator to go over any details, as you'll be unreachable for much or all of your travel day.

○ **BE IN TOUCH WITH THE WEDDING PARTY.** Reconfirm when each member is arriving and make sure he or she knows how to reach you.

○ **PICK UP TUXES.** Make sure all of the elements of the groom's look are ready to go. Page 82

○ **CALL THE AIRLINE.** Reconfirm all of your flights and arrange for transportation to the airport.

○ **FINISH PACKING.** Double-check documents and put them in a sturdy container like a leather portfolio, then pack them in your carry-on luggage. Page 204

○ **GET CASH.** Don't rely on using ATMs once you arrive—they may limit you to daily withdrawals of just a few hundred dollars.

○ **CREATE A RECEPTION RUNDOWN.** Determine who will be toasting, which dances you'll do, and when you'll cut the cake. Page 132

3 to 4 days

Upon Your Arrival
(2 to 3 Days Before the Wedding)

○ **MEET WITH YOUR COORDINATORS AND ANY VENDORS.** Go over any last-minute details and reconfirm load-in times.

○ **INFORM YOUR KEY PLAYERS.** Distribute wedding day directions, schedules, and contact lists to all parents, attendants, and vendors as you meet with them.

○ **CHECK IN WITH HOTELS.** Make sure they're ready to greet your guests and distribute the welcome bags.

○ **HAVE A FINAL TASTING WITH THE CATERER.** If you haven't done so already, have a tasting of the wedding meal and cake so you can request last-minute adjustments if necessary.

○ **TOUCH BASE WITH YOUR OFFICIANT.** Confirm the rehearsal details and wedding day schedule.

○ **FINALIZE PARTY PLANS.** Confirm details for the bridesmaids' lunch, welcome party, rehearsal dinner, and morning-after brunch.

○ **HAVE A HAIR AND MAKEUP TRIAL.** Even if you had a trial on an earlier visit, it's a good idea to try it out with your veil and other accessories. Page 75

○ **GET DRESSES STEAMED (IF NEEDED).** Determine the separate locations where bride, groom, and attendants will dress for the wedding.

○ **HAVE A FAMILY DINNER.** If the rehearsal dinner will be large, this is the time to have an intimate family-only dinner.

○ **ORGANIZE YOUR FINAL PAYMENTS.** Put final balances and cash tips in marked envelopes and give them to your planner or a male attendant (since guys have pockets, it's easier for them to hold the envelopes) to distribute on the wedding day.

The Day Before Your Wedding

○ **HAVE A BRIDE-AND-GROOM PREWED-DING BREAKFAST.** This may be the last time you have a moment alone, particularly if you plan to sleep in separate rooms on the night before the wedding.

○ **THROW YOUR ATTENDANT OUTING.** Thank everyone before the other guests arrive with a special sailboat ride, a golf game, or a croquet match. Page 104

○ **DO A WALK-THROUGH.** Tour the grounds of your ceremony and reception locations with your coordinator and make any last-minute adjustments.

○ **GET A MANICURE AND PEDICURE, A MASSAGE, ETC.** Pamper yourself after all your hard work planning. It's also a great bridal party activity.

○ **GREET AND ENJOY YOUR GUESTS.** Relax and participate in a welcome party or other fun activities you've arranged for guests. Page 102

○ **APPLY SUNSCREEN.** We're serious— you don't want to get an ugly burn or weird tan lines that will be memorialized forever in the wedding photos.

○ **WRAP UP DETAILS AT THE REHEARSAL.** The officiant and an attendant should have extra copies of your vows and of all readings. Page 105

○ **SORT OUT THE RECEIVING LINE.** When you have the key players assembled at the rehearsal, tell them your plan for the receiving line (if you'll be having one), including where they should stand and what order they should stand in.

○ **SIGN THE MARRIAGE LICENSE.** This is typically done at the rehearsal, though your officiant might have you do it on the wedding day, depending on local procedure.

○ **RELAY INFORMATION.** At the end of the welcome dinner, have the wedding planner or best man make key announcements, such as reiterating what time everybody needs to assemble the next day.

○ **GO TO BED EARLY.** You'll want to look refreshed and feel rejuvenated for your big day!

Turn to page 190 for your minute-by-minute Wedding Day Timeline.

{contents

INTRODUCTION 1

1 PREPARE FOR TAKEOFF: ENVISIONING YOUR EVENT 5

Seaside or Slopeside? Determining Your Style 6
Intimate or Everyone? Deciding on Size 11
How Much? Setting Your Wedding Budget 13

2 YOU ARE HERE: FINDING THE PERFECT SPOT 23

Deciding on a Destination 25
The Best Places to Say "I Do" 27
Doing Your Homework 30
Shopping for Your Location 32
Scoping Out Destinations in Person 37
Visiting Your Location 39
Making Your Final Decision 41
The Contract: Signing on the Dotted Line 42

3 ASSEMBLING YOUR "A" TEAM:
HIRING VENDORS FROM AFAR 49

The Art of Interviewing 50
Who's Playing Wedding Planner? 52
Calling All Caterers 57
Who Bakes the Cake? 63
Finding a Florist 66
Mastering the Musicians 68
Picking a Photographer and a Videographer 70
Hiring Hair and Makeup Artists 74

4 BE MY GUESTS: WHO TO INVITE AND HOW 79

Your VIPs: The Wedding Party 80
Creating Your Guest List 86
Invitations and All: Spreading the Word 87

5 PLAYING CRUISE DIRECTOR: ORGANIZING THE WEEKEND ACTIVITIES 101

Hello There: Orchestrating the Arrivals 102
Good Stuff: It's in the Welcome Bag 102
Quality Time: An Outing with Your Attendants 104
The Preview: A Rousing Rehearsal Dinner 105
Come Together Now: Where's the Welcome Party? 107
Keep It Going: After-Party Principles .108
Wake-up Call: Morning-After Munchies 109
The More the Merrier: Group Activities 110

6 DESTINATION "I DO": DESIGNING YOUR CEREMONY 115

Making It Legal 116
Choosing a Ceremony Style 117
Finding Your Officiant 120
Working with Your Officiant 122
A World of Ceremony Ideas 123
Setting Your Service to Music 125
Put It in the Program 125

7 PARTY ON: PLANNING YOUR RECEPTION 131

The Defining Moments of a Reception 132
Create a Mood 134
Focus on the Food 138
Get Serious About Seating 142
Let's Dance: Mastering Your Music 144
Enjoy Every Minute 146

THE DESTINATION DIRECTORY 151

DESTINATION WEDDING WORKSHEETS 189

RESOURCES AND CREDITS 210

ACKNOWLEDGMENTS 213

INDEX 214

introduction

Every wedding is a special event, but a destination wedding is a unique adventure. After all, instead of climbing into a limo for a ride to the local reception hall, you're boarding a plane, dress and passport in hand, en route to an exotic locale that's reflective of your style. There's no pedestrian rehearsal dinner for your wedding party; you have two days (and maybe more) with your guests to enjoy pre-wedding activities, from golf to sightseeing tours to dinners on the sand. And in place of a standard ceremony, you're saying your vows in a completely breathtaking setting. Best of all, the moment you're pronounced husband and wife, you'll already be on your honeymoon.

There are as many reasons to have a destination wedding (DW) as there are couples who have them. For some, it's a chance to make their wedding day stand out by hosting it in an exotic or off-the-beaten-path locale that most of their guests have never visited. A DW is also perfect for brides and grooms who grew up in different places, met while away at school or after moving around in their early years, and consequently have family and friends scattered across the country. If most of your guests are traveling to your wedding anyway, why not give them the chance to fly somewhere exceptional? While there, couples get to spend quality time with their nearest and dearest, and those guests who have never met before often walk away from the experience with newfound friendships. And believe it or not, a DW can even save you money in some instances: If you live in a pricey area like New York City, your wedding dollars won't take you as far as they will in someplace like Mexico or Jamaica (yes, that includes airfare and hotel).

Of course, all of these benefits come with some complexities. First off, there's the guest list: A weekend-long destination wedding may not fit into everyone's schedule—or budget—and travel can be hard on some (think elderly) guests, so be prepared for a pared-down list when the RSVPs come in. Hey, at least you'll know that you can show those who do make the trip a really good time. And a larger "can't make it" pile might actually be a blessing in disguise if you're trying to control a ballooning budget, too.

You'll also have extra tasks on your to-do list: taking a scouting trip to your location, coordinating guests' travel and activities, organizing additional events like the welcome party. And, since you're planning from hundreds if not thousands of miles away, you'll need to learn how to relax about some of the details. For the laid-back couple who's looking for a stress-free approach, a DW is perfect; for the control freaks among us, it may cause a few minor panic attacks.

Putting together a destination wedding can seem like a daunting task, but there's really no reason to fear. In fact, once you have the vision of the wedding you want—plus the proper timeline, budget, and assistance to plan it—the process can be half of the fun. So turn the page and let us help you plan the destination wedding of your dreams. The adventure is just beginning!

Ch. 1

prepare for takeoff:
envisioning your event

The first step in planning your fantasy destination wedding is to start visualizing the event. Are you thinking thirty guests or three hundred? By the waves in Hawaii or castleside in Scotland? These first factors—the who, what, when, and where—will drive all of your planning decisions.

The beach wedding where guests sip piña coladas poolside is the classic notion of a DW, but throw out your preconceived ideas. If you don't see yourselves swapping vows with sand between your toes, you could do it instead in one of a zillion quaint country inns, classic lakefront resorts, or ski chalet–style mountain lodges. Remember, there is no such thing as a "traditional" destination wedding. (We'll get more into specific destinations in chapter 2.)

seaside or slopeside? determining your style

You want your guests to walk away from your wedding weekend saying, "That was so *them*!" Your wedding elements—not just location, but also activities and overall vibe—should say something about your personal style and your passions. Did he propose on vacation in Paris? Then why not host a swank wedding on the French Riviera complete with laid-back afternoons spent in medieval villages and late nights in cafés? Are you obsessed with food? Think about having your crew gather in a place like Tuscany or the California wine country and engage in foodie activities like cheese tastings and wine tours. Are you adventure-seekers? Bring everyone to an eco-friendly spot like Costa Rica, where they can ride a zip-line through treetops before the rehearsal dinner. Choose a place that means something to you and let the details of the wedding—your colors, your stationery, your attire, the weekend events—speak for your location.

The City Chic Wedding

If your most memorable times together always had an urban backdrop—seeing plays, seeking out "hidden gem" restaurants—don't stray too far from your first love.

WHY YOU'LL LOVE IT A rooftop cocktail hour with a view of the skyline; a rehearsal dinner at a celebrity chef's restaurant; the perfect setting for a sleek modern gown; dozens of top vendors at your fingertips.

WHY GUESTS WILL LOVE IT With so many museums, historical spots, and shopping destinations to hit, there's never a dull moment. They will also appreciate easy airport access, endless lodging options, and, of course, world-class entertainment: theaters, comedy clubs, nightclubs. Look into arranging group discounts.

SPOTS TO CONSIDER
New York City in autumn
San Francisco in spring or summer
Miami year-round
Paris in spring or fall
London in summer

The Ski Wedding

What's more romantic than sipping hot toddies by a roaring fire? If you two are the Tyrolean types and think your guests would love some alpine action of their own between festivities, consider a wedding slopeside.

WHY YOU'LL LOVE IT Arriving at the ceremony in a horse-drawn sleigh; gorgeous vistas filled with snowcapped mountains; alpine wedding images like pinecones and evergreen trees; a white velvet/fur shrug for your gown; timbered lodges for your reception; a steaming soup bar for your cocktail hour; "Just Married" decals for your skis or snowboards.

WHY GUESTS WILL LOVE IT Group ski and snowboarding lessons; snowshoeing through the woods; romantic nights of their own in their wood-paneled suites.

SPOTS TO CONSIDER
Aspen or Vail, Colorado
Okemo, Vermont
Swiss Alps
Park City, Utah
Sun Valley, Idaho
Whistler, British Columbia (Canada)

TIP

Consider your entire guest list when deciding which style of wedding makes sense. For example, elderly guests may have trouble getting around slushy streets and up snowy steps.

The Island Wedding

Palm trees, the sound of the sea, and the sun setting at your back make a tropical locale a laid-back, picture-perfect place to say "I do."

WHY YOU'LL LOVE IT A sunset ceremony; an outdoor moonlit reception dinner; plenty of signature island drinks (a Bahama Mama, a Hawaiian rum punch, or a perfect margarita); being serenaded by the sounds of a steel drum band; taking windswept, sun-kissed photos; exotic flowers in your bouquets; watching the sun rise over the sea.

WHY GUESTS WILL LOVE IT An excuse to take a warm-weather getaway? Who could refuse! They will enjoy fishing outings, spending downtime at the beach, a multitude of water sports, working on their tans, and extending their trip into a full-blown vacation.

TIP

The marriage license requirements of many locales can make getting legally married difficult. Know these details before you set your heart on a destination. See the Destination Directory starting on page 151.

SPOTS TO CONSIDER

Florida Keys

United States Virgin Islands

Bahamas

Cayman Islands

Jamaica

Bermuda

Hawaii (any of the islands)

Southeast Asia

Mexico

The Old-World European Wedding

For the stuff of fairy tales, whisk your betrothed and a few special guests away for a grand wedding in a castle or celebrate among ancient ruins in a romantic European city.

WHY YOU'LL LOVE IT Arriving in a horse-drawn carriage; working your family tartan into your wedding party's attire; enjoying meals with ingredients grown within a mile of where you eat them; having your reception in a thousand-year-old castle; taking advantage of the chance to honor your family's ancestry; learning a foreign language; hiring authentic local musicians to play at your ceremony; reenacting the most romantic scenes from your favorite movies.

WHY GUESTS WILL LOVE IT They will appreciate the incredible opportunity to see some of the world's greatest historical sites, partake in authentic local cooking classes, and sample local wines.

SPOTS TO CONSIDER

Florence or Lake Como, Italy

Athens, Greece

Scotland

Loire Valley, France

Montreal, Quebec

The New England Wedding

Whether you have family ties to this part of the country or its nature-focused vibe just suits your style, the fresh air and open spaces of New England make a perfect summer wedding setting.

WHY YOU'LL LOVE IT Garden ceremonies; bouquets of local wildflowers; tented lawn receptions; antique four-posters in historical bed-and-breakfasts; fireflies at night; rehearsal dinner clambakes.

WHY GUESTS WILL LOVE IT They'll enjoy hiking through the forests, swimming in the lakes, and great golfing options—not to mention easy access from major cities in the Northeast.

SPOTS TO CONSIDER
Newport, Rhode Island
Bar Harbor, Maine
Lakes Region, New Hampshire
Berkshires or Cape Cod, Massachusetts
Catskills, New York

The Wine Country Wedding

Oenophiles can celebrate a passion for wine by taking guests to the bucolic wine country and sharing your favorite vintage with the people you love most.

WHY YOU'LL LOVE IT Backdrops of grapevines and terra-cotta earth; a beautiful vineyard ceremony; warm days and cool nights; a wine-tasting cocktail hour; bottles of local wine as favors; locally grown produce for your reception meal; a hot air balloon ride on the first day of your honeymoon.

WHY GUESTS WILL LOVE IT They will relish the road trips they can take when the festivities wind down, and the wine-tasting options everywhere they turn.

SPOTS TO CONSIDER
Napa or Sonoma, California
Tuscany, Italy
Bordeaux, France

The Cruise Wedding

In true cruise fashion, every detail is attended to from the moment you step off the plane. All you need to worry about is making the most of your time with your guests and each other.

WHY YOU'LL LOVE IT Waking up every morning in a different port or country; eating breakfast out on your balcony overlooking the sea; working a nautical theme through your invitations, menus, and programs; having all your guests in one place; spending time alone or with the group.

WHY GUESTS WILL LOVE IT It's nice to unpack once and get to visit many different countries or ports of call. There's also plenty of onboard activities, and everything is included.

SPOTS TO CONSIDER
Caribbean
Hawaii
Mediterranean

> **TIP**
>
> It's a myth that any ship's captain has the automatic authority to marry people. In order to do so, he or she must hold a civil title such as judge, magistrate, justice of the peace, county or court clerk, or notary public. (For more on cruise ship weddings, see page 36.)

The Adventure Wedding

You two have a hard time sitting still, and so do most of your family and friends. Share your love of adventure and exploration by hosting a wedding in an exciting place.

WHY YOU'LL LOVE IT Star-filled skies; fresh air; backpacks full of trail maps and excursion suggestions as welcome bags; bonfires at night; barbecue rehearsal dinner.

WHY GUESTS WILL LOVE IT There's always something to do—canopy tours, wilderness hikes, treks to view local flora and fauna, horseback riding—never a boring moment.

SPOTS TO CONSIDER
Costa Rica
Colorado
Montana
Hawaii
Mexico

it's in the
details

images from real destination
weddings to inspire you

diana and john
seaside, florida

Charming Seaside, Florida, was a frequent childhood destination of this bride, so tying the knot on the beach of her favorite resort town was a no-brainer for Diana and John. The couple said "I do" by Seaside's Savannah Pavilion beneath an arbor covered in palms. The beach-chic vibe—mixed with a hint of Creole flair, a nod to the mother of the bride's Southern background—carried over to the casually elegant dinner for 150 set under a tent on the croquet lawn, featuring turquoise hues and warm candlelight.

[A] Spiky palms lined the ceremony aisle. In cool, beach fashion, John, his father, and the groomsmen sported soft green linen pants, blue and green striped shirts, and navy blue blazers. [B] Paintbrushes tied with a turquoise ribbon were on hand to dust sand off everyone's feet after the beach ceremony. [C] Bright turquoise lanterns and tablecloths brought the color of the ocean into the reception tent. [D] Guests received beach bags trimmed in aqua blue filled with a Frisbee, a Seaside welcome guide, a lottery ticket, an umbrella, and a flashlight. [E] The lush white peonies, soft-blue hydrangeas, and touches of greenery carried by the bridesmaids were echoed in the tables' casual floral decorations [F]. [G] White, wave-shaped place cards displayed against a turquoise background added a whimsical touch to the reception, [H] a theme that also found its way onto the three-tiered cake.

PHOTOS BY SHAWN CONNELL/CHRISTIAN OTH PHOTOGRAPHY

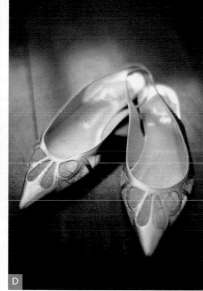

tracy and brad
round hill, jamaica

Round Hill, Jamaica, certainly speaks for itself. Tracy and Brad knew they wanted a beach wedding—and a vacation—but the renowned resort's laid-back yet professional vibe (with the added bonus of direct flights from their New York hometown) stopped their location scouting on the spot. So when it came time to plan their wedding, they naturally wanted the surroundings to do the same. Steel drummers, menu selections (a local whitefish), potted orchids, and palm fronds added Jamaican flavor to their traditional day.

[A] The pair exchanged vows on a lawn in front of the resort's spa, a nineteenth-century plantation house that overlooks the sea. [B] Lining the aisle, woven pouches filled with wild orchid arrangements decorated modern white chairs, while [C] standing arrangements of lush white orchids marked the altar area. [D] [E] For Tracy, comfort was key—and her stylish flats and light, airy Angel Sanchez gown fit the bill. [F] The hot pink lily and lime green cymbidium orchid bridal bouquet picked up on the gown's modern lace appliqués. [G] The wedding's tropical-inspired style continued to the reception on the resort's Georgian Terrace, where [H] a single orchid stem was placed in each napkin atop the menu card. [I] The yellow cake with white fondant was covered in the day's signature bloom: orchids.

PHOTOS BY FRANCESCO MASTALIA

lindsay and thomas
block island, rhode island

It wasn't hard for Lindsay to convince Thomas to throw a Block Island destination wedding. Yes, it's where she spent her summers growing up, and the island's classically New England chic style suited them to a tee, but the pair also met in Providence, making the entire state of Rhode Island close to their hearts. Shell accents and a lighthouse motif (the island is dotted with seafaring landmarks) captured the essence of the wedding location, while a modern—not to be confused with patriotic—color scheme of red, white, and light blue pulled it all together at the Spring House Hotel.

After a church ceremony with simple décor— [A] white flowers in galvanized pails— [B] the couple made their grand entrance on the hotel's lawn. [C] In light blue dresses, the bridesmaids carried peony and rose bouquets complete with shells. [D] A seashell added texture and a beachy twist to a traditional boutonniere. [E] Several low, small floral arrangements and coral frames displaying the table names added visual interest to the sophisticated tables. [F] The white, three-tiered, round cake received a kick of color from hydrangeas and berries in the wedding's colors. [G] Menu cards, imprinted with seashell and lighthouse motifs, did double duty as place cards, while [H] seashells, direct from the seashore, indicated where guests could find their tables at the reception.

PHOTOS BY KRISTIN CIOFFI DUARTE/KRISTIN STUDIO

You made it!

We are happy that you got in safely. Since ___ wi___ few days, we put together this packet to ___ ___ ___.

Welcome

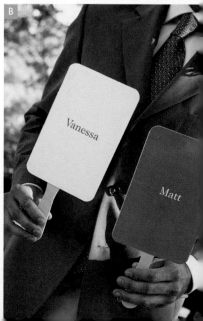

Vanessa

Matt

vanessa and matt
sonoma, california

A wine country wedding is appealing for so many reasons: the gorgeous landscape, the local libations, and the self-contained vineyard theme. For Vanessa and Matt, all those reasons applied—except the last. The creative couple used their graphic backgrounds to design an intimate celebration at her sister's home in Sonoma that highlighted the area's beauty in a modern, orange way.

For their backyard ceremony, the couple passed out [A] parasols and [B] personalized fans in the modern orange palette. [C] Vanessa carried a bouquet of orange-shaded roses and greenery before moving on to the seated reception for seventy. [D] Chinese lanterns cast a romantic glow over the outdoor reception area, while heat lamps were on hand for the cool California night. [E] Boxes at every place setting on the children's table were filled with balloons, candy, airplane gliders, and other fun toys. [F] Images of hands were used as table numbers. [G] In lieu of a cake, guests helped themselves to cookies that were iced to match the wedding colors and placed in large glass jars or [H] cupcakes dotted with orange icing.

PHOTOS BY JULIE MIKOS

heather and christopher
pienza, italy

Heather and Christopher knew Italy was the perfect location for their wedding—after all, that's where they met and fell in love (both had coincidentally moved to Rome from the U.S., he from Los Angeles, she from Boston). The pair chose Tuscany because of its romantic and exotic nature—not to mention that it's the perfect place to throw a great party for their friends and family! The festivities kicked off with a birthday party for Christopher's father on Wednesday night, and continued through the weekend with a Thursday lunch and Friday evening rehearsal.

[A] The ceremony took place at Sant'Anna in Camprena, a former monastery. Half of their 130 guests traveled to Italy from the U.S., many for the first time. [B] As a sentimental touch, the couple wrote the Italian celebration ceremony, which involved friends and family. (They were legally wed in the U.S.) [C][D][E] In order to personalize the event, Heather designed and assembled many of the wedding details, including the table cards, programs, and menus, all with beautiful calligraphy. [F] Heather's lace gown featured a wide pink sash, which inspired the wedding's pink and green palette. [G] Heather carried a bouquet in shades of pink and green featuring roses and peonies; table centerpieces took on the same color and mix of blooms. [H] White votive candles lit the tables, creating a warm glow beside the majestic elegance of Sant'Anna.

PHOTOS BY SUZY CLEMENT

A

C

E

D

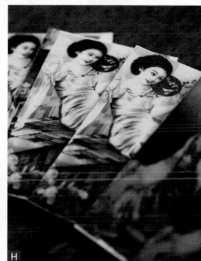

F

G

H

B

eileen and dean
salt lake city, utah

With its gorgeous mountain views and rustic woodwork, the Sundance Resort outside Salt Lake City is a great wedding destination for any outdoors-loving couple. Yet Eileen and Dean put their own cultural spin on the scenic site, famous for its film festival. The look was *Crouching Tiger, Hidden Dragon* meets *A River Runs Through It*: reds and gold mixing with wood and stone in understated, subtle elegance.

[A] Eileen and her bridesmaids entered the mountainous outdoor space through two screens of red and gold cloth and walked down a red-carpeted aisle. [B] White and red rice-paper parasols were handed out for the hilltop ceremony. [C] Hundreds of large, round red Japanese paper lanterns decorated the reception room, where tables were adorned with [D] pale pink cherry blossoms and white orchids in a cylindrical glass vase flanked by Black Magic roses. [E] [F] [G] From the red-trimmed escort cards and the thank-you notes with the couple's signature stamp to the red place cards fashioned like fortune cookies, the paper products highlighted the Asian fusion theme. [H] Handcrafted tissue packets featured vintage Asian prints.

PHOTOS BY CAROLINE YANG PHOTOGRAPHY

laila and eric
south maui, hawaii

How do you have a small wedding with big impact? For San Franciscans Laila and Eric, Hawaii was the answer. Once they laid eyes on the White Orchid House, a private home in South Maui, they never looked back. A mix of tropical blooms and Hawaiian traditions—think Hawaiian prayers and customized leis for each of the thirty guests—gave this destination wedding a homespun feel.

[A] Married by a Hawaiian minister—and wearing traditional leis—the pair walked down an aisle of hot pink rose petals. [B] [C] Both the bridal and bridesmaid bouquets featured hanging accents: tiny white blooms for Laila and pink ribbons for her girls, while [D] the flower girls carried pink and white pomanders. [E] Replicating the ceremony setup, banquet tables and lei-covered chairs [F] were set under fabric canopies overlooking the ocean. [G] Cool black river rock and white and pink orchids surrounded cylinders of water served as centerpieces. [H] The three-tiered wedding cake was accented with white and pink orchids and a buttercream pearl trim. [I] Cocktail hour delicacies (like chicken satay with peanut dipping sauce) were served on wood trays decorated with tropical blooms.

PHOTOS BY ANGIE SILVY PHOTOGRAPHY

intimate or everyone?
deciding on size

A destination wedding for 20 guests is a very different event from one for 120. A small wedding has the relaxed and intimate feel of a family vacation, while a wedding with a hundred or more guests has all the excitement of summer camp. The planning is also very different: Size affects what type of resort you research, how much guest-coordinating you need to do, and, of course, the amount of money you spend. There's no need to finalize the guest list at this stage (more on how to do that in chapter 4), but a solid first step is to decide roughly how many people you want to witness your vows.

The Inner Circle Wedding

WHO Up to thirty people: just the two of you, your families, and your very closest friends.

WHAT YOU NEED TO KNOW A tiny gathering is by far the easiest type of destination wedding to plan. Because you will need to find only one hotel, there are fewer travel plans to keep track of, and you'll be able to spend quality time with everyone. You can exchange your vows anywhere with your nearest and dearest gathered in a circle around you, followed by an intimate dinner at the best restaurant in the area. If you choose this type of gathering, it is a good idea to plan a postwedding party back home so that the rest of your friends and family can share in the celebration. (For more on planning a party at home, see page 96–97.)

> TIP
>
> For a large-scale destination wedding, you need to hire a wedding planner or a group travel agent (see page 52 for more details).

The Friends and Family Wedding

WHO Thirty to eighty people: friends, extended family, a few coworkers.

WHAT YOU NEED TO KNOW This is the most common size for a DW. With more than fifty guests, your wedding will truly feel like a celebration, complete with a reception of eight to ten tables, a busy dance floor, and enough people to stay up late to after-party with you. A bridal party of three to four bridesmaids and groomsmen is appropriate. Arranging activities and handling the concerns for a crowd of this size is a manageable undertaking, though you might need to book rooms at more than one hotel to cater to guests with different budgets. A simple cocktail party will do the trick to celebrate your nuptials back home, since so many friends will have been at your DW.

The Everyone Wedding

WHO Eighty to two hundred people: everyone you want to invite, including parents' friends, business associates, and extended family.

WHAT YOU NEED TO KNOW Coordinating details for eighty to two hundred guests or more is a serious enterprise, but the fun of having everyone you can imagine present at your wedding and the surrounding celebrations will more than make up for the extra work required. Keep in mind that the farther away your destination is, the more likely it is that some of your invitees will have to decline. So if you have your heart set on a huge wedding, you may want to consider a locale close to where most of the invitees live, one that is easy and affordable to reach.

stamp out scheduling conflicts

You're asking guests to set aside more than just a Saturday night for your destination wedding—many will need three, four, or even five days. Use these tips to keep your guests in mind when picking a date for your nuptials.

Choose long weekends. Presidents' Day, Memorial Day, Labor Day, etc., are all good options because people already have three-day weekends and won't have to take much (if any) time off from work or school to attend. However, these weekends are hectic and more expensive times to travel, and many people are busy with family obligations and their own vacations, so weigh those considerations against the convenience.

Confirm with the VIPs. List the guests without whose presence the wedding simply couldn't take place (close relatives, best friends) and ask them if they have any prior, can't-miss commitments during the period you're considering. Then block out those dates on your calendar.

Avoid awkward times. Do any of your guests have specific needs or limitations? To maximize the likelihood that they'll be able to attend, think about scheduling conflicts before you set the date: college graduation, grad school finals or bar exams, tax time. Also consider key cultural and religious holidays: Rosh Hashanah and Yom Kippur in the fall, Chinese New Year, Easter weekend.

how much? setting your wedding budget

There's no magic formula for figuring out how much a destination wedding will cost. Depending on how many people you invite and how high-end you go, your nuptials could ring up to $15,000, $50,000, or upwards of $1.5 million. The only real place to begin is to determine how much you and your families can afford to spend. If done right, a destination wedding can cost no more—and maybe even less—than hosting the same party at home. (For example, if you live in a U.S. metropolitan area where event facilities are in high demand, then holding your wedding in Mexico will likely be less expensive than doing it at home, even when you factor in airfare and hotel expenses.) But costs can easily spiral out of control when you fly in photo and video professionals or decide that you must have peonies for the centerpieces—even though it's winter in the Caribbean.

Budget Basics

Even if money is no object, it is still essential to have a budget figure to use as a guide for your decisions (you can always decide to increase the allocation for any item). A DW budget is best thought of as four different budgets. Before you book a site or buy your ring, you need to have a total number in mind for each of these categories of expenses.

TIP

Use our handy budget worksheets (see page 194) to calculate and keep track of your basic budget numbers. Feeling technical? Use the form as a basis for a spreadsheet, or use The Knot budget tool to keep track of wedding expenses online: theknot.com/mybudgeter.

WEDDING BUDGET All expenses relating to the ceremony, reception, and after-party, including the services of a makeup artist, need to be separated out so that they can be managed. Here's an easy-to-remember loose formula that provides perspective before you pull out your credit card to buy that gorgeous gown: 40 percent of the budget devoted to the meal (food, drink, service, rentals), 10 percent toward travel (not only yours to and from the location but guests' on-site travel as well), and about 10 percent to each of the following: attire, music, photo/video, flowers/decor, and details (rings, invitations, etc.). Reallocate funds based on your priorities (a desperate love of orchids might trump the purchase of a couture gown).

GUEST ACTIVITY BUDGET Calculate expenses for all the events and activities you will be treating your guests and attendants to—the welcome party, bridesmaids spa

Do the bride and groom pay for everything? What about hotel rooms and airfare for their guests?

The bride and groom (and/or their parents) are expected to pay for:

O The wedding reception (whether it's a five-course meal or a beer-and-burgers bash)

O A rehearsal dinner

O A welcome party

O A morning-after brunch (a friend or a family member may volunteer to host this for you as a gift)

We highly recommend the hosts also cover:

O Selected activities (a group sailing trip, a tour around town)

O Transportation to and from the ceremony and reception sites

O A shuttle to pick up your guests at the airport when they arrive

O Attendant hotel rooms. According to tradition, the bride or her family should cover lodging for the bridesmaids; the groom or his family should do the same for the groomsmen. If these expenses will burst your budget, tell your attendants their presence is their gift to you. (Keep in mind: If hotel room rates are $400 a night, that may be more of a present than they intended to give!)

O Travel expenses for VIPs with no other means to make it to the wedding (think: elderly relatives or the starving-artist bridesmaid)

Guests should expect to pay for:

O Their plane ticket to and from the destination

O Their hotel room stay

O Any meals or beverages that aren't part of the wedding festivities

O Any nonwedding activities they choose to participate in

Attendants should expect to pay for:

O Travel to and from the destination

O Formalwear and accessories

O Hair and makeup or spa appointments

O Food and drinks that aren't part of a wedding event

party, departure-day brunch. Factor in food and beverage, facility rental, entertainment, and individual participation fees for golf or other outings as well as tips for tour guides and the like.

HONEYMOON BUDGET Will you be flying to another location for the honeymoon? In addition to the room rate at your hotel, factor in your daily food and entertainment expenses, as well as activities.

POSTWEDDING PARTY BUDGET A party to celebrate the wedding for friends back home should really have its own budget. Never assume there will be money "left over" from your DW.

Extra DW Expenses

There are added expenses specific to destination weddings.

IMPORTING KEY VENDORS. If you decide that you absolutely must have a top photographer and your hometown minister, you will pay for their airfare, rooms, and meals (and possibly for the photographer's assistant's airfare, rooms, and meals), which can be a significant additional expense.

WELCOME BAGS. Since your guests will be coming from out of town, you'll want to show your thanks when they arrive. The bags don't have to be lavish, but since you're making dozens of them, the costs will start to add up. (Turn to page 102 to find out what to put in your welcome bags.)

ADDITIONAL ACTIVITIES. Since you're playing host for multiple days, you might want to arrange extra events for your guests—a welcome party, a postwedding brunch, some organized group activities. You don't need to underwrite everything, but even super-low-key activities can have some associated costs. (Get more info on these extras in chapter 5.)

TRAVEL COSTS FOR YOU AND YOUR PARENTS. Your travel and lodging costs during the event add a line item to your wedding budget. Keep in mind that you'll also need to visit your destination at least once (and up to three times) as part of the planning process. (A detailed itinerary for the planning trips is on page 31.)

SUBSIDIZING GUESTS. You certainly aren't obligated to pay for anyone but yourselves, but if you want to chip in toward some of your guests' expenses—by hosting extra breakfasts and lunches, for example, or by covering one night of room fees—be sure to factor your largesse into your budget.

TIP

If you make casual plans with a group of people ("We're having dinner at X spot tonight if anyone wants to join us"), be certain to tell the restaurant or activity company in advance that you aren't paying for everyone. This way they can be responsible for keeping separate tabs or collecting payment from each individual, sparing you an awkward situation.

Prepare for Takeoff

12 ways to save—without sacrificing!

1. Avoid high season and Saturday night. Many locations are just as gorgeous in their off-season (Aspen in the spring or Paris in the winter). And by having your event on a Friday night your guests can have more time to vacation with you after the wedding.

2. Look for travel bargains. Work with a travel agent to get a reduced group rate on airfare for yourselves, your family, and your wedding party.

3. Go local. Using vendors from the area will be more cost-effective than importing your own. Their styles may differ, but consider that part of the adventure.

4. Cut back on decor. Rely on the backdrop of the land and the surrounding foliage instead of involved floral arrangements. Don't rent your own chairs, china, and linens; live with the ones offered by your location.

5. Simplify the photo/video. Hire a professional photographer for only part of the evening— perhaps the ceremony and the first few hours of the reception. Consider filming just the ceremony.

6. Keep food and drink casual. Serve three courses instead of five, have a beer-and-wine-only bar, or limit your dessert offerings to a delicious cake. It doesn't matter how many options you give your guests, as long as the food tastes great and the wine keeps flowing.

7. Host all events "on location." If your rehearsal dinner, ceremony, reception, and brunch are all held within walking distance, you can save the expense of booking buses for your guests.

8. Practice DIY. Do the calligraphy for the envelopes and escort cards on your computer, make the favors, or create your own aisle runner. Give the day a personal touch.

9. Use e-mail when possible. Instead of making your mailing bulky with hotel particulars, direct guests to your website, where they can access lodging options and save-the-date details. E-mail is also a better way to communicate with your vendors than telephoning, since you'll have a record of your correspondence.

10. Simplify the invitations. Use thermography or plain offset printing instead of engraving or letterpress, and limit your use of extras (special ink colors, decorative envelope linings) that can drive up the price. For responses, use postcards instead of cards with envelopes, or consider having RSVPs online as a feature of your website.

11. Plan more casual activites. Substitute expensive guest outings like golf or sailing with frill (and more inclusive) activities like volleyball, ultimate frisbee, or a sand castle–building contest.

12. Stay put for your honeymoon. Instead of jetting off to yet another destination after your wedding, stick around to further enjoy and explore the spot you're in. If you want to leave the ceremony behind, switch to another hotel or head to a neighboring town or island that's a quick trip from the one where you said your vows.

How Far Will Your Money Take You?

In the most general sense, it's important to know how certain choices will affect cost, so do some preliminary research. Call a wide variety of venues to find out how much they charge. Go to a bridal salon that carries your favorite designer and find out the price range. Start adding up some costs, and see where your calculations take you.

THE DESTINATION. If you choose one of the pricier Caribbean islands (Anguilla or St. Barths, for example), everything—from airfare to the reception food and drink to what you pay for a bottle of water on the beach—will probably cost more than it would on an island with less pricey accommodations (Jamaica and the Bahamas are two islands where you can often find bargains, though they certainly have their selection of posh places, too).

YOUR VENUE'S EXPERIENCE. The more experience your venue has with throwing events of this type, the less you're likely to spend on additions. For instance, if they routinely do weddings on the beach, they might have an altar or a chuppah you can borrow (and decorate), saving you the cost (and the trouble) of renting or procuring one through other means.

THE EXCHANGE RATE. If your destination is in a foreign country, consider the exchange rate—your American dollars will buy way more wedding in Mexico than they will in England.

Adjusting Your Budget—or Expectations

If, after doing your research, you realize that you can't pull off the wedding you want with the budget you have, consider waiting until you've saved enough, borrowing money, or scaling back on your guest list. Or simply adjust your vision of what you want—go more casual, pick a closer location, skip the prewedding luau.

When you plug in the numbers, start by figuring out your fixed costs. If you have already decided on your location, then enter the amount of the big, non-negotiable items, such as the food for the reception and your airfare and hotel rooms. That way you'll be able to see how much you have left to spend, so you can decide where you'll scrimp and where you'll splurge. (Off-the-rack dress and pricey letterpress invitations? Or custom-fitted couture and stationery created on your ink-jet printer?)

destination dresses

No doubt you'll want to start shopping for your wedding dress right away, but choosing one for a destination wedding is a little different.

Pick your location first. Your dress should blend harmoniously with the setting. Weddings in tropical destinations should have a more casual feel. You don't have to wear a sundress, but a beaded satin ball gown on the beach would strike the wrong note. If your ceremony is seaside, forgo both the long train, which will accumulate sand, and the cathedral veil, which can become unruly in the ocean breeze. Stick with styles that feel tropical or beachy, like slip dresses, mermaid shapes, or even layers of wild ruffles (even though you're not going formal, you can still be ultra-festive). The same principle applies to weddings in country and rustic mountain settings—bypass glam sequins and royal wedding–style poufs in favor of fabrics and lines with elegant simplicity.

But if you're walking down the aisle in a medieval chapel or a European castle, a more formal look involving yards of rich fabric and intense embroidery will suit the old-world setting.

Respect the tone and time of the ceremony. A featherweight dress is not appropriate attire for a candlelit ceremony in a centuries-old church, even if the church happens to be in the Dominican Republic. And if you're getting married in a garden at noon you may need to relinquish your fantasy of elbow-length gloves and a mile-long veil, even if the garden is on the grounds of a fancy five-star hotel.

Remember the weather. Select a fabric that will be comfortable to wear in your destination's climate. Are you headed to a steamy tropical paradise? Choose lightweight materials like airy silks that breathe, such as chiffon, organza, charmeuse, or crepe, and avoid heavy weaves like satin and brocade. Fabrics that wrinkle or pucker are poor choices if it's humid, as is heavy beading, which weighs a dress down. Are you getting married at the top of a ski slope on New Year's Eve? Reverse those rules: Choose a weightier fabric and pair it with a cashmere wrap or a fur stole.

Will it travel? Before you purchase a massive swagged ball gown with a cathedral train, consider how you'll get it to your destination. Avoid lost-luggage issues by carrying your dress with you. Some fabrics (linen, satin, and organza, for example) wrinkle severely when packed; upon arrival, you may need a professional to press or steam your dress. Soft fabrics like lace, silk chiffon, or charmeuse are easy to pack.

Flatter your figure. Regardless of where your wedding takes place—on a beach or in a ballroom—you need to choose a style that flatters your figure. Try on a variety of silhouettes (sheath, A-line, Empire waist) to find the one that plays up your assets and makes you feel gorgeous. If the cut that looks best on your body feels too formal for your destination—for example, you really like a strapless bodice with a full skirt—look for other ways to tone down the dressiness. Choose a matte fabric free of beading or other ornamentation, and exchange the tiara for a simple hairstyle. On the other hand, if you feel most comfortable in an unadorned sheath but your destination calls for something fancier, dress it up with eye-popping jewelry.

Remember your accessories. The dress is just the base of your wedding day look—your accessory choices can transform the feel of your outfit. A dramatic necklace or chandelier earrings can make a simple dress more spectacular. A long veil can make a slip dress look more traditional during the ceremony. And the right underpinnings are essential to ensuring your gown doesn't slip, twist, or reveal the wrong parts. To the right is a complete list of every accessory you need to consider.

Before you go . . . Call the airline in advance to inform them that you'll be carrying on your attire (this notice is especially important if your dress is oversize). There may be an extra fee, but it's worth it. Once you board the plane, ask the flight attendants to place your outfits in the closet in the first-class cabin (even if you're not seated in first class—don't worry, everyone will indulge you since it's your wedding). For details on how to pack your dress, go to page 206.

style sheet for bride

Use this checklist to account for all of your fashion essentials.

o Veil
o Tiara/headpiece
o Wrap or stole
o Purse
o Shoes
o Gloves
o Bustier/bra
o Panty hose
o Thong or slimmer
o Garter
o Slip
o Petticoat/crinoline
o Bracelet
o Rings
o Earrings
o Necklace
o Handkerchief

CHERI & JASON · VATICAN CITY

Hometown: New York, NY
Guests: 17

The Destination Decision: History buff Cheri always dreamed of marrying in the country where one of her ancestors was raised. "Italy was the perfect choice," she says. "It would celebrate Jason's Italian heritage and the Catholic side of my family."

Planning Pointer: Find a wedding planner who has tastes similar to yours and is fluent in the language. "That way the planner will be able to add the special touches that bring the wedding up a notch," Cheri says.

The Definitive Detail: In the course of their research, they came across an interesting option, having their ceremony at the Vatican. "We were like, we can get married at *the* St. Peter's?! No one really seems to know about it," marvels Cheri. But you must be flexible—the Vatican gives only two months' notice on the actual date. (There are extensive requirements for a Vatican wedding. See SantaSusanna.org.)

Ch. 2

you are here:
finding the perfect spot

The location of your wedding determines not only the mood (sporty, rustic, sophisticated, etc.) but also the travel, time, and expense required to pull it off.

Your destination decision actually consists of two parts: the locale itself and the venue (the resort, villa, or local ballroom where the festivities will take place). Often they go hand in hand—for example, at an all-inclusive island resort everything is taken care of for you. More often, though, you're only halfway home once you've settled on a geographical area.

Step 1: Figure out whether a certain type of setting or a specific place in the world is more important to you. What do we mean? Well, if your dream is to be wed on a white-sand beach, it can come true in any number of places, from Hawaii to the Hamptons. But if you envision an authentic Tuscan experience, traveling to Italy is your only option.

My future in-laws are really excited for us to have a destination wedding—at their beach house. We'd rather go somewhere that doesn't belong to either family. How can we tell them and everyone else that we're making this decision on our own?

Deciding where to host your wedding is going to be topic A in many of your conversations with friends and family, and you'll be overwhelmed by others' opinions. One friend will try to convince you that Hawaii is the only way to go, while another will warn you not to expect guests to skip through more than one time zone. Resolve to listen to these opinions politely, and thank them for their input, but don't let yourselves be too influenced. If anybody gets pushy, say something diplomatic like, "Every destination has its pros and cons, but I'm sure we'll find the one that's right for us."

You may find your parents struggling with your decision to have a destination wedding. Traditionally it is their party to host, so having it in a distant location puts greater pressure on them.

As for your in-laws, simply tell them that you're incredibly grateful for their generous offer to let you use the beach house, but that it's your dream to start your new lives together in a destination that's new for both of you—not someplace that's been in one of the families for years. Although they may be disappointed, they shouldn't argue with that.

Step 2: Once you've decided on a setting or a specific place, pinpoint a particular type of venue, from oceanside restaurant to stately castle. The great news is that you can have your East Coast–style, classic ballroom wedding virtually anywhere. You just need to find the right hotel.

deciding on a destination

Think you know which destination is right for you? Before making a final decision, consider these important factors:

EASE OF GETTING THERE. Accessibility correlates directly to the number of guests who will be able to make it, though you may equate remoteness to exclusivity—just the vibe you're going for. To get a sense of the travel and cost involved, run a few online flight searches.

EXPENSE: Price will be a consideration for most guests, no matter how much they love you. It can also affect how much they enjoy themselves when they get there—if they are stressed about the expense, they are not likely to indulge in all the location has to offer. Focus on how much it typically costs to reach your potential destination from your friends' and relatives' departure cities.

TIP

Use a travel search engine such as Sidestep.com or Kayak.com, both of which allow you to search multiple airlines and discount travel sites at once.

CONVENIENCE: How often flights leave and how many airlines fly to your location are essentials to understand. The most important detail is whether flights are direct. Two-flight destinations create additional hassles—missed connections, lost luggage, long layovers—that may affect your guests' experience. Factor in jet lag, as well.

TOTAL TRAVEL TIME: Think about on-site transportation. How long does it take to get from the airport to the town or resort? Are taxis readily available, or will you need to rent cars? What will guests' total travel time (flight plus ground transportation) be? (Some destinations, like St. John and Nevis, are accessible only by boat or small plane.)

EASE OF MARRYING THERE. The legal side of tying the knot in a different country can be complicated. Many countries have a "residency requirement" (for example, twenty-four hours in the Turks and Caicos and seven days in England), which means you must reside in the country for a certain length of time before your ceremony. Although this is usually just a few days, it can be longer: France

legal ease

ON THE EASY END

Some destinations have made a special effort to simplify the wedding requirements to attract more out-of-town brides and grooms. Here are a few of the most hassle-free locations:

Las Vegas: no waiting period

Hawaii: no waiting period once marriage license has been issued

The Bahamas: must be on the island for one day before obtaining a marriage license; after that, no waiting period

Jamaica: twenty-four-hour waiting period after marriage license is issued

ON THE MOST COMPLICATED END

They're not impossible, and the result is worth the effort, but if you're set on getting legally married in any of these five destinations, be aware of the lengthy residency requirements:

French Polynesia: 30 days

France: 40 days

St. Maarten: 10 days

Ireland: 15 days

Kenya: 20 days

Many destinations (such as Italy and Thailand) also require extensive document translations or approvals from the embassy. Make it easier on yourself and work with a wedding planner.

requires you to arrive at least forty days before you marry!

THE BEST TIME TO BE THERE. You probably already have an idea of when you want to get married, but before you choose the date, be sure to look into:

THE WEATHER. The Caribbean is a high-risk destination from July through October because of hurricane season, while Hawaii's rainy season makes it less welcoming from November to March. Italy can be uncomfortably hot in July and August, particularly in the central and southern regions. Check the high and low temperatures, as well as the average rainfall, for all the places you are considering, particularly if you have your heart set on an outdoor ceremony. Optimal times to visit various locales are given in the Destination Directory on page 151.

THE CROWDS. Most locations have a "high season," when they're most crowded, and a "low season," when they're less popular. Keep that in mind when pairing your date with a destination.

THE AVAILABILITY. Hotel rooms can book up at unexpected times: spring break, local festivals, or heavy corporate off-site season. The same goes for flights.

the best places to say "i do"

Looking for a recommendation? Whether you crave warm beaches, lush fall foliage, outdoor activites, or after-dark action, here's your insider's guide to the perfect destination:

BEST BEACHES

Anguilla, Turks and Caicos, Florida, Saint-Tropez (France)

MOST SCENIC

Aspen, Napa, Italy, St. Lucia

MOST SECLUDED

Tortola, Kauai, Virgin Gorda, Mustique (the Grenadines)

BEST ALL-INCLUSIVES

Jamaica, Mexico, Bahamas, cruise ships

MOST EXOTIC (DESPITE THE ADDED DIFFICULTY OF MARRYING THERE)

Tahiti, Morocco, Maldives, Seychelles

BEST FOR PRIVATE VILLAS

Antigua, Jamaica, Anguilla, Santorini (Greece)

BEST FOR GOLF

Scotland, South Carolina, California, Hawaii, Bermuda

BEST NIGHTLIFE

Miami, New York, Brazil, Las Vegas, Barcelona (Spain), Puerto Rico

BEST FOOD

Italy, France, Anguilla, San Francisco, New York

BEST FOR FALL FOLIAGE

Lake Placid, New Hampshire, Vancouver (Canada), Mackinac Island (Michigan, U.S.)

BEST OUTDOOR ACTIVITIES (HORSEBACK RIDING, FISHING TRIPS, ETC.)

Cabo San Lucas (Mexico), Lake Tahoe, Jackson Hole, Bahamas

BEST SKIING

Canada, Colorado, France, Switzerland, Utah, Vermont, Taos (New Mexico, U.S.)

BEST SCUBA/SNORKELING

Australia, Belize, Bonaire, Cayman Islands, St. Lucia, Cancun

BEST FOR KIDS

Hawaii, Jamaica, Orlando, cruise ships

BEST WATER ACTIVITIES (SAILING, WINDSURFING, ETC.)

Capri (Italy), Hawaii, St. John (U.S.V.I.), Sardinia (Italy)

BEST SPAS

One&Only Ocean Club (Bahamas), The Spa at Mandarin Oriental (New York and Elbow Beach, Bermuda), The Palms (Turks and Caicos)

BEST PRIVATE ISLANDS FOR RENT

Guana (BVI), Moody's Nena Island (Fiji), Little St. Simons Island (Georgia, U.S.)

BEST SHOPPING

Miami, Milan, Honolulu, Paris, Vegas

(If you want more in-depth evaluations, flip to the Destination Directory on page 151.)

the best times to go to ...

FLORIDA

Go: High season is December through April, though the summer months are also beautiful and may be less expensive.

Don't Go: Hurricane season runs from June to November; fall months are most risky. Spring break destinations such as Miami and Fort Lauderdale are craziest in February and March.

HAWAII

Go: Anytime. Year-round temperatures are in the 70s and 80s during the day. Dry season runs May through October, but even in winter, rain showers are short and mild.

Don't Go: If you're looking to save a little cash, avoid winter and early spring, when tourist season is in full swing.

LAS VEGAS

Go: March, April, and May offer the most temperate climate, and the summer sizzle cools in September or October. The temperature can really drop at night, especially in the winter, but it's nothing unbearable, and the first three weeks in December are when you'll have the most luck with availability and good rates.

Don't Go: Vegas is in the desert, so the summer heat can be beastly, especially in July and August. Holiday weekends, Valentine's Day, and Cinco de Mayo are some of the most crowded times. So are the days surrounding major sporting events like the Super Bowl, the NCAA Final Four, and so forth. Try to avoid the week between Christmas and New Year's, too. By most accounts, it's the busiest time of the year, so you and your guests might not get the kind of attention from the staff that you would at other times, and traffic will be a mess.

NEW ENGLAND

Go: Summer is warmest and busiest—and the most popular. To avoid the crowds, consider the shoulder months (May and September). Temperatures are still comfortable, the scenery is still gorgeous, and rates are slightly cheaper.

Don't Go: New England winters are notoriously freezing, and storms come quickly, causing major transportation problems.

NEW YORK CITY

Go: Anytime. Most of the city's main attractions are indoors, so it doesn't matter much what the weather is like.

Don't Go: Heat and humidity in July and August make being outside especially uncomfortable. Holiday season, though beautiful, is crowded, but it could be a perfect time for guests to sample some of the city's most famous attractions.

NORTHERN CALIFORNIA

Go: Late spring, summer, and early fall are best, with highs in the 70s and 80s.

Don't Go: Winters are chilly and rainy.

PUERTO RICO

Go: December through May. Temperatures are fairly constant (highs between 75 and 85).

Don't Go: June to November (hurricane season).

THE ROCKIES

Go: For beautiful winter landscapes, November through March. However, if you have guests traveling by plane, keep in mind that major snowstorms could cause serious flight problems.

Don't Go: In the late spring. Beautiful winter snow will turn to slush and mud—not ideal for a long white gown.

AUSTRALIA AND NEW ZEALAND

Go: Summer months—December through February (remember, their seasons are reversed)—are great. Spring starts in October, which also brings warm temperatures, tons of sunshine, and beautiful wildflowers.

Don't Go: In winter (June through August) a blustery wind blows through the region, and as in North America, natural scenery is minimal.

BERMUDA

Go: Mid-April through early September are warm and sunny months.

Don't Go: Don't expect tropical weather in the winter—Bermuda rests on the same latitude as North Carolina but is sometimes confused with the Bahamas.

THE CARIBBEAN

Go: The best (and busiest) time is December through March, though April and May are great options if you want to avoid the crowds and save some cash.

Don't Go: Avoid the hurricane season, which runs from June through November, and don't forget about spring break in February and March—some areas may become crowded with college-age partiers.

GREECE

Go: Between April and mid-June, before the high season, popular sites are relatively uncrowded and rates are reasonable. Fall is also an excellent time to enjoy scenic landscape and comfortable temperatures.

Don't Go: Prices skyrocket from mid-June through August, temperatures are high, and crowds are overbearing.

ITALY

Go: Seaside towns are best weather-wise in summer, even though tourism is at its peak. Try early spring—it's especially warm in the south, and you'll avoid the tourist rush. If you're planning to wed in Rome or Florence, think fall—temperatures are cooler and the cities are manageable but lively.

Don't Go: Cities are crowded and hot in the summer, while coastal towns are virtually deserted in the winter.

MEXICO

Go: Winter months are best, but crowded, with sunny, 80-degree days. April and May are traditionally slower months for tourism, and the weather is still great.

Don't Go: Rain is heaviest in June and October, with the possibility of hurricanes through November. Spring break season runs from late February through March—especially popular in Cancun and Cabo San Lucas.

SOUTH PACIFIC

Go: May is the peak of dry season, but book early to avoid crowds and hefty price tags. Plus, ocean breezes keep the air from being too stuffy.

Don't Go: To avoid rain, don't go during January and February—humidity peaks during these months.

UNITED KINGDOM

Go: Summer highs reach into the 70s, and rain is less likely during this time.

Don't Go: Spring and fall weather can be fickle—some spring days are warm and sunny, others cold and rainy.

doing your homework

Now that you've narrowed down your destination options, use the following resources to start looking into potential venues:

INTERNET. Travel sites and the websites of specific resorts or hotels can be helpful, but *always* double-check to see when the information was published. Just because a photo is online doesn't mean it's up-to-date—you could be looking at shots taken years ago.

TOURIST BOARDS. The official websites and wedding planning kits for your target destinations are packed with useful info, but keep in mind that the featured hotels and restaurants probably paid for the promotion. To find "hidden treasure" places that don't advertise, do extra online digging or talk to a wedding planner who is familiar with the area.

GUIDEBOOKS. Travel guides written for the everyday tourist probably won't be as much help as wedding-specific guides. Books from the more reputable names in travel (Fodor's, Frommer's, etc.) can definitely give you a good overview of the area and its climate and culture, as well as a general idea of the reputations of hotels and resorts.

PERSONAL RECOMMENDATIONS. Word of mouth is definitely your friend. Advice and tips from friends or relatives who have traveled to the area will give you an uncensored version of what things are like. And don't forget to check out what other couples have to say about a particular destination or resort on our message boards at TheKnot.com/destinationboards.

REAL WEDDINGS. Consulting friends of friends who have had weddings in your locale is an obvious step, but another resource for site referrals are the "real weddings" featured in magazines, on wedding websites (TheKnot.com/weddings), and in this book. Better than straight listings, these editorial, photo-driven wedding stories will give you a true picture of what your ceremony and reception will look like at a specific location. And because most of these featured weddings list the name of the site, photographer, and florist, you'll be able to get a head start on the rest of your hiring. Real weddings are also a perfect jumping-off point for finding an event planner—the best source of all for finding wedding-friendly resorts.

TIP

If your dream destination has a long residency requirement, a civil ceremony performed at home either before or after you go may be neccessary. (This is not the best option for the ultratraditional.) Read more about these legalities on page 26.

planning your site visits

THE ONE-TRIP PLAN

WHEN TO GO: 8 to 10 months out
HOW LONG TO STAY: at least 3 days
WHAT TO DO: pick your place

O Pick your location ASAP. Do your homework before you go and visit no more than three venues. Try to make a final decision by the end of the first day.

O Check out the various ceremony and reception spots at the time of day you'll be using them.

O Plan to meet with as many vendors as possible—prioritize the vendors you care about most (make the planner a must)—and handle the rest from afar on recommendations.

O Meet every person on the properties who will have a managing role in your wedding: the wedding planner, the site coordinator, the chef, and the general manager are musts. Having a face to put with an e-mail address can simplify communication.

O Use your experience as a "first-time guest" to uncover the things your guests may need to make their time more enjoyable. Scope out any potential problems (difficulty tracking down cabs at the airport, for example) and put finding solutions for them on your to-do list.

THE TWO-TRIP PLAN

Refer to the one-trip plan.
Trip Two
WHEN TO GO: 3 to 4 months out
HOW LONG TO STAY: a long weekend
WHAT TO DO: get down to details

O Visit your property.

O Check out the ceremony and reception spots at the time of day you'll be using them. Do a run-through and make sure you're happy with the locations.

O Have your caterer/reception manager show you what your tables will look like with linens and place settings.

O Do a tasting.

O Request a trial centerpiece from your florist.

O Collect any local items for your welcome bags. Bring any decorations or supplies to the resort that you want the manager to store for you until the wedding.

THE THREE-TRIP PLAN

Refer to the one-trip and two-trip plans.
Trip Three
WHEN TO GO: 1 to 2 months out
HOW LONG TO STAY: 2 days
WHAT TO DO: refine the details

O Make any last-minute decisions.

O Walk through the room where you'll be spending your wedding night and make any special requests.

O Bring any remaining decorations or supplies to the resort.

O Test-drive hair and makeup.

shopping for your location

When you have a short list of hotels or resorts that interest you, call each place and ask to speak with the wedding coordinator or catering manager. Be prepared with a list of questions that include the following:

HOW EXPERIENCED ARE YOU WITH WEDDINGS? HAVE YOU DONE MANY EVENTS OF MY SIZE?

POINTER: Wedding experience is not essential—large corporate off-sites, conferences, or parties have similar logistics and needs.

WHAT IS ONE OF THE BEST FEATURES OF A WEDDING AT YOUR FACILITY VERSUS [GIVE THE NAME OF ANOTHER HOTEL YOU'RE CONSIDERING]?

POINTER: Show them you are serious and give them the opportunity to point out the distinctive features of their facility.

DO YOU OFFER PACKAGES OR IS EVERYTHING CUSTOM OR À LA CARTE?

POINTER: Find out exactly what's included in a package so that you'll be able to make realistic cost comparisons.

ARE YOU FLEXIBLE REGARDING CUSTOMIZATIONS? HOW MUCH LEEWAY WOULD I GET WITH MENUS, MUSIC, FLOWERS, PHOTOGRAPHY, AND THE LIKE?

POINTER: If you're very picky about a certain vendor (for example, you definitely want to bring in your own photographer), or if you have specific needs (like a kosher or vegetarian meal), be sure the site can accommodate you. If getting what you want will cost you, you need to know up front, so that you can determine whether the site fits your parameters.

WHAT TYPES OF SPACES ARE AVAILABLE FOR BOTH THE CEREMONY AND THE RECEPTION?

POINTER: Loving the looks of a spot isn't enough—you also need to know that it will fit your wedding! After all, your intimate crowd of thirty will be lost in a big ballroom.

CAN I SEE MORE PHOTOS OF THE FACILITY?

POINTER: Sure, there are probably amazing images on the website, but amateur pics will give you a much better idea of what the place really looks like.

IS THERE AN ON-SITE WEDDING COORDINATOR?

POINTER: A wedding coordinator who's part of the package is often one of the biggest pluses of an all-inclusive site. Not only will this person have lots of experience with weddings at the venue, he or she will also be invaluable when it comes to recommending local vendors. Make sure the coordinator will be available to run things on the day of your wedding.

CAN YOU GIVE ME REFERENCES FROM RECENT CLIENTS?

POINTER: No references? No dice. You need to know that they stand by their work, and references will give you the inside scoop on any problems to anticipate. If possible, try to talk to people who've had events that were similar in style or scope to yours. Better yet—ask to see their wedding photos.

DO YOU HAVE SPECIALLY PRICED WEDDING PACKAGES? WHAT'S INCLUDED IN EACH PACKAGE?

POINTER: Many larger hotels and resorts will offer you deals with many of the big-day details included. Find out exactly what is being provided (and what you'll have to bring there yourself) before you sign on the dotted line. The same goes for anything you want to bring in on your own—if you've got a baker and the wedding cake is included in your package, find out if you can subtract the cost of the cake from the total or substitute it for other desserts (or something else that you really want).

TIP

Your best bet budgetwise is the "shoulder season," the month on either side of the high season when the weather is still great but the crowds are gone. Although not at their lowest, resort rates are significantly reduced.

TIP

Hire a wedding planner who specializes in your destination to do the legwork finding the perfect location. Find out how to hire one on page 52.

You Are Here

IF THERE IS NO WEDDING PACKAGE, HOW ARE WEDDINGS PRICED? IS THERE SIMPLY A PER-GUEST PRICE, OR DO YOU CHARGE AN ADDITIONAL FEE FOR RENTING THE SPACE? HOW DO PRICES VARY ACCORDING TO SEASON, DAY OF THE WEEK, OR TIME OF DAY?

POINTER: It might seem like a pain, but comparison shopping—even at the same site—can definitely be worth it. Saturday night is prime time for weddings and parties, but since all of your guests will be around (and free) for a few days, there's no reason you have to wed at a traditional hour. An off day or time is likely to save you.

HOW MUCH OF A DEPOSIT IS REQUIRED TO RESERVE MY DATE? WHEN WOULD I NEED TO MAKE THE NEXT PAYMENT?

POINTER: Even if the site is definitely within your budget, you need to double-check on not just how much you'll need to pay but when, so that you'll have the cash on hand when the balance is due.

DOES THE HOTEL HAVE ENOUGH ROOMS FOR ALL OF MY GUESTS ON THAT DATE? DO YOU OFFER GROUP DISCOUNTS? IF YOU DON'T HAVE THE CAPACITY TO HOUSE ALL OF MY GUESTS, CAN YOU SUGGEST ALTERNATIVES FOR THE OVERFLOW?

POINTER: While having all your guests in the same spot might not make for tons of wedding night privacy, it does make it a lot more convenient for all of your wedding activities—everyone has plenty of opportunities to meet up and mingle, plus it's much easier to get the whole crew together for group fun. If they can't all stay in the same hotel, make sure the alternative accommodations are close enough so that no one is stuck paying too much for cabs or hoofing it for miles.

WHAT TYPES OF ACTIVITIES DO COUPLES USUALLY ORGANIZE FOR GUESTS? WHAT'S ON THE PROPERTY? WHAT'S NEARBY?

POINTER: An on-site coordinator may be better able to answer this question than a catering manager, but the latter should be able to provide you with a few suggestions. Find out if the resort will coordinate these activities for you.

HOW FAR ARE YOU FROM THE AIRPORT? DO YOU OFFER A SHUTTLE SERVICE? WILL GUESTS NEED TO RENT CARS?

POINTER: Mobility is definitely something to keep in mind, since you don't want your guests schlepping on their own any more than is absolutely necessary. The venue's ability to provide transportation from the airport is a big plus, because even if the airport is close to the site, this is usually the most expensive trip your guests will have to take.

ARE CHILDREN ALLOWED?

POINTER: Some all-inclusive resorts, like the popular Sandals, are adults-only. Some exclusive resorts simply frown on children because it isn't the vibe they are trying to create for their clientele. If you plan to include younger guests in your celebration, pick a spot that is family-friendly.

ARE ANY OTHER WEDDINGS SCHEDULED TO TAKE PLACE ON MY WEDDING DAY?

POINTER: If the place is large and spread out, multiple weddings on a single day aren't a big deal—but if there isn't enough room to handle two events, and other people's guests can wander into your reception, then it's an issue. If you won't have exclusive use of the facilities, ask about their procedures to keep confusion to a minimum, so that you won't be able to hear strains of "YMCA" from someone else's reception.

HOW FORMAL IS THE HOTEL? WHAT IS THE STANDARD ATTIRE AT THE HOTEL RESTAURANT?

POINTER: You need to suss out whether the hotel will really fit the style of your wedding. If you're looking to have a laid-back party, a jackets-required dining room probably isn't for you. If you want to go upscale, avoid the hotel where bathing suits and flip-flops are acceptable guest attire.

> TIP
>
> A nothing-but-the-best budget is great if you can afford it, but some of your guests may not be able to splurge. Don't force anyone to stretch beyond his or her means—offer one or two nice but budget-friendly hotel options.

your love boat: the ins and outs of cruise ship weddings

THE LEGAL PART

In Port

Many cruise weddings actually happen while the ship is docked in a harbor. Your marriage license is issued from that port of call, and you are subject to the marriage requirements of that country.

At Sea

Very few cruise lines will actually marry you at sea—Princess Cruises is one of the few that can marry you in the open ocean. Your marriage license will be issued from Liberia, which is where many of the Princess ships are registered, so you'll want to confirm that your state recognizes a Liberian wedding license.

THE CELEBRATION

Whether or not you get legally married on one of their ships, most cruise lines offer wedding packages that include flowers, photographers, special meals, and luxury accommodations. (If you have the chance to spring for a room with an outside balcony, do it—it's well worth the extra expense.) When you book your cruise, ask your reservations agent to put you in touch with the line's wedding coordinator, who will take care of you.

YOUR GUESTS

An all-inclusive cruise ship wedding can be a great bargain for both you and your guests. (One important caveat: At most land-based all-inclusive resorts, drinks are free; on a cruise, you pay for each drink.)

CRUISE WEDDING RESOURCES

Princess Cruises
www.princess.com
866-444-8820

Celebrity Cruises
www.celebrity.com
866-535-2352

Royal Caribbean International
www.royalcaribbean.com
888-WED RCCL

Norwegian Cruise Line
www.ncl.com
800-392-3472

Holland America Line
www.hollandamerica.com
888-475-5511 (North America and the Caribbean)
877-580-3556 (Europe)

scoping out destinations in person

If at all possible, you should visit your destination before you book. (A detailed to-do list for your visit is on page 31.) While you *can* plan everything via phone and the Internet, nothing beats being there for getting a sense of whether or not a certain place is really right for you. Let the event coordinators at the places you're visiting know when you will be arriving, and make sure they set aside a number of hours to show you around the properties and answer all of your questions.

When you first arrive at your destination, pay attention to every detail of the travel experience: You and your guests will repeat it en route to your wedding. Focus on the following particulars:

○ Is the airport easy to navigate?

○ Do you have to go through customs, and if so, how long does it take?

○ Are you greeted by a representative from the resort at the airport? If you need a taxi, how easy is it to find one?

○ Do the airport workers and taxi drivers speak English? If they don't, how easy is it to communicate with them?

○ If you rent a car, how easy is it to make your way from the airport to your hotel?

○ Are the road conditions good or bad?

○ Are the hotel amenities acceptable? Are the rooms big enough? Are they clean?

○ Is the hotel staff friendly and accommodating?

○ Is the hotel big enough to host both the ceremony and the reception? Can it handle other wedding-related events?

○ Does the area surrounding the hotel seem safe?

○ Are there plenty of dining options for guests when they will be on their own for meals?

TIP

Just because a room offers an "ocean view" doesn't mean you won't also have a view of something else, like the pool or the building across the way. Every hotel is different; ask to see a room in every price range so you know what your guests will be walking into when they arrive.

TIP

Try to time your site visit to coincide with another wedding on the property—you'll get great ideas for what you do and don't want to do.

You Are Here

the pros and cons of "all-inclusive" venues

All-inclusive hotels and resorts are venues where pretty much everything—food, drink, and recreational activities—is included in the room fee. Such resorts are most commonly found in Mexico and the Caribbean, and many cruise ships are all-inclusive, too.

PROS

You save money. Since all of your guests' food and drink is included in the price of their rooms, you probably won't have to pay for either at your wedding reception (although some resorts require you and your guests to stay for a minimum of seven days in order to receive this perk). (However, if some of your guests are staying at other resorts, you'll have to pay for their event meals.) If you remain at the resort for your honeymoon, you may be able to get some or all of the other wedding fees waived.

Simplicity rocks. Both you and your guests will appreciate the ease of an all-inclusive venue. Once you arrive, you don't need to open your wallet or give a moment's thought to how much anything costs, so you can say, "Next round of mai tais are on me!" every night if you feel like it.

CONS

Options are limited. If you are a control freak, an all-inclusive venue may not be ideal for you, because some don't allow you much choice in terms of what food and drink will be served at the wedding or which vendors you can work with.

Your "guests" pay their own way. Even though you've made all the arrangements and sent out the invitations, your guests are essentially sub-sidizing the affair because their room rate includes their food and drink on the property. Your nearest and dearest will understand your budgetary constraints and will be happy just to share this special occasion with you, but you need to make sure you're comfortable with this dynamic. Robust welcome bags in guests' rooms and extraspecial favors at the reception are ways to show your appreciation, especially if the resort is not charging you for your reception as a result of all of the business your wedding brings in.

QUESTIONS TO ASK ALL-INCLUSIVE RESORTS

O Will my guests' food and drink be covered during wedding activities even if they aren't guests at the resort?

O Do we have to use your vendors for flowers, food, cake, entertainment, etc.?

O How are the charges for the ceremony and reception broken down?

O Are there plenty of included activities for all of my guests during their entire stay?

O Do you offer reduced-price or free weddings with honeymoons of a certain length?

O Are there any other weddings on-site on that day?

O Can I choose the ceremony wording or personalize my vows? Can I bring my own officiant?

O Where can I get married at the resort? Is anything off limits?

O Are there enough rooms available for my guests on those dates?

visiting your location

When you meet with the event coordinator for the first time, be prepared with a big list of questions:

CAN YOU SHOW ME WHERE I CAN GET MARRIED ON-SITE? IS ANYWHERE OFF-LIMITS? WHAT HAPPENS IF IT RAINS?

POINTER: Make sure your venue offers a Plan B. If you want to say "I do" outside, find out if there is an indoor room to accommodate you and your guests if it rains. A nominal fee may be charged to hold the room, but it pays to be safe. You'll be less stressed should the forecast call for a few scattered clouds.

ARE ANY RENOVATIONS SCHEDULED ON MY WEDDING DATE? WILL THEY BE DISRUPTIVE?

POINTER: Renovations always last longer than anticipated. If you are worried that a particular venue will not be ready in time for your big day, either move the party elsewhere or have a fallback plan in place.

CAN YOU ARRANGE FOR AN OFFICIANT TO PRESIDE OVER MY CEREMONY AND COORDINATE THE LEGALITIES?

POINTER: The site's wedding coordinator should be able to arrange for an officiant, but to make your ceremony more personal, consider inviting your own minister or rabbi to perform the ceremony. Or ask a family member or friend who is licensed to preside over the ceremony.

CAN SOMEBODY ON STAFF ORGANIZE GROUP ACTIVITIES AND OUTINGS FOR MY GUESTS?

POINTER: Resorts with on-site wedding planners will arrange activities for you and your guests. If the hotel you have chosen is booked through a tourism agency, such as Apple Vacations, the company may provide a host or a hostess to welcome your guests and coordinate group activities. If no one else is available, the hotel concierge will be able to make recommendations and direct visitors to the local hot spots.

WHAT TYPES OF DECORATIONS OR THEMES DO YOU OFFER? HOW MUCH DO THEY COST? ARE THEY SET OR CUSTOM?

POINTER: Some venues allow you to change the entire look of the space. (If you want a pink wedding, go ahead and remove the old floral drapes and hang up soft, pink sheers.) Others may want you to stick with what's there. Their flexibility is a good way to gauge how much experience the site has with weddings.

IF THE RESORT USES SPECIFIC VENDORS, CAN I SEE THEIR WORK BEFOREHAND? WILL YOU GUARANTEE IN WRITING THAT THE SPECIFIC VENDOR I CHOOSE WILL PROVIDE SERVICES ON MY WEDDING DAY?

POINTER: Check the resort's website: You may be able to access different vendors who work with the venue. A contract can guarantee that you get the vendor of your choice for your wedding day. (Hiring vendors is dicussed in chapter 3.)

FOR A BEACH RESORT: IS THE BEACH EXCLUSIVELY FOR HOTEL GUESTS OR OPEN TO THE PUBLIC? IF THE BEACH IS PUBLIC, DO SOLICITORS ANNOY GUESTS?

POINTER: If the beach is public, and you are saying "I do" right by the ocean, there may be uninvited guests at your ceremony. A public beach cannot keep away beachcombers or children frolicking in the sand. Check with your destination's visitor center for a list of private and public beaches before booking your site.

HOW MANY ROOMS WILL YOU BLOCK OUT FOR MY GUESTS? HOW LONG WILL YOU HOLD THEM?

POINTER: If rooms are available, most hotels won't have a problem reserving a block for large groups (often at a discounted rate). However, that deal is usually good for a limited time, so make your guests aware of any deadlines.

making your final decision

Ideally one location out of the many you've investigated will stand out as the absolutely *perfect* place to hold your wedding. Most likely, though, no single venue will offer every desire on your fantasy wish list. Here's how to make the final decision:

ORGANIZE ALL THE INFORMATION. Compile all the research you've collected into one document; use categories such as "overall vibe," "service," "flexibility," and "budget."

TALK IT THROUGH TOGETHER. Once you have pulled all the info together, sit down with your sweetie and discuss the pros and cons of each option. Carefully weigh your findings against the priorities you defined at the beginning of the process.

DON'T SOLICIT MORE OPINIONS. Although it may be tempting to poll friends, family, and random passersby on the street, try to keep the conversation between the two of you and your parents so that others' input won't cloud your true desires.

LET YOUR INTUITION KICK IN. After you've talked it over, agree to a "cooling off" period, anywhere from forty-eight hours to a week, where you try not to obsess about it and just focus on which option *feels* right. Picture yourselves meeting at the end of an aisle—which setting comes to mind first? Think of looking at your wedding album decades down the road—which venue will you be happiest to see in the background? When you mull over the different options, does a certain one stir more excitement than the others? If all things are equal, was there one on-site planner with whom you'd rather work?

RESERVE YOUR DATE. When you've made your decision, move quickly. Call your contact, tell them you are committing to the location, and ask how to make it official. Be very clear that you are not debating but have actually decided, so that they do not offer your date to another couple.

> TIP
>
> Ask the hotel to comp your room—many will agree since they're eager for all the business your wedding will bring. If the answer is no, push for a discount or other perks, like a free upgrade to a suite.

You Are Here

the contract:
signing on the dotted line

Know this: No matter how many friendly conversations you have with a location's staff, and no matter how many times they verbally agree to host your wedding on a certain date, nothing is guaranteed until you have it in writing. Even if a handshake is the local standard, you'll feel much more at ease when you sign a binding contract. (For negotiating tips, go to page 58.)

GET A PROPOSAL Before you commit to a location in writing, ask the venue to draw up a document stating the specifics of everything included in your wedding package (officiant, flowers, music, cake, marriage license, photography, video, salon services, candlelit dinner, massage, etc.). If an element is not included, find out if the venue can arrange it and have it written into the proposal. Remember to get answers to these questions:

O What deposit amount will reserve your day?

O What is the payment schedule?

O Is the site providing vendors, or are you bringing them?

O How many guests can attend the ceremony?

O Is there a charge for guests who are not staying at the resort?

O Are children allowed to attend?

O Does the property have enough rooms for your guests on that date?

O Is a group discount offered, and at what rate?

O Can the site arrange a seated reception if you want one? Where? What are the costs per person?

O Do per-person rates vary by the time of day or by day of the week or by month? What do they include?

O Can you choose the menu?

CONTRACT POINTERS The following items should be listed in your contract:

O Total cost and line-item breakdown of what's included

O Amount of deposit and when it was paid

O Outstanding balance

O Payment schedule

O Exact date and time of your wedding

O Exact location of your wedding (e.g., "in the main gallery," "in the presidential ballroom")

O Detailed list of everything the venue will provide (tables, chairs, linens, etc.)

O Name of the site rep who will be on hand on your wedding day, and the name of an acceptable substitute

O Proof of liability insurance and liquor license

O Cancellation/refund policy

O Anything else you agreed to orally that you want set in stone

planning your honeymoon escape

Although it may feel as though having a far-flung wedding is enough of a honeymoon in itself, you'll definitely want to schedule some time after the festivities to wind down and celebrate your union in private (preferably with some kind of cocktail in hand). Whether you linger at your wedding location a little longer or whisk yourselves off to yet another fabulous locale, here are five honeymoon options to consider.

STAY-WHERE-YOU'RE-AT HONEYMOON

Since you're already someplace fabulous, why leave? Instead, spend the next week, ten days, or as long as you can finagle enjoying your wedding property at a less-frenetic pace.

Pros: No travel time. As soon as the last guest leaves the reception, you're magically already on your honeymoon. You may also enjoy significant accommodation discounts from your resort if you choose to stay on.

Cons: The qualities you look for in a destination wedding location (good for groups, accommodating to all guests, and so on) may not be the same qualities you look for in a honeymoon spot. And then there are your guests—hopefully if they're also lingering after the festivities, they'll realize that now is not the time to tag along.

Tip: Book a day trip early on, if not the first day, of your official honeymoon. It will kick the week off to a fun start, give you some alone time, and free up "vacationing" guests to pursue their own adventures.

CLOSE-BUT-NOT-TOO-CLOSE HONEYMOON

Why not take the opportunity to change your environment—just a little? Instead of staying at the same resort or hotel where you swapped vows, rent a car, take a short flight, or board a ship and rack up some other experiences. If you're getting married in Montego Bay, Jamaica, maybe head off to Negril. If you've said "I do" in Tuscany, maybe now is the time to tour Rome.

Pros: Very little travel time. Since you're already so near your final destination, you don't lose much vacation time (or vacation budget) in transit. Also, chances are since the distance you're traveling is short, the climate is similar, so there will be less to pack.

Cons: You may want to hang out a little longer with the wedding guests who have traveled to be with you.

Tip: Wherever you plan to go—far away or back home—if at all possible, choose flights that leave in the afternoon if not a full twenty-four hours after your wedding—you don't want to be rushing back to your room to pack on your wedding night in order to leave at the crack of dawn.

A-WHOLE-NEW-WORLD HONEYMOON

As soon as you get the rings on your fingers, take off for someplace completely different and fabulous.

Pros: You get to see more than one destination over the course of a few weeks and still only take one big chunk of time off work.

Cons: You may be a little tired from your wedding, and the extra traveling so soon afterward may not be so welcomed. You'll also have to pack for a lot of different events and situations. Thinking about all of that in the hectic weeks before your wedding can be tough.

NOW-AND-LATER HONEYMOON

Instead of skipping the postwedding honeymoon altogether, stay at your wedding spot a few days after to unwind and then plan a totally different honeymoon for sometime later in the year.

Pros: You get the best of both worlds: relaxation time after the event (plus more time with any guests who've traveled to see you) in addition to a tailor-made honeymoon to look forward to after you go home. The festivities never end!

Cons: You'll likely have to take a larger chunk of time off work, and you'll spend more overall time in transit.

POSTPONED HONEYMOON

Maybe you really want to rack up more vacation days to put toward that three-week honeymoon, or maybe you've gotten in some good R&R during the wedding festivities already. Whatever the reason, you come home after the far-flung wedding and then plan something spectacular down the line.

Pros: You go to both your wedding and honeymoon locations at ideal times for each. If you get married in New England and want to honeymoon in the Caribbean, you can still have that fabulous Vermont summer wedding, and then wait until after the hurricane season is over to jump on a Barbados-bound flight. You also get to look forward to another amazing event in the coming weeks and months.

Cons: Being at work the Monday after you say I do.

Tip: Promise to make your first week back home feel like a honeymoon. Go into work late one or two mornings. Meet each other for lunch. Send sweet e-mails. Make romantic dinner reservations to celebrate being married for a full seven days.

EMILY & BRIAN · VAIL, CO

Hometown: Los Angeles, CA
Guests: 300

The Destination Decision: A connection to the location led Emily and Brian back to Vail for their wedding held over Valentine's Day weekend. It's where Brian had proposed the year before. He had hired a photographer to capture his mountaintop proposal, and the two used that photo in their save-the-date cards.

Planning Pointer: Embrace your location. The jet-setters didn't let cold weather and snow put the slightest damper on their chic wedding aesthetic. Emily donned furry white après-ski boots with her strapless Badgley Mischka gown. Elbow-length white leather gloves and a white mink stole complemented her ski-bunny-bride look. Bridesmaids and flower girls received gifts of white down parkas embroidered with the wedding logo, which they wore to the ceremony. Groomsmen wore their gifts of black car coats. Of course, the couple traveled in style as well, arriving in a horse-drawn carriage.

The Definitive Detail: Emily and Brian wanted their reception to reflect the location, so a production team draped yards of billowy white fabric throughout the ballroom for a snowy setting. Hundreds of crystals, more than six thousand white roses, and dozens of candles completed the romantic indoor winter wonderland.

Ch. 3

assembling your "a" team:
hiring vendors from afar

You've found the perfect place for your wedding; now you need the perfect people to ensure that your big day goes off without a hitch.

While booking your band, florist, and other vendors at a distance may seem like mission impossible, you actually have access to vast resources—many more than you may realize. Once you are armed with a list of recommendations, the Internet, and the right questions to ask, finding the right people should be a piece of fondant-frosted wedding cake.

Our checklist on page 200 gives you an idea of all the vendors you may need. Tailor it based on which vendors come with your location: Some venues prefer to use particular pros or even require you to use certain people contractually (often a florist, a cake baker, and a lighting pro, among others). Having that knowledge beforehand will save time.

Visit websites (including TheKnot.com and the tourist board site for your destination) and search online to learn about vendors in the area. Do you know a couple who was married at your location? Find out which vendors they used. Were they satisfied? Do they have any advice to share?

the art of interviewing

Vendors in demand book up quickly, so the sooner you start making calls, the better. Your wedding planner (we talk about hiring one of those up ahead on page 52) can meet with potential vendors on your behalf, then send you detailed e-mails about your options. But if you're doing the planning solo, you'll have to interview vendors via phone and e-mail.

REVIEW THEIR WORK. Most vendors will have websites and digital portfolios, so you won't have to make a decision in the dark. If a vendor isn't online, ask him or her to overnight or e-mail work samples for you to review.

GET REFERENCES. Vendors should have no problems giving you the names of past clients and contact information. Ask these references to describe what they liked about the vendor and to name some of his or her weaknesses (hey, everyone's got one or two). Would they recommend this vendor to a good friend?

MEET IN PERSON, IF POSSIBLE. Ideally you'll be able to make a prewedding visit to your destination to finalize vendor decisions. (How to plan your site visit is discussed on page 3.) If a visit just isn't in the cards (or budget), your wedding planner can help you make the final decisions.

GET A DETAILED WRITTEN PROPOSAL FROM EACH VENDOR. This document should contain every aspect of your relationship with your vendor, including all items to be delivered (how many bouquets, entrées, or table linens), details about each one if applicable (bouquets with eight to ten Black Magic roses, three dahlias, and gardenia leaves, stems wrapped with burgundy silk satin ribbon), how long services last (five hours for the band, eight hours for the photographer, etc.), and any other details you've discussed. For bands, photographers, or other vendors whose work is provided on an hourly basis, be certain this proposal includes their overtime rate. And don't forget to ask for a deposit amount and a payment schedule, so that you know when the vendor requires payments.

NEGOTIATE. Use your charm, wit, and knowledge to get the most from your vendors. There is almost always room to negotiate a price reduction or the addition of a little something extra at the proposed rate. This negotiating should take place after you have received proposals from two vendors so that you can compare the costs.

ALWAYS HAVE A WRITTEN AGREEMENT. After the proposal, you move to the contract stage. All of your written vendor contracts should include each of the following items:

* Business name, address, and phone number

* Contact person

* Person responsible for your event

* Date of the wedding (double-check this one!)

* Complete description of product or service, down to the minutiae (for example, "band" is unacceptable; be specific: "16-piece band, including 1 drummer, 2 saxophonists, 2 violinists . . ." and so on)

* Exact start and finish times, including setup and breakdown

* Exact prices, including tax, service/tip, delivery fees, payment schedule, and hourly overtime rate (make sure your vendor will be available for overtime)

* Staff dress code that's appropriate for your wedding

* Cancellation/refund policy

* Return/cleanup policy (who is responsible for picking up the equipment, etc.)

who's playing wedding planner?

Planning a destination wedding weekend requires hours of research, hundreds of e-mails, extensive coordination, and, ultimately, the right resources. One of the many reasons to hire a professional wedding planner is that a good one will be familiar with—or be able to find—a wide variety of local vendors. He or she can also describe the pros and cons of each, judge their skills appropriately based on your wedding vision, and provide insider tips on how to get the most out of them. Plus, a planner will have direct contacts and the best scoop about how to track down the most talented, in-demand vendors. To figure out if you need the extra help, consider these four factors:

THE COMPLEXITY OF YOUR EVENT. If you're planning a celebration for 50 guests two states away, you'll probably need less help than if you're planning a party for 150 in another country where you don't speak the language. If your wedding has a large guest list, a unique, involved vision, or multiple off-location events, help from an experienced professional is critical.

YOUR EXPERIENCE AND AVAILABILITY. If you are in marketing or public relations and plan events for a living, chances are you could pull off the affair on your own. But the crucial question is: Do you really have the time? Given the travel required, unending negotiations, and days needed before the wedding to finalize the plans, DW planning can become a second job. Be honest about whether or not your schedule will permit you to handle the details effectively.

THE SERVICES PROVIDED BY YOUR SITE. If your location provides an on-site planner who is on call to arrange the entire event *and* activities—and you are comfortable handling all prewedding invites and RSVPs—you probably don't need additional help. The same holds true if you're booked at a resort that offers complete wedding packages.

YOUR BUDGET. A wedding planner's services are an additional expense (either an hourly/daily fee or a percentage of your total budget) at a time when you probably already feel swamped with expenses, so evaluate carefully. In most instances, planners more than cover the cost of their fee by protecting your budget. They have the experience, connections, and contracted obligation to understand how much things cost, create a realistic budget, and make sure you don't exceed it. In addition, they often have the relationships to get deals that you don't.

TIP

If you do decide to hire extra help, try to earmark part of your budget (about 10 percent of the total) for a wedding planner or a destination wedding consultant.

Who's Who and What They Do

There are three types of professionals you can work with to plan your wedding: on-site event coordinators, professional wedding planners, and travel agents.

ON-SITE EVENT COORDINATORS

What they do: On-site coordinators are often salaried employees of the hotel or resort where you're having your celebration, and their responsibilities vary widely. Some will help you plan from the very start; others won't want to get involved until just a few months or weeks before the event. At the very least, on-site coordinators should be able to recommend vendors they've used in the past and put you in contact with couples who had their weddings at the property (they are great resources!). On the actual day of your wedding, they should act as your coordinator for all details.

What they don't do: On-site planners won't help with small-picture particulars like coordinating RSVPs or guest activites. They may not have much experience with vendors other than those used regularly by the resort, so if you want to hire a florist you discovered yourself or have an outside caterer do the food, you may want a planner with extra expertise. If you decide to employ an outside event planner, you can still use the services of the venue's on-site coordinator. He or she knows the inner workings of the place like no one else, and will be an invaluable resource for site-specific details when your wedding day arrives.

Who it works for: Couples looking for local help toward the end of planning. You may still need to take one scouting trip to meet the coordinator and share your vision.

Approximate price: Free–$ (usually factored into the cost of the wedding; the only additional cost is a gratuity).

TIP

Be sure to clarify: Is the on-site coordinator truly an experienced wedding planner or simply a catering manager who handles weddings? The latter seldom assists with anything other than the food-related events.

PROFESSIONAL WEDDING AND EVENT PLANNERS

What they do: Also known as wedding consultants, planners are pros at arranging every last detail of your wedding. No matter how far you're traveling, how large your guest list, or how specific your needs, you can trust that your consultant has tackled even more complex affairs. Planners work in different ways: You can hire them by the hour, by the day, or from start to finish (in which instance planners usually charge a percentage of your total budget).

Planners should be able to handle anything you throw at them, from vendor suggestions to bridal party and guest travel coordination to getting save-the-date reminders designed and in the mail. Discuss everything up front with your planner so that together you have a clear understanding of expectations and of the work involved (which will be reflected in the fee).

What they don't do: Very little. For example, if your future father-in-law needs a constant supply of the best-quality cigars at his disposal, a planner can usually accommodate your request.

Who it works for: Just about everyone, from couples who want a few hours of consultation at the start of planning to make sure they're on the right track to those who are hosting huge affairs and need every detail carefully thought out and managed. If you hire someone for the duration of your planning, you may not need to take a single scouting trip, but your planner will, and it will be factored into your cost.

Approximate price: $–$$$$ (depending on the contracted services).

TRAVEL AGENTS

What they do: Travel agents schedule travel, lodging, and transportation for your guests. They will let you know who has booked and who hasn't, and can also help you secure group discounts on airfare or lodging. Agencies experienced with group travel will be able to procure tickets to local events, book restaurant reservations, and organize tours.

What they don't do: Unless your agent specializes in weddings—and an increasing number do—he or she won't assist you with hiring vendors or any of the wedding day specifics.

Who it works for: This option is great for couples getting married at an all-inclusive resort, where guests spend their entire stay in one place, and for couples planning small weddings. If you use a standard travel agent, plan to do most of the real wedding work yourself or in conjunction with another kind of planner.

Approximate price: $–$$. Most travel agents charge per-booking service fees; if they assist with your wedding arrangements, they may also charge a "planning fee" of several thousand dollars. In addition, they sometimes get kickbacks from resorts, which allow them to lower the fee they charge you.

TIP

Because of cultural nuances, you want to hire someone familiar with the practices and work style of your destination so that you can cut through any red tape you encounter.

Questions to Ask

Seek out word-of-mouth recommendations, ask the resort for referrals, and search online. Ask candidates for references from other couples who had destination weddings similar to yours in size or style. Review portfolios of the weddings they have worked on, particularly if you expect them to coordinate event design. Be sure to ask the following questions:

TIP

Given their connection to travel wholesalers, agents often have access to airline seats and hotel rooms that would be considered "sold out" to consumers or even wedding planners. This can be a critical advantage if your event is held during a locale's high season.

DO YOU CHARGE BY THE HOUR OR BY THE PACKAGE? ACCORDING TO DESTINATION OR WEDDING SIZE?

POINTER: Think about how much time you'll need from your planner. It may be better to hire a planner for a couple of consults along the way plus a day-of coordination package than it would be to hire one from start to finish for a larger fee.

HAVE YOU PLANNED WEDDINGS IN THIS DESTINATION AND VENUE BEFORE?

POINTER: Although firsthand knowledge is always best, don't worry if your coordinator hasn't done a wedding at your resort before. Do try to find someone who's done a wedding in your state or country, however, to make sure they're familiar with the local customs, vendors, and/or language.

HOW MANY WEDDINGS HAVE YOU DONE THERE? IF NONE, HAVE YOU DONE WEDDINGS IN SIMILAR DESTINATIONS?

POINTER: Recommendations are indispensable in this situation. Ask the coordinator to put you in touch with couples whose weddings he or she has coordinated in locations similar to yours. Ask them about the coordinator's attention to detail, creativity, professionalism, and accessibility.

DO YOU HAVE PARTICULAR VENDORS YOU LIKE TO WORK WITH?

POINTER: Many event planners have their go-to sources for certain services—two or three photographers whose work and professionalism they prefer, a local transportation service that has never let them down. Don't expect them to share names (that type of info is a trade secret), but listen for their enthusiasm and confidence about their resources.

why you need wedding insurance

It's extremely important that you have insurance for a destination wedding. Although you don't want to think about it, serious problems (natural disasters, medical emergencies) can arise. But if the worst does occur, you'll be comforted knowing you won't suffer a financial loss as well as an emotional one.

You can purchase wedding insurance policies from a handful of different companies (visit TheKnot.com/insurance for a current list of resources). The cost will vary depending on the level of coverage you buy, but plan to spend between $200 and $800. Although that may sound like a lot of money to spend on something you probably won't have to use (fingers crossed), you'll realize it's worth it when you consider the following list of worst-case scenarios wedding insurance can protect you against:

Natural disasters. Not only should you protect against the possibility that your venue could be destroyed in a hurricane or a fire—forcing you to reschedule the wedding—but a huge storm closer to home could prevent you or the majority of your guests from getting to the destination (even if the destination wasn't affected). In either case, you'll need coverage so that your expenses will be reimbursed.

Personal illness. If you or a family member gets seriously ill and the wedding has to be postponed, insurance will cover your deposits and reimburse you for many of your costs.

Vendors who let you down. Insurance can reimburse you if a vendor fails to show up or perform and you have to make other arrangements: For example, the bus slated to take people from the ceremony to the reception never materializes and you have to charter a fleet of taxis for three times the price, or your photographer falls ill and you have to hire a more high-end replacement.

Loss of or damage to wedding essentials. If the bridal gown or any other key items have to be replaced at the last minute, insurance can cover the cost.

Personal liability. This covers any expenses you might be responsible for if somebody is injured at your wedding or property at the wedding site is harmed by you or one of your guests. Check to see if your venue is insured against such possibilities (most large or reputable resorts will be). In that case, you probably don't need to buy extra liability insurance.

CAN YOU HELP ME WITH MY HONEYMOON ARRANGEMENTS?

POINTER: It is an especially nice perk if your coordinator is an expert in the destination and you plan to take your honeymoon near where you're getting married. He or she will likely know all the luxury properties in the area and be able to pull together the perfect trip. Ask whether this service is included in the fee.

WHAT IS THE FEE TO START THE PROCESS? IS A DEPOSIT REQUIRED?

POINTER: When you're ready to sign a contract, list as many of the items you want your planner to help you with as possible: handle group travel arrangements, assemble welcome bags, plan activities, and so on. Take a look at the to-do list on pages vi–xviii to help you identify these tasks. Make sure everything you expect is noted in the contract.

calling all caterers

Ensuring that the food is absolutely delicious is one of your foremost priorities.

GO LOCAL OR IMPORT? Go local. In most instances, you'll be working with an in-house caterer, but even if you need to hire somebody from outside, it's still smart to stick with a local vendor.

Questions to Ask

WHAT'S INCLUDED IN THE PRICE?

POINTER: Most catering is priced per head and includes the food and drinks. But some caterers will charge additional fees for services such as room setup, food carvers (if you have stations), specialty linens, cake cutting, and bartenders. Be sure to get all of these details in writing.

TIP

Even if you have enlisted the services of a planner who will be delivering vendors and negotiating contracts, you need to know what questions to ask. Details on each category—from caterers to makeup artists—begin below.

TIP

Using in-house catering doesn't mean you can't make special requests, so the chef should be open to tweaking the menu. Remember, the venue as a whole—including the caterer—has a job: making you happy. (Learn how to spice up your wedding day menu on page 139.)

Assembling Your "A" Team

the art of negotiating

Know the market. Find out what other vendors at your destination charge, and use this as leverage. Ask about everything included in your package. Would eliminating any extras you're not interested in reduce the cost (e.g., the caterer's price includes printing menus, but you'd rather have your stationer do it or skip it altogether)?

Practice makes perfect. Try your hand at negotiating the little things (the room rates) before taking on the biggies (the band).

Get creative with pricing scenarios. A vendor may be willing to cut a deal as long as you agree to something additional (a photographer may charge less per hour if you include an extra two hours of shooting). Confirm that the compromise won't actually cost more in the end.

Be clear about your budget. If a vendor is excited to work with you, he or she will try to work within your budget and suggest creative alternatives such as replacing imported blooms with equally stylish seasonal ones.

Appear indifferent. You need the vendor to believe that if he or she won't meet your offer, you will walk away. Of course, don't threaten to walk if you really want to hire that person—the threat won't necessarily make the vendor want to work with you. Respect the vendor's talents and believe it when he or she says, "I can't do that."

Know when to hold 'em. If your vendor has negotiated in what you think is good faith by taking 10 percent off or upgrading your linens, don't keep pushing. If you feel you've both compromised and are within your budget, get ready to sign your contract. There's truth in an old business rule: You always want the person working for you to make a profit—you'll get better work.

WHAT ARE THE RECOMMENDED MENUS?

POINTER: Many venues can give you a preplanned catering list before you book to give you an idea of their sample fare for a wedding party.

CAN YOU RECOMMEND SOME REGIONAL OR KITCHEN SPECIALTIES?

POINTER: Recommended menus are designed to be the most pleasing to the most people, but you can still get better or more interesting food for close to the same price. Your catering manager may be able to recommend an alternative, like a seasonal vegetable, a traditional island dish, or a gourmet entrée he or she likes that didn't make the basic menu, just for the asking. And you can also ask how the chef would upgrade a dish or two to evaluate if it's worth the extra expense to add a course, a meat choice, or a specialty dish.

WILL YOU ARRANGE FOR A TASTING BEFORE BOOKING?

POINTER: If you've already fallen in love with and booked an all-inclusive location, this is probably a done deal, but if you're working with an outside caterer, try to fit in a tasting. If for some reason you can't get a preview, ask for references of other couples who wed there. Sure, everyone's taste is different, but they should be able to give you some perspective about what to expect.

Q & A

I want to hire a babysitter to look after guests' children on the night of my reception. How do I go about it—and politely tell guests that their kids aren't welcome at the party?

To find a great babysitter, ask your wedding planner, on-site coordinator, or hotel concierge (or all three) for a referral. Look for somebody with lots of experience with children (i.e., not the catering manager's teenage daughter) and check references.

Let guests know early on that children aren't invited to the reception by indicating both in the save-the-dates and on your wedding website that babysitting will be available on the night of the wedding. Then, when you send out the official invitations, put only the names of adults on them. A follow-up phone call from a member of the wedding party verifies that everyone is clear about the arrangements being made.

Although it's absolutely your prerogative to have a kid-free reception, know that some of the parents on your guest list will be uncomfortable about leaving their children with a stranger, especially if your destination is a foreign country. To calm their nerves, arrange for the babysitting to take place at the reception site if possible (in a hotel suite, perhaps), so that parents can steal away from the festivities for a few minutes to check on their kids. Assure them that the sitter comes highly recommended and that you've checked references.

HOW WILL YOU ADDRESS MY SPECIAL NEEDS?

POINTER: If you require kosher meals or a specific type of ethnic food, your location will most likely let you use an outside caterer who specializes in your chosen cuisine. However, they will probably charge you an extra fee for each meal served by your outside caterer, so be sure to get those details in writing in advance.

ARE YOU WILLING TO WORK WITH ME ON THE MENU TO INCLUDE FAVORITE RECIPES OR MENU SUGGESTIONS?

POINTER: Personalizing your menu is a great way to make your meal memorable. That said, some caterers might not be amenable to deviating from their own recipes or usual menus. If you can't convince yours to work in a big change, think smaller: Add a couple of your favorite cookies to the dessert course, or get a garnish for the main course that matches your wedding colors.

WHAT TYPES OF LINENS, TABLES, CHAIRS, AND DINNERWARE ARE INCLUDED IN THE FEE?

POINTER: It's always a good idea to double-check your contract to make sure your vendor's provisions are up to snuff. Many to-be-weds have special ideas for their decor, and basic white ballroom tablecloths may not fit that design scheme. Including elements like Chivari chairs, specialty linens, slipcovers, custom-dyed table runners, and antique silverware may require a whole new vendor. Your caterer or site can supplement any basics you lack, but ask your florist, your wedding planner, or an outside event planner to help you carry out highly detailed design elements. (For more on choosing your decor, go to chapter 7.)

ARE YOU WORKING OTHER WEDDINGS ON THE SAME WEEKEND?

POINTER: This is not a deal breaker, but it is something you'll want to know. You're really asking, "Will you be focused on my event?" Will they be available to deal with any last-minute questions? And feel free to ask them how many weddings they've successfully pulled off on the same weekend—it may be the norm for a large, well-organized company to juggle multiple events. If that's the case, they can give you references: Check with other brides to make sure they didn't feel neglected.

ARE THERE CORKAGE OR POURING FEES IF I PURCHASE THE LIQUOR, OR CAKE-CUTTING FEES IF I BRING IN AN OUTSIDE CAKE?

POINTER: Fees like these (which are usually no more than $1.50–$3 per slice of cake or $10–$20 per bottle of wine) are sometimes built into your contract as, yes, a little punishment for not letting your site provide the liquor or cake. Alcohol markups are a huge profit center for the food service industry, and you're likely to have to pay that cost one way or another. Bottom line: getting your own bottles may not be as much of a steal as you think.

IS A CHAMPAGNE TOAST INCLUDED?

POINTER: Many all-inclusive sites include a round of bubbly to toast the newlyweds. Check in advance whether you're getting one—it will help you figure out what you need to stock the bar. If for some reason you don't want one, find out if the toast can be nixed and the cost lowered accordingly.

HOW EXTENSIVE IS YOUR WINE LIST?

POINTER: If you're able to choose beyond the basic red and white, go for it! Selecting the wines yourselves—even from a prescribed menu—adds a personalized touch to any meal. Most caterers are responsive to the growing importance of wine at weddings, so don't assume that what's on the menu is all that's available. Some companies are willing to work with you to provide a certain vintage that you want to serve for sentimental, geographic, or plain old taste reasons. You may incur corking or pouring fees, even if you use the company's selections. Watch out for unanticipated service charges. Negotiate all gratuities and other service fees (some caterers charge a percentage of the wine's cost and a restocking fee for unused bottles) in advance, and include them in your contract so you won't be surprised by extra labor costs.

> **TIP**
>
> If you're set on a cake from an outside baker, then don't even question the venue's per-slice service costs. Cutting fees are just another item to absorb into your budget—and a small price to pay for getting the cake of your dreams.

> **TIP**
>
> If your caterer's fancier creations don't taste five-star to you, ask the kitchen to create simple, classic fare instead. The majority of your guests will be thrilled with basics like roast chicken and mashed potatoes or burgers and fries—dishes that are incredibly hard to screw up.

tips on importing your pros

Whenever possible, choose local florists, musicians, and caterers. But for more control over services like photography and video, consider flying in a professional. Here are a few details to anticipate:

Be prepared for the added expense. You'll be expected to pay for airfare, transfers, meals, and hotel rooms for your vendors (and often for their assistants). Some charge their day rate for each travel day. Fees for a rental car or toting their equipment may also be your responsibility.

Honor their travel requests. Some vendors insist on making their own travel reservations. While you do not have to pay for first class, you should respect their airline preferences: Many professionals have established relationships with specific carriers and other companies based on their needs—for example, a good insurance policy in case equipment/baggage is damaged or accommodations for a fragile cake.

Investigate visas. In some countries your vendor may have to apply for a special visa or work permit in order to service your ceremony. Rather than encourage him or her to work around this "inconvenience," recognize that attention to bureaucratic red tape is the sign of a true professional.

Ask for an early arrival. Arranging to have your vendors arrive in town twenty-four hours ahead of time is always a good idea, even if it adds a day to their fees. In case of inclement weather or other unforeseen glitches, your pro will still have time to make alternative travel plans or hop on a later flight.

Get detailed estimates. Ask questions up front about what your vendor expects in regard to time and expense so you aren't stuck with any unpleasant surprises (as in out-of-your-budget bills) after you get home from your honeymoon.

Agree on a per diem. Establish dollar limits for meals each day. If you know your photographer has agreed to spend only $50 a day on food, you won't panic when you hear him ordering an expensive cognac at the end of the night. He's probably doing it on his own dime.

Include them in your calculations. Calculate your photographer, officiant, or planner into your head counts for events like the rehearsal dinner and lunch onboard the boat. If your budget allows, it will be easier than having them run off to find their own food during the evenings' festivities.

who bakes the cake?

Having a beautifully designed, delectable wedding cake will be, well, like the cherry on top of the cake of your day. Fortunately, talented pastry chefs can be found in every corner of the world.

GO LOCAL OR IMPORT? The caterer you're working with will no doubt be able to supply a great cake, but if it's your dream to have a luxe cake from a well-known baker in the States, it is in fact possible to have it flown in (usually accompanied by someone to assemble it). Regardless of who makes your cake, your first step should be to have a tasting—ask to try several different options. If you don't like the way a cake tastes, no matter how nicely they ice or stack your tiers, it's not for you.

Questions to Ask

HOW MUCH DOES YOUR AVERAGE CAKE COST?

POINTER: At many resorts, the cake is included in the catering fee. For other locations, cakes are most often priced per slice, and the more complex the decorating, the more expensive it gets. Keep in mind that many pastry chefs won't bake a wedding cake for fewer than fifty guests.

WHAT INGREDIENTS ARE USED?

POINTER: Expect the standard fare, but always ask in case you have any food allergies (especially to nuts) or if there's a potential substitution you feel strongly about (for example, you want real butter and absolutely no margarine). Depending on where you're marrying, you may need to be a bit flexible. If you really like a baker's work but you're not wild about the cake ingredients, do a tasting. Can you really notice the difference?

HOW FAR IN ADVANCE ARE CAKES PREPARED?

POINTER: Here's the timeline you want to shoot for: Most of the time, cakes are baked the day before a wedding. Complicated decorations like sugar flowers are prepared earlier, since they're time-consuming and often need time to

TIP

Many non-American bakers may not be experienced with fashioning elaborate decorations such as sugar flowers. Don't try to convince them to attempt a cake style beyond their skill set; work with what they know.

TIP

Make sure every little thing you want your guests to put in their mouths—from crudités at cocktail hour to petits fours served with the after-dinner coffee—is clearly spelled out in the contract. Keep in mind that American-style, three-course fare is not the norm everywhere. In Italy, for example, a traditional wedding meal is light bites in the afternoon.

harden or dry. It's okay (and totally normal) for your cake to be sitting around overnight—but it probably won't be at its tastiest if it's ready more than two days in advance.

WILL YOU WORK WITH MY FLORIST TO MATCH STYLES?

POINTER: If you plan on using fresh flowers to decorate your cake, you might want to put your florist in touch with your baker to be sure that they're both on the same page designwise. You should let your baker know that you plan on adding blooms to your cake. Tell your florist that the flowers are for a cake (they need to be well cleaned and pesticide free). Whoever is cutting your cake should be told whether or not the flowers are edible, so that blooms intended for decoration only can be removed and set aside instead of winding up on your guests' plates.

WHAT ARE YOUR MOST POPULAR FLAVORS OR FILLINGS? DO SOME COST MORE THAN OTHERS?

POINTER: Keep your mind open to fun flavors that may feel special and reflect your location. Be prepared to pay extra for some choices. Why? Your baker will have to buy different ingredients (and may have to put in more hours) to create something that's not your basic white wedding cake. The same goes for fillings: Variations on a basic buttercream will usually fall within a pretty small price range, but more exotic fillings like fresh fruit preserves or liqueur-infused spreads may get pricey.

WHAT IS THE DELIVERY PROCESS?

POINTER: Your cake is going to be a center of attention at your reception, so you need to make sure this guest of honor gets there on time and unscathed. Your baker will know the best way to transport it, even if it's fully decorated in tiers and needs to be completely assembled on-site by the pastry chef who's flying in with the confection. (Yes, you may be responsible for another vendor's airfare and day rate if your cake comes with a baker in tow.) Put the cake delivery on your wedding day schedule, and if it's coming from off-site, give the baker the name of a contact at your venue who will know where the cake should go and how it should be set up (special table decoration, refrigeration, etc.). Be sure to ask if there is a fee.

managing your vendors from afar

Hiring vendors and handling these relationships can be very tricky when the people you're working with are in a different city or country or on a different continent—especially when cultural and even language barriers stand between you. Use these pointers to bridge the spoken and unspoken distances:

Find out the best way to communicate. Don't assume it is e-mail. It may seem strange to us when someone doesn't check e-mail every five minutes, but for an on-the-go vendor without a PDA, once a day might be a lot.

Show, don't tell. Whenever possible, try to find a way to communicate your desires with examples, not just words: e-mail digital photos of centerpieces you like to your florist; send CDs of your favorite songs to your band or DJ. Keep written records and printouts so that you can refer back to them.

Have a final in-person meeting. As soon as you arrive at your destination before the wedding, have a final in-person meeting or walk-through with each vendor to make sure nothing was lost in translation during your long-distance dealings. Bring your records and images with you so that you can easily resolve any last-minute confusion over what you want. If any of their plans aren't to your liking, you'll still have time to make changes.

Be understanding, but be understood. When you are dealing with professionals for whom English is a second language, you need to be careful. Even though communication may at times be frustrating, don't treat them disrespectfully and assume people are less intelligent—it will get you nowhere. Instead, stick with simple language ("green" not "chartreuse"), find someone to act as translator (your coordinator or their assistant), and keep as much communication as possible in writing (the fax machine may be your new best friend).

finding a florist

TIP

Spell out in your contract
with the florist all flowers
and/or foliage you definitely
do not want included in your
floral design. For instance,
to reduce the chance that
the arrangements look like
something made for Secre-
tary's Day, stipulate that you
don't want any carnations,
daisies, mums, or baby's
breath.

Whether your decor involves decking out a tent and a huge ball-room or simply adding a few blossoms to table settings, you want the bouquets and boutonnieres to be stunning.

GO LOCAL OR IMPORT? It makes sense to use a local florist, unless your budget is well into the six figures. Many florists in foreign destinations may have a pretty generic, FTD style that won't be up-to-the-second stylish. This doesn't mean you have to settle for substandard blooms—you simply need to take a very hands-on role in directing the design of the arrangements. Send lots of photos of bouquets and centerpieces you like, and stick with simple ideas that highlight your wedding's look and its physical setting. Going gaga over the latest trend from a celebrity floral designer will add little to your day except an inflated bill and flowers that may not match their surroundings.

Questions to Ask

HOW WOULD YOU DESCRIBE YOUR STYLE? WHAT ARE YOU MOST KNOWN FOR?

POINTER: You want to find a floral designer who has a vision and is excited about his work. Ask him to describe and show you some of his creations from recent weddings.

HAVE YOU DONE WEDDINGS AT MY CEREMONY/RECEPTION SITE BEFORE?

POINTER: If the answer is yes, great! Ask to see pictures, and follow up with questions about how the florists dealt with any site-specific issues you may have noticed (e.g., view-obstructing columns, low ceilings). If the answer is no, ask them to take a look at the site beforehand (ideally with you, so you can point things out and tackle any problems together). Either way, you're looking to hear what ideas they have for your site.

HOW WILL WE WORK TOGETHER?

POINTER: Since the flowers are a big part of your wedding's decor, you no doubt want to check out the florist's vision for your wedding before the big day. Most will design sample center-pieces for you to look at and make changes based on your feed-back. Arrange for this on one of your visits. If you're not making a prewedding trip, the florist can take photos and e-mail them to you, or you can arrange to meet with him or her when you first arrive at the destination right before the wedding.

TIP

If your favorite flowers turn out to be the priciest ones (and isn't that always how it is?), ask about substitutions with the same look or in the same color scheme that create a similar effect. Splurge on your expensive favorites for your bridal bouquet. (Which blossoms work best for your destination? Find out on page 137.)

WILL YOU BE INVOLVED IN SITE SETUP AND WORK WITH THE VENUE ON THE EVENT DESIGN?

POINTER: You want your florist to be hands-on. Blooms delivered to workers at your venue on your wedding day may not be set up exactly as you'd imagined (yes, even if you've sent detailed instructions). Likewise, you want the florist to be in touch with your site during the planning to work out scheduling and compromise on any potential issues (for example, if you want rose petals sprinkled everywhere and your site manager's fretting about the mess).

WHO WILL BE PRESENT ON THE DAY OF THE WEDDING?

POINTER: If the florist you're meeting with won't be around to set up, it's not a deal breaker. The key is to have your designer of choice build the actual arrangements, and if he or she has trusted assistants who can follow the setup instructions to a tee, the rest is easy. That said, it is still preferable to have your actual florist pitching in on the big day, since he or she is the one who really knows the plan inside and out.

ARE THERE CERTAIN BLOOMS YOU LOVE TO WORK WITH? ANY TO AVOID?

POINTER: Listen for a knowledge of what flowers are in season, easy to get in the location, and stand up well to all local conditions.

Skip the penalty clause in
band and DJ contracts that
imposes a fee if they inad-
vertently use songs on your
"do not play" list—maybe
that ear-cringing version of
"Macarena" was actually
requested by your great-
aunt, who's still excited that
she knows how to do it.
Instead, make sure the musicians have a list of what
they must play, and work
from there.

mastering the musicians

You want to engage a band or a DJ who will get your guests up
and moving, while creating the exact mood you have in mind for
the occasion. In addition to reception entertainment, you may also
want to hire separate musicians for your ceremony, cocktail hour,
and even after-party.

GO LOCAL OR IMPORT? Paying for an entire band to travel, along with
their equipment, to your destination is probably prohibitively expensive. However, if you can't get married without KC and the Sunshine
Band or a hometown band you and your friends are absolutely nuts for
in attendance, it may well be worth it. Overall, though, you should be
able to find a local band or a DJ who will do a great job, but you'll
probably need to give very clear instructions to avoid musical misun-
derstandings. If you're using a DJ outside the United States, there's a good chance his
or her selection of the latest tunes may not be up to your standard, so be prepared to
supply some of the music.

Questions to Ask

HOW LONG WILL YOU PLAY?

POINTER: The answer depends on a number of factors: how long your party will
be, what kind of set the band usually does, and whether your site imposes any
restrictions (either about noise after a certain hour or about the amount of
time you're allowed to use the space). Find out beforehand how much time is
included in their basic contract and the cost of overtime if you're planning a
longer reception. Chances are you'll pay less if you plan for an extra hour up
front rather than have to beg for it on the night of your celebration.

HOW MANY BREAKS DO YOU TAKE, AND FOR HOW LONG?

POINTER: The party's just heating up and then . . . break time. A good DJ or MC
should be able to avoid an abrupt halt to the festivities, but finding out when
the breaks are scheduled also helps to keep the party flowing no matter what
the music. The duration and number of breaks will depend on what kind of
entertainment you have and how long your party goes. If you want to keep

the house rocking all night long, trust us, the band is going to need some time off! Also, don't forget to schedule in one break that will allow your musicians time to eat dinner.

TIP

Ensure that your band doesn't show up with substitute musicians: Write the names of the musicians you saw and heard when you hired them into your contract. Require advance notice and approval if one of them will not be present at the wedding. (Have your guests boogying all night long with the tips on page 144.)

WHEN YOU'RE ON A BREAK, WILL YOU PLAY A CD? DO I NEED TO SUPPLY IT?

POINTER: Chances are the sound system won't go silent, but find out beforehand if you are responsible for providing the tunes. If they supply the music, ask for permission to pick songs that fit your vibe.

WHAT WILL YOU BE WEARING?

POINTER: It sounds weird, but think about it: If they're wearing tuxes and you're down with that, fine. But if your twelve-piece band shows up in gold lamé, you might not be so thrilled. Don't be afraid to ask about their wardrobe—and if you're not happy about it, feel free to request alternative garb. Your musicians will be front and center, so they should fit the look and feel of your wedding.

HOW LONG DO YOU NEED FOR SETUP?

POINTER: Find out how much time it will take them to get everything ready and do a sound check, then ask your venue if it's cool for your musicians to be in your space beforehand (that way, you won't have to subject your guests to a half hour of "testing . . . one, two, three"). If your site is hosting multiple weddings that day and there is a time crunch, this may not be an option, so figure out where everyone needs to be (maybe you can keep the cocktail hour outside?) to ensure that the setup is snag free.

HOW MUCH SPACE DO YOU NEED?

POINTER: Space for the band or DJ should be one of your considerations when choosing your site (an orchestra will overwhelm a small site, a string trio's sound may get lost in a cavernous hall). Determine exactly how much space the band and its equipment will occupy so you can figure out where to put them. Are there any must-haves—outlets, extension cords, etc.—for the performance? Be sure your site will provide them.

Assembling Your "A" Team

picking a photographer and a videographer

Your wedding will last only a few hours, but you'll want memories of it forever.

GO LOCAL OR IMPORT? If you fly in only one vendor, make it the photographer. Since so many of the dealings with your shutterbug will take place *after* the wedding (seeing negatives, ordering prints, assembling albums, etc.), it's actually more convenient to have that professional based near you. And if you use a local photographer in another country and something goes wrong (worst-case scenario: He or she loses the film), you'll have little or no legal recourse. Also, as a stylistic consideration, American wedding photographers tend to have a much more journalistic style than many of their foreign counterparts (who often take more traditional, posed photos), so if you're marrying abroad and would like your photos to have a natural, candid look, you may want to fly in a photographer. The same considerations would apply to your videographer, though importing both could get pricey. You may want to decide which medium is most important to you, then import that pro and hire the other locally.

Questions to Ask

WHAT FORMAT DO YOU SHOOT IN?

POINTER: Photographers should be using a 35mm professional SLR (single-lens reflex) camera or better. If they shoot in digital, make sure you'll get quality pictures by checking out the black-and-white shots—they should have the same beautiful varieties of tone you'd expect from black-and-white film. Shooting in digital has become the norm in wedding videography, and the industry standard is a three-chip DV (digital video) camera.

CAN I SEE ALBUMS/VIDEOS FROM SIMILAR WEDDINGS YOU HAVE SHOT?

POINTER: Reviewing the body of work of a photographer or videographer will give you a good sense of his or her style. Ask to see entire albums or videos rather than just a portfolio or a highlight reel to get a much better idea of how the cameraman captures a wedding as a whole.

WHAT IS YOUR PHILOSOPHY ABOUT SHOOTING WEDDINGS?

POINTER: Asking this touchy-feely question will help you to gauge the pro's passion and enthusiasm for his or her work. It's also a good way to determine whether your style meshes with your vendor's.

WILL I GET NEGATIVES, OR DO I HAVE TO ORDER ALL PRINTS THROUGH YOU?

POINTER: Though they are photos of your wedding, the images you get may not be your wedding photos, so to speak. Read over your contract carefully to find out who owns the rights to your photos and what the deal is when it comes to reprinting them. You will get at least one copy of all of your photos as prints, but if you want reprints you may need to go through your photographer to get them if you don't own your negatives.

IF YOU'RE USING SOMEONE LOCAL: CAN I GET NEGATIVES OR PROOFS BEFORE I LEAVE THE DESTINATION?

POINTER: Getting the negatives or proofs from a local photographer while you're still at your venue will speed up your time frame and make everything easier—for you, that is. Your photographer may not be able to accommodate your request, especially if you're not sticking around long after the wedding. Try to get a time estimate before the wedding so that you'll know what to expect.

HOW DO YOU DETERMINE PRICE: BY HOUR, NUMBER OF PICTURES, PROCESSING TIME, OR A COMBO?

POINTER: If you love a photographer's work but don't need as much from him or her as is quoted in the package, ask about ordering à la carte or lowering the base fee in exchange for the additional cost you'll be paying for travel time. Photographers should be able to give you an estimate based on the length of your event, the number of guests, and the amount of time they'll be in transit, which are the stats they usually use to figure out what their services will cost for your wedding.

> TIP
>
> The pace of things at some destinations tends to be more laid-back and the service, well, slower than what we're used to in the United States. Ask brides who've been there or local coordinators for an honest perspective of how "on time" works at your destination. If flexible schedules are the norm, definitely schedule your wedding day hair and makeup for earlier than you would otherwise. It's better to be sitting around for a few extra hours looking divine than rushing half-done into your own ceremony!

IS THERE AN ASSISTANT OR A SECOND CAMERA, AND IF SO, IS THERE AN ADDITIONAL FEE?

POINTER: If you are having an especially large event or if your pro is bringing a lot of equipment, there's a good chance he or she will want to bring an assistant, either to provide more complete coverage of your wedding or just to have someone there as a right hand. It's generally to your advantage to have the assistant around, but find out beforehand how much it will cost for the sake of your budget.

HAVE THE PHOTOGRAPHER AND VIDEOGRAPHER EVER WORKED TOGETHER BEFORE?

POINTER: A team that has is ideal because they know each other's wants and needs. If they haven't, it's a good idea to introduce them prior to the event if possible. The final walk-through before your wedding is a good time to do this—that way, they can plan out where they'll stand in order to get the best shots (without one winding up in the other's shot).

HAVE YOU EVER SHOT/FILMED A WEDDING AT MY SITE?

POINTER: Don't worry too much if the answer is no—but do find out if they can take a quick spin around the site with you so that you can show them where key stuff like the grand entrance or cake cutting is happening. It's a good idea to do this at the time of day when your wedding will take place so they can get a sense of the lighting. If they've worked at the site before, ask for their opinion on the pros and cons of shooting there—if you're happy with the answers (they seem to know their stuff), skip the tour.

WILL YOU ACCEPT A LIST OF MUST-TAKE SHOTS?

POINTER: If there are certain moments you really want to include in your wedding photos or video, find out ahead of time how much direction your photographer and videographer are willing to take. You don't want to infringe on their artistic license (you probably picked the wrong person if you feel compelled to); you just want to be sure that they will listen to what you want.

destination beauty rules

The bride's beauty strategy needs to be a bit specialized for a destination wedding: Beauty secrets that never fail to create a stunning look at home may fall short in other climates.

WARM CLIMATES

If you're not careful, heat and humidity can be harsh on your appearance, triggering rashes, oily skin, makeup meltdowns, and haywire hair. These practical tips can help you keep your cool:

Be scrupulous about SPF. Starting the second you arrive, use sunscreen with an SPF of at least 15 every time you step outdoors. It's much easier to fake a glow with bronzer than to try to cover up a burn.

Work with your hair's natural texture. A blowout that turns your corkscrew curls into pin-straight strands won't maintain its silkiness beyond the ceremony if the weather is super-steamy. Opt for a style that doesn't fight what your hair wants to do.

Switch to summer products. If your skin tends to get shiny, switch to lighter skincare products for the duration of your stay. Use a gel cleanser instead of a cream, add a shine-fighting toner to your regimen, and stick to oil-free moisturizers.

Stick with waterproof makeup. It will stay put longer in humidity.

Fight shine on the fly. Stash a packet of blotting papers in your bridal bag for quick shine-banishing fixes.

Consider wearing your hair up and off your neck. You'll feel cool and look elegant.

COOL CLIMATES

Mountain regions and other cool, dry climates can present their own beauty challenges: Think dry, chapped skin and flyaway hair. Use these tips to cope:

Get smooth and soft from head to toe by exfoliating all over in the shower with a sugar scrub (the natural enzymes in sugar are powerful sloughers that won't irritate skin), followed by a postshower application of rich body butter. If you take baths, add moisturizing oils to the water.

Before bed, rub a rich moisturizer or a petroleum jelly product on your nails, feet, and elbows. Wear thick socks over your feet to help it soak in.

Get weekly pedicures in the month leading up to your wedding, and keep your feet soft by smoothing them with a pumice stone in the shower.

Battle chapped lips with an SPF-spiked lip balm.

Deal with dry facial skin by using rich lotions and a biweekly moisturizing mask. Consider buying a moisturizing foundation for your wedding (but test it out before you arrive at your destination to see how your skin reacts).

Add a little extra drama to your makeup effect. During your trial run, test out dramatic hues, a glossier mouth, and playing with a touch of shimmer on your eyes or cheeks to create a radiant, lit-from-within look.

hiring hair and makeup artists

TIP

Finding one person who can do both hair and makeup will cost less than hiring a separate hairstylist and makeup artist. You can also save time and dough if your bridesmaids arrive with their hair blow-dried and their basic makeup already done. Then the pros can put the finishing touches on their dos and faces rather than start from scratch.

You can look drop-dead gorgeous on your wedding day, even if you're getting married halfway around the world.

GO LOCAL OR IMPORT? Unless your hairstylist is a friend who would be at the wedding anyway, skip paying the travel costs of your hair and makeup team. Hire local stylists instead and arrange a trial session or two on one of your planning visits to be sure you are comfortable with their approach. If you aren't able to have an in-person trial, photos are essential. Have your hair and makeup done at home and take photographs to e-mail to the local hairstylist and makeup artist you'll be using; ask them to take before-and-after pictures of their clients to show you their skills (take special note of their ability to work with your type of hair—say, transforming curly hair into a sleek updo or volumizing limp hair with extensions). Have a trial session with them a few days before the wedding once you've arrived at your destination.

Questions to Ask

HOW WILL THE CLIMATE AFFECT MY HAIR AND SKIN?

POINTER: An in-the-know artist will be able to explain the potential havoc the local weather can wreak on certain types of hair and skin. A savvy stylist can tell you what to factor in—dryness, frizziness—before you choose a style.

HOW LONG WILL MY MAKEUP LAST?

POINTER: You want to stay fresh-faced, especially in hot and humid areas. Ask for an estimate of how long the makeup will hold up, as well as tips on refreshing it (don't take "Don't worry about it" for an answer here).

WHAT ARE THE BIGGEST CHALLENGES YOU'VE FACED WITH A BRIDAL CLIENT?

POINTER: Don't expect stylists to dish dirt on their clients, but ask them to be honest about problems they've encountered: a hairdo that wilted between the car and the church, mascara that ran during a bride's tearful vows, a bride who changed the orders for her attendants' hair after half of them had been styled. Their tales of woe will give you insight into how they handle crises.

HOW MUCH TIME SHOULD BE SET ASIDE FOR EACH PERSON?

POINTER: If the stylist has been involved in weddings before, he or she should be able to give you a realistic estimate of how long it will take to make you and your bridal party look fabulous (don't forget about your mom and future mother-in-law, too!). Our advice: Always add on an extra half hour.

WILL YOU STAY THROUGH THE FIRST PART OF THE RECEPTION FOR TOUCH-UPS?

POINTER: Many brides need a touch-up after the ceremony (especially if you're taking formal pictures during the cocktail hour). Though your hair and makeup team probably won't stay for the whole wedding, find out if they can wait through the ceremony to do just a quick pick-me-up before it's time to party. If they can't stay, ask them to show your mom or maid of honor what to do. This is especially important if you need to remove your veil after the ceremony, so make sure they know how to do it without mussing your coif.

IF I'M SUPPLYING MY OWN MAKEUP, WHAT EXACTLY DO YOU NEED ME TO BRING?

POINTER: Packing your own makeup means you don't risk the horror of having a bad skin reaction to a new product on your wedding day. That said, your stylist might still give you a shopping list of products that you don't generally use, like a heavy-duty foundation, to test on your skin before the big day. You should also be sure to ask about who will be providing other tools like makeup brushes and straightening irons so that you know to bring along anything they can't provide for you.

bridal beauty tips

Follow these pointers to ensure your stylist will be able to do her very best work on your wedding day.

O Wear a white robe or button-down shirt when you get your hair and makeup done so you can slip out of it without pulling it over your head and messing up your hair or face. (If you wear white, your cosmetician can see how the makeup will look with your dress.)

O For your makeup application, natural light is best. If possible, set up a table near a window. If there's no natural light available, use a superbright lamp.

O If you're getting ready at a hotel, ask for a high bar stool so you can be on eye level with your makeup artist.

O When getting your hair styled, sit in a low-backed chair in front of a low counter with a mirror so your stylist will have easy access to your tresses. And make sure there are electrical outlets nearby for appliances such as hair dryers, curling irons, and electric rollers. For extra insurance, bring a few extension cords.

O Ask your stylist how they'd like you to prepare for your makeup application and hair transformation. Should you arrive mascara-free and moisturized? Should you wash your hair that morning or not?

SANDRA & KEVIN · KAUAI, HI

Hometown: San Francisco, CA
Guests: 200

The Destination Decision: The couple chose Hawaii for their "beach chic meets haute couture" wedding. Sandra, an interior designer, had a hands-on approach to the wedding's look: She planned the entire thing from the mainland, had Thai silk shantung fabric runners custom-made, designed her own dress, and developed a decidedly un-beachy palette of ivory, champagne, coral, and deep red.

Planning Pointer: A natural organizer, Sandra tried to get everything booked as early as possible. She soon learned that her type A approach wasn't effective in long-distance negotiations. "Vendors in Hawaii have a much more relaxed approach and didn't confirm details until very close to the wedding date. It was probably a good thing—it taught me to have patience!"

The Definitive Detail: Sandra limited the use of orchids so that the wedding wouldn't look "too Hawaiian," but the islands' flair was everywhere. The couple exchanged vows in front of four beachside palm trees instead of an altar. Sandra's brothers wrote songs that they sang, and one of her brothers even learned to play a Hawaiian staple, the ukulele, for the performance. Each table at the reception was named after a different Hawaiian island. Tiki torches and mai tais dotted the reception. Favors were chocolate-dipped macadamia nut shortbread cookies from Big Island Candies.

Ch. 4

be my guests:
who to invite and how

A destination wedding requires lots of proactive and detailed communication with your guests *before* the event. Your goal is to make everything having to do with the wedding as easy as possible for them—from deciding whether they can make it to figuring out the most convenient way to get there, from finding lodging that fits their tastes and budgets to locating a great salon for prewedding primping.

You need to consider yourself travel agent, concierge, and cruise director from the day the save-the-dates go out until the moment you kiss the last guest good-bye. But—and this is *key*—the whole process needs to be easy, and actually enjoyable, for you, too: The second your guests see you stressed, they'll feel uncomfortable, which is the total opposite of the effect you want your wedding to have on them. Sound impossible? Well, it's not—with proper planning and a little help from the right people—and we can prove it.

your VIPs: the wedding party

The most important part of your guest list is your wedding party. These chosen few will share in the most intimate moments of your wedding day, from fastening the bride's bustier to calming the groom's nerves before he heads down the aisle. Their job as attendants is to assist with certain parts of the wedding planning, such as helping to pick out invitations or hauling the dress back home.

Decide on the perfect members for your party as early as possible. While you can have two or ten attendants, a good rule of thumb is one (on each side) for every twenty-five guests. Keep in mind that having more people involved doesn't necessarily mean less stress—all those personalities to manage, and too many well-meaning people asking how they can help, can actually become a bad thing. It's quality, not quantity, that counts: You want the *right* attendants.

PREPARE YOUR PARTY. Give your chosen few an honest idea up front of what you'll need from them. In addition to the traditional duties, attendants at a destination wedding should expect to:

ARRIVE EARLY. Most members of the wedding party should arrive at the destination a day or two in advance (no later than the day before the rehearsal dinner) to help you get organized and to get the lay of the land before the other guests descend.

PLAY SHERPA. A few of them will need to pack materials for your wedding (anything you're not buying locally) in their luggage so you don't have to send it all ahead or haul it yourselves. In addition, they should help you to assemble favors, welcome bags, and so on.

HEAD UP GROUP ACTIVITIES. Name one member of the wedding party to be the point person for each activity you arrange. He or she will be in charge of finalizing details with the vendor or guide you hired for the event and greeting guests when they arrive for the activity.

COORDINATE TRANSPORTATION. Put another bridesmaid or groomsman in charge of liaising with any drivers or bus companies you hired to ferry your guests around the area.

GREET GUESTS. For each pre- and postwedding event (the welcome party, the morning-after brunch, etc.), assign a couple of bridesmaids or groomsmen the task of getting to the venue fifteen minutes early and greeting guests as they arrive. You will be too busy to be the perfect host for every second of every event, so it's smart to enlist your friends to make everyone feel welcome.

Be a Good Leader

Your attendants will require lots of clear information from you. Follow these rules of communication from the time you ask them to participate in the wedding until the band or DJ plays the last song.

MAKE THE CONNECTION. Your bridesmaids and groomsmen have many details to coordinate among themselves. Make a formal group introduction via e-mail and include each bridal party member's name, relationship to the bride or groom, and contact information.

KEEP THEM INFORMED. Give them travel and lodging information as soon as you can and ample time to buy the right outfit. Let them know what roles you want each of them to play in the wedding as soon as you decide on the details.

BE DIRECT. Do you want your attendants to arrive the night before the rehearsal dinner? Should the bridesmaids' shoes coordinate and the groomsmen's ties match? Don't make them guess—tell it to them straight.

timeline for bridesmaid dresses

O Allow three months' delivery and alteration time for the bridesmaids' dresses.

O A month after ordering, call the shop to reconfirm the delivery date.

O Have all bridesmaids schedule a local fitting based on the delivery date.

O When the dresses arrive, the maid of honor should pick up dresses for out-of-town bridesmaids and ship them to each one.

O Touch base with all bridesmaids (or ask your maid of honor to) a month after delivery, to make sure fittings and alterations are on schedule.

attendant attire

FOR THE BRIDESMAIDS

Use this list to cover all of the fashion basics for your right-hand ladies.

O Dress

O Wrap

O Purse

O Bracelet

O Necklace

O Earrings

O Hair accessory

O Shoes

O Undergarments

FOR THE GROOMSMEN

Keep the men in check with this wedding day wear checklist.

O Tuxedo/suit

O Vest/waistcoat

O Cummerbund

O Tie

O Cuff links/studs

O Shirt

O Shoes

O Socks

BE SENSITIVE TO THE EXPENSE. Bridesmaids and groomsmen must set aside a serious budget for the honor of being in your wedding: the dress; the shoes; the shower; the drink and debauchery at the bachelor party. A DW requires the additional outlay for airfare and accommodations. If possible, cover part of their travel and lodging—or at least tell them you don't expect a wedding gift.

STREAMLINE YOUR COMMUNICATIONS. Don't shoot off an e-mail to the wedding party every time a little detail crosses your mind ("What do you girls think about pink pearl earrings?"). Send fewer e-mails (every two weeks, once a month) that are packed with more information. If the info comes in dribs and drabs, your attendants won't be able to keep track of it.

DON'T TURN INTO A DICTATOR. It should go without saying that your attendants are friends doing you a big favor, not employees to boss around at will. Even though planning a destination wedding can be stressful, don't take it out on the people who are there to help you.

SHOW YOUR GRATITUDE During the run-up to your wedding it's easy for the bride and groom to be a little self-absorbed and wear blinders when it comes to others' needs. That's especially true if those others are the wedding party—after all, they're supposed to help you out, right? Well, yes, but if you want your relationship with them to emerge unscathed, consideration needs to be a two-way street. The members of your wedding party have a right to expect:

To relax and have fun! They are spending money and, most likely, a chunk of their limited vacation days

styling the groom and his guys

The groom should adhere to the same rules of DW dressing as the bride: Choose an outfit appropriate to the location, ceremony style, and weather, but make sure you feel comfortable in it. Heed these tips on tuxedos and other fashion options:

Stay home. If you're renting or buying a tuxedo, don't plan to do it at the destination. The styles and even the sizes are often limited, especially in foreign countries. Find exactly the tux you want at home, rent it or buy it, and bring it with you.

Be consistent. All the groomsmen should get their tuxes at the same shop so you'll match perfectly. (The store may even give you a discount.) If they live in various parts of the country, ask them to get measured by a local tailor and send their measurements to your shop.

Ask a friend. To avoid paying exorbitant late fees, ask a trusted friend or a relative to return your rented tux to the shop back home since you'll be going on to your honeymoon.

Style right. Black tie will look over-the-top in casual environments, so if your wedding will be on the beach or in a country field, ratchet the formality down a notch or two. (However, if you're hosting your affair in a ballroom that happens to be near a beach, black tie may still be appropriate.) To give your tux a hip and slightly more casual look, swap the bow tie for a black necktie, or wear the jacket over a tone-on-tone shirt set, such as a gray oxford and a long platinum tie (blues, greens, and purples look great, too).

A suit is an option. A dark suit is one of the most flexible styles for a groom, dressy enough for formal environments (and able to stand up to the most elaborate bridal gown) but a step down from black tie, so it doesn't look out of place in casual settings.

For a look that's laid-back enough for a casual setting, but still crisp and clean, opt for a suit in an informal color, like khaki, or fabric, like linen. A navy blazer with khaki pants, either with or without a tie, is often the go-to choice for grooms who want a classic, preppy look that's appropriate for weddings in laid-back destinations.

Casual is cool. Of course, if you're getting married on the beach or in any very casual setting, you can throw out the rules and wear anything you want: a white linen shirt untucked over a pair of khakis or jeans, or a Hawaiian shirt and shorts. But do make an effort to look well groomed, as a sign of respect for your guests.

Double up on the shirt. No matter what style you're going for, buy two wedding shirts and have the extra on hand during your wedding day so you can change into it quickly if you sweat through the first one (this is especially important at hot and humid destinations, though it can happen anywhere—you'll be nervous!).

fashion advice for your entourage

MAID OF HONOR AND BRIDESMAIDS

If your destination is warm or tropical, consider having your attendants wear more casual dresses (cotton with knee-length skirts) or two-piece ensembles like fluttery skirts with beachy halter tops. Laid-back cuts and fabrics will be more comfortable for them in the heat, easier to transport, and probably less expensive. And if you're getting married on the beach, definitely let them wear sandals so that sand won't get stuck in their shoes. In cooler climates, more traditional bridesmaid attire is appropriate—but you can consider adding a pashmina wrap or cashmere cardigan to keep your ladies warm and give the ensemble a more casual and comfortable feel.

JUNIOR BRIDESMAIDS AND FLOWER GIRLS

It makes sense to let your younger attendants wear comfortable, more casual attire at a destination wedding. Flower girls will look just as sweet in cotton piqué or eyelet dresses as they would in satin. Dresses for junior bridesmaids are often made of the same fabric as the older attendants' dresses, but in a less sophisticated cut that's appropriate for preteens. However, for a laid-back look, you can have your junior maids wear entirely different dresses (maybe cotton sundresses in a pretty print) that coordinate with the look of the rest of the wedding party.

GROOMSMEN

If you want to make it really easy and inexpensive for your groomsmen, let them wear their own clothes—say, khaki pants, blue blazers, and white shirts—and give them matching ties. The ties and their boutonnieres will create a cohesive look (and you can take it a step further by having them wear matching pocket squares, too).

Of course, if an ultraformal DW suits your style, don't hesitate to ask the guys to wear black tie. Make tuxes look a little more laid-back by swapping long ties for bow ties, wearing simple unpleated, lay-down collar white shirts, and avoiding formal touches like tails.

RING BEARERS

At a warm-weather destination, the little guy will look great in a seersucker or linen suit or, if your ceremony is taking place seaside, a sailor suit. But if your setting is more formal, dress him in a mini tux, a velvet suit (if it's a cold climate), or a dressy color like navy blue or dark green. Just make sure he's comfortable.

THE MOTHER OF THE BRIDE

Help your mom understand the vibe of your destination so she can choose an outfit that will fit your nuptial style. If she's never been there, show her lots of photos of both the destination and the specific location where the reception will take place, and give her detailed info about what the wedding party will be wearing, what the wedding colors will be, and what types of flowers your florist plans to use.

Although you can't dictate what she wears (your wedding is one of the biggest days in her life, and she probably has some strong opinions about how she wants to look), you can give her clear guidelines. If your wedding will be somewhat casual, and you're hoping she'll go with a knee-length look free of any elaborate sequins or beading, say so, and go shopping with her so you can gently guide her toward outfits that will fit the tone of the event and the style of the destination. And as soon as your mom has decided on a dress, give a heads-up to the mother of the groom so she can use it as a guideline.

on your wedding, so it shouldn't feel like a freelance event-planning job. Tasks you assign to each member of the wedding party should not be *too* burdensome.

Help with the travel arrangements. Give all your guests logistical assistance with travel and lodging, but make it especially easy for your wedding party. Reserve their rooms for them, research flight options on their behalf, and make sure they don't need to worry about getting around once they arrive at the destination.

A token of your appreciation. Since a destination wedding will require extra effort—and expense—on the part of your attendants, reward them with extra-nice thank-you gifts.

Dress Them in Style

Whether it's black tie or bandeau top, your attendants' attire sets the tone for the entire wedding. Consider the following:

CLIMATE. Consider both temperature and humidity levels at your location before settling on an outfit. A bridesmaid won't appreciate the cutest, most "wearable after the wedding" dress if she's sweating buckets in it during the ceremony.

PACKABILITY. A slinky silk dress or shirt may be lightweight for traveling, but it will come out of the suitcase with more wrinkles than a shar-pei. You don't have to base your fashion decisions solely on how the garments will travel, but at least consider the downside—and make sure the hotel concierge can arrange to have multiple irons, ironing boards, or steamers on hand for your crew.

LOCAL CULTURE. In some countries, it's considered inappropriate for women to enter a house of worship without covering their heads or with bare shoulders; other cultures frown on low-cut dresses worn in public. If your ceremony will take place in a religious institution, ask the officiant what you should know about customary clothing. Your local wedding coordinator or hotel concierge should also be able to clue you in to any cultural differences you need to observe. (And once you know, make sure to add it to your wedding website and newsletter, so other guests don't unwittingly wear something viewed as disrespectful.)

TIP

There are many ways besides "beach bikini" to incorporate your wedding locale into your attendants' actual clothing: mandarin collars for the groomsmen or kimono-print sashes on your bridesmaids' gowns can help contribute to the overall destination experience.

TIP

Consider getting your attendants a standard thank-you gift (jewelry for the girls and a tie or cuff links for the guys). Then also give each one a gift certificate for something he or she can indulge in after the wedding—spa treatments, a luxurious dinner, time at the driving range.

SCHEDULED ACTIVITIES. Coordinate ahead of time if you want your wedding party to look uniform at other activites—for example, "Please wear wild Hawaiian prints to the rehearsal dinner." And don't forget to be specific about shoes! You'd be shocked at how many people would consider an embellished flip-flop "formal attire." What you may think is obviously dress-down may seem perfectly appropriate to your attendant, and there's no reason for you both to feel bad when you realize the misunderstanding at the event.

creating your guest list

Compile an official guest list before you verbally invite your boss or your second best friend from high school—not a vague idea, but an actual list of names and a final count. You'd be surprised at how few people fifty is.

TIP

Make the list of people you plan to invite to the post-wedding celebration at the same time as your guest list. For more on organizing a party back home for extended friends, go to page 96.

KNOW YOUR NUMBER. You need a general idea of how big you want your wedding to be before you pick a location. If you plan to host a huge group, choose a destination with the capacity to handle it in terms of hotel rooms, restaurants, and amenities. If you want a small wedding, a far-flung destination is ideal, since the distance will keep your numbers down. How to decide on the size of your wedding is discussed in chapter 1, but the general categories are:
Inner Circle: Up to 30 guests
Friends and Family: 30 to 80 guests
Everyone: 80 to 200 guests

WRITE AND REVISE. Ten months to a year before the wedding draw up your initial guest list—everyone you can imagine inviting to the event. Let this list settle for a while before you go in for a second pass—there may be names you've forgotten. Before you make your final edit, cross-reference all lists to make sure there is no duplication. Strive to have the ultimate list of names ready by eight months before your wedding.

DIVIDE THE LIST. It's customary for the guest list to be divided three ways: a third of the guests are from the bride's family, a third are from the groom's family, and a third are made up of friends of the couple. If the couple is paying for the wedding, the percentages shift to half for the bride and groom and a quarter for each family. Be sure everyone is clear on their guest allowance to avoid last-minute additions.

FEEL FREE TO OVER-INVITE. Once you have determined your ideal number, there's a unique math for figuring out how many people to invite to your event. For a hometown wedding, planners will tell you to expect 80 percent of your invitees to attend, but for a faraway DW the acceptance rate is typically closer to 50 percent. Since it's impossible to know for sure, and it's always better to over- than underestimate, be prepared for 70 percent of people to accept. Forget last-minute "B-list invites" that local brides and grooms issue to fill the seats. DW guests need to make their travel plans well in advance of receiving the official invitation.

Don't be offended if some of your close friends or relatives can't attend. Some invitees simply won't be able to swing the expense (and don't assume you know who can afford it and who can't—you never know the inner workings of other people's finances).

BE OPEN—IT'S EASIER. If you are having an intimate wedding, be verbal with friends about the fact early on to avoid uncertainty and hurt feelings.

invitations and all: spreading the word

You need to let everyone know about your plans for a destination wedding as soon as possible. Here's a list of crucial communications:

Save-the-Dates

WHAT THEY ARE. These announcements let your guests know the date and location of your big day. They're essential to give your guests extra time to schedule vacation, arrange for child care, and shop around for a competitive airfare.

fun save-the-date ideas

○ For a beach wedding, create a "message in a bottle." Roll up your documents, tie them with a bit of twine or a tiny rope, and put them in a bottle with sand and seashells.

○ For a winter destination wedding, mail out customized snow globes with a picture of you two and the details.

○ If you're asking guests to travel to a luxe links resort or a country club in your parents' hometown, have golf balls engraved with your personal information. Cut out a tiny square of Astroturf or fake grass and send each in a box with the golf ball on top.

○ Send postcards from the town where you're holding the affair. For bonus points, send them in one envelope to a local planner who can mail them—that way, they'll have a destination postmark.

○ Lay local color over your invites by including paper currency, exotic greenery like a banana leaf, or a vellum sheet printed with a historical map of the town.

○ Send cards that match your formal invites but add a locale-themed twist, like a drawing of a local landmark or a stamp celebrating the state.

WHEN TO ORDER. Most paper products take four to six weeks to produce and print, so try to place your order eight to ten months before your wedding day.

WHEN TO SEND THEM. Ideally you should mail them out just as soon as the ink is dry on your location contract, or six to eight months before the wedding. If you are marrying on an extremely busy holiday weekend, consider sending your announcements out even earlier—but never more than a year before the date.

WHO GETS THEM. Only send save-the-dates to your A-list friends and family who will definitely be on your final guest list. Once someone has received this announcement they are officially invited —there is no taking it back.

WHAT TO INCLUDE. Obviously the date and location are the key pieces of information to communicate. If the information is available, also include:

Hotel options: List hotels in the area, and be sure to note the places where you've negotiated group rates or reserved blocks of rooms, as well as the dates when those rates or room blocks expire. Include the hotels' phone numbers and websites, along with details such as price and how close they are to the wedding location.

Flight information: Tell guests which airlines offer direct flights to the destination from major cities, and whether you've arranged any discounted or group rates. If there is more than one arrival airport to choose from, explain the difference.

The 411 on the destination: Include a bit of background on the locale, especially if people may not be very familiar with it. Exchange rates, area codes, and even a small map will help guests get a sense of where they'll be going.

Dress code: Your guests can start their fashion strategizing early if you give them a heads-up on whether the wedding will be black tie or casual. However, if you haven't decided yet, you can omit this info for now and post it on your website when you make the call (and include it on the invitation, of course).

Where to go for more info: Give the link for your website and the contact info for your wedding planner. Say that you'll be updating the website frequently with more specifics, such as transportation at the destination, group activities, dress codes for various events, and everything else your guests will need to know.

destination dress codes

Some of your guests may have never attended a destination wedding, leaving them clueless about what to wear. And unless your wedding invitation carries the clear catchphrase *black tie* (which may not be the best option for an outdoor tropical celebration), they'll look to you for advice. Here are some standard what-to-wear guidelines, translated to your location.

Black tie optional: Yes, this is a formal wedding and you need to dress up. No, he doesn't have to wear a tux and she can go light on the hair and makeup. Other ways to word this: "black tie very optional," "formal dress," "cocktail attire."

Beach formal: Great for an elegant beach wedding; it implies colorful semiformal dresses and summer suits (think a high-end restaurant on a summer day), but lets them know there is no need to break out the stilettos. Other ways to word this: "beach chic," "island festive," "summer semiformal," "festive attire," or "jackets required" (especially if your venue has a definite dress code).

Flip-flops required: You guessed it, flip-flops paired with informal but wedding-appropriate wear like sundresses and khakis with white linen shirts. Be forewarned: guests could show up in T-shirts and shorts. Other ways to word this: "beach casual," "sarong style," or "tropical attire."

How do you get the word across? You can print one of these destination-worthy dress phrases on the bottom of the invitation or list the info on your wedding website. The latter allows you to be as specific and as in-depth as possible—consider adding some "what to wear" questions to the FAQ page on your site. Here, you can provide answers to questions such as "What is everyone wearing to the rehearsal dinner?" or "What exactly does 'festive attire' mean?" You can then answer: "Other guests are wearing summer cocktail dresses and sports coats without a tie." You can also include important info like "sunglasses required" for a daytime outdoor ceremony or "shawls suggested" for a nighttime one.

organizing your stationery order

This list includes the total run-down of every piece of stationery you might need—choose what fits your wedding style and budget. It makes sense to work with a single vendor for all your stationery needs. Once you have established a style with your save-the-dates, the execution will be simpler. Plus, working with one professional may also entitle you to a package discount!

THE BASICS

O **Envelopes**
Outer envelope: mailing envelope, addressed with full names and addresses

Inner envelope: optional packaging envelope, unsealed, contains all materials

Reply envelope: self-addressed stamped envelope in which guests return RSVPs

O **Invitation**
Includes all the "when and where" details and indicates who's hosting.

O **Reception Card**
This optional card lists information for the reception if it's not in the same place as the ceremony.

O **Response Card**
Your guests return it, indicating whether they'll attend (and their menu choices, if requested).

ADVANCE EXTRAS

O **Save-the-Dates**
These are typically sent for destination weddings and weddings that will take place on popular holidays or in major cities.

O **Travel Information**
Printed maps, directions, or location information may be sent with the save-the-date or the invitation.

O **Welcome Kits**
This packet includes an itinerary and information on activities and is usually given to guests when they check in to their hotel rooms.

WEDDING DAY OPTIONS

O **Wedding Programs**
May include information about the ceremony, the names of the bridal party (and perhaps their relationship to the bride or groom), the order of events, and the titles of readings and songs.

O **Menu Cardss**
These cards, generally displayed at reception tables (either one per table or one per place setting), give guests a taste of what's to come.

O **Escort Cards**
Direct guests to their tables.

O **Place Cards**
Inform guests which chair to sit in.

O **Favor Tags**
Personalized labels to make gifts for your guests a bit more memorable.

THE MOST IMPORTANT PIECE OF ALL

O **Thank-you Cards and Envelopes**
Be prepared to send out thank-yous no later than one month after your honeymoon for gifts received on the day of your wedding. You should ideally send thank-you notes out immediately for any gifts received before your wedding day.

We both have big families, so our wedding parties are all sisters and brothers, and sisters-in-law and brothers-in-law. We'd have more fun sitting with our friends at the reception, but is it horribly rude not to have the wedding party at the head table?

Although it *will* break with tradition if you fill your reception table with friends who aren't attendants, it's not a major breach of etiquette. The most important thing is for you two to have a great time, so if you'll have more fun seated with friends than family, then go for it. But be sure to seat your attendants at tables in close proximity to yours, and place them together or with other close family members so they won't feel snubbed. You may want to explain to the key members of your wedding party why they won't be seated with you. Simply say that you have a number of close friends whom you weren't able to include in the wedding party, so you're choosing to honor them with positions at the head table instead.

wedding announcements 101

If you're not planning a second party back home—and a lot of your friends and acquaintances aren't invited to your DW—you may want to send out a wedding announcement.

FORMAL WORDING

Mr. and Mrs. John James Smith

are pleased to announce

the marriage of their daughter

Lauren Elizabeth

to Michael Eric Brown

February 11, 2010

Los Cabos, Mexico

CASUAL WORDING

We tied the knot!

February 11, 2010

Los Cabos, Mexico

Lauren & Michael Brown

WHEN TO SEND

If you are not at all superstitious, you can have these printed prior to your departure for your wedding. Leave them at home to be sent out while you are on your honeymoon, or get them printed and send them yourselves upon your return.

Invitations

WHAT THEY ARE. The formal announcement of your ceremony and party, the actual invitations for a DW can look much the same as they would for a hometown wedding.

WHEN TO ORDER. Custom invitations can take up to three months to design and print. Order yours six months before your wedding.

WHEN TO SEND THEM. Send the invites out a bit on the early side (ten to twelve weeks instead of the standard six to eight for a hometown wedding) and ask to receive RSVPs no later than six weeks before the wedding date. A large number of the RSVPs will be a formality since many guests will have already told you whether they're coming and made their travel arrangements before they received the official invite in the mail.

WHAT TO INCLUDE. The basic facts about your wedding—who's hosting it, where it will be, the time, the date, and your names. You don't need to include too many specifics since you'll be keeping your guests up to date on the logistics through your website and newsletter.

Your Wedding Website

WHAT IT IS. An online resource for your guests that provides more extensive information than you offered in the save-the-date. Guests who are serious about attending should be able to log on and see frequently updated details about your wedding as they become available.

WHEN TO SEND THE URL. Your site should be up and running—even if it only says "More details will follow"—by the time you send out your save-the-dates. Those cards should include the website address so guests know right away where they can go for planning help.

WHAT TO INCLUDE. Links to local hotels, typical weather conditions at the time of year when your wedding will be held, a list of local sights and activities you suggest your guests check out on their own, a list of the activities you'll be organizing for them, and info on the dress code for various events.

> **TIP**
>
> If you haven't heard from invitees once the "please reply by" date has passed, feel free to send them an e-mail or give them a call to follow up. Rather than just say, "Are you coming or what?" ask them politely if there's any further information you can give them about the event.

> **TIP**
>
> Don't forget less web-savvy guests, such as grandparents. Put a parent in charge of communicating with those guests.

Be My Guests

PRACTICAL ADVICE. Definitely post any important tips, like whether they'll need passports, where they should change currency, and the time zone difference between their hometowns and the destination.

LOCAL COLOR. You may also want to include a bit of information about the destination—its history, its customs, and interesting facts about its culture and cuisine. All of this will entice your guests to come and get them excited about the journey. On your website, ask guests to give you an e-mail address where you can send them updates.

Newsletter

Since you can't count on guests to check your website every week for updates, send an e-mail newsletter out when you have a new chunk of info to share (when you've finalized the details of transportation from the airport to the hotels, or decided that the welcome party will be a *Pirates of the Caribbean* costume affair) and when you need to remind them of a deadline (when it's their last chance to reserve one of the hotel rooms for example).

Another clever way to share information is to compile a list of guests' frequently asked questions, with answers. Some of the FAQs will be specific to your destination, but here are a few general ones to include:

* Why did you choose this destination for your wedding?

* What will the weather be like?

* What's the time difference?

* What's the local language and currency?

* What do we do for transportation once we arrive?

* What are the must-see sights in the area?

* How far are the various hotel options from where the wedding will be held?

*. How many days should we plan to stay?

* Is there anything special we should pack?

TIP

Make life easier by creating one guest group in your e-mail program so that with one click you automatically e-mail all of your invitees. It may take a minute to learn how—ten at the most. Just click on "about" or "help" in your e-mail program and search for "mailing list" or "create group." Ultimately, it will be more efficient than going down the list name by name each time you have an update.

the rules of registering

There's a fine art to registering for gifts for a destination wedding.

Register for more items. When your wedding's far away, some people who aren't invited may still want to buy you gifts. So if you plan to invite 100 people, and 80 of them will be coming as couples, you may think you need to ask for only 60 gifts (40 from the couples and 20 from the single guests), right? The truth is, you should actually register for around 120 to allow for noninvitees who want to get you something, as well as extras such as engagement and shower gifts.

Register in two stages. If you're worried that registering for too many gifts at once will result in your not getting the things you most want, start with a smaller registry of the items you really crave (say, 50 gifts instead of 120). As your favorites get snapped up, you can add more.

Pick items in a wide range of prices. Guests may spend a little less on a gift since they're shelling out for travel costs, but invitees who decline may get you an especially nice gift out of guilt (and since they're saving dough by not attending, they may feel as if they can splurge).

Let everyone know. Place your registry information in a prominent spot on your website, along with links to the online registries. Ask anyone who throws a shower or prewedding party for you to include that info in the invitation.

Don't feel guilty. Some couples feel awkward registering for gifts when their guests are already going to great expense attending the wedding. If that's the case, simply add a line somewhere in your planning materials, in the FAQs on your website, and at the registry links stating "Your presence is present enough." But you should be prepared with a registry anyway—most people will still want to buy you a gift and you are better off making it easier for them.

Be prepared to pack it. Even though gifts should be sent to your home, some guests will buy a gift in advance and bring it with them to the wedding. Have extra luggage on hand to accommodate the new loot.

wedding redux? throwing a second party back home

Are you worried that friends not attending your wedding will feel left out? Does not getting to celebrate with everyone you love make you sad? Then host a postwedding party back home a few weeks or months after you return from your honeymoon.

Why you'd want to do it: A party back home allows you to have it both ways—you get your fantasy destination wedding without sacrificing the chance to let a broad circle of friends share in your joy. It keeps the crowd you didn't invite to your DW from feeling left out and takes the pressure off others to make the trip if they feel they can't afford the time or expense.

What it entails: Your options are endless. If your destination wedding was a casual, barefoot-on-the-beach affair, you may want to use this later celebration as a chance to go swankier and do a sit-down dinner complete with all the fine linen and crystal you passed on earlier. You can also keep it simple and throw an elegant cocktail party, a buffet luncheon, or a backyard barbecue. A wedding cake is a nice symbolic touch but certainly not required.

What to wear: Any party attire is appropriate, but many brides do wear their wedding dress again. It helps the celebration feel like a wedding: Everyone always wants to see a girl in her gown, and you'll get more mileage out of your purchase. The groom can simply wear a suit unless, of course, the party is black tie!

A word on gifts: Don't expect them. Guests are only obligated to give you a gift if they were invited to the actual wedding. Many will want to, though, so it is still a good idea to register in advance of the event.

Show off the event: A digital slide show of your wedding photos will help your guests feel more included in the big event. Leave a copy of your album out or play a video of the two of you exchanging vows. If your albums aren't ready, ask your photographer in advance to give you a second set of proofs to leave in little frames around the event.

Hire a photographer: Have a professional take pictures of you and friends at the event. Set up a digital photo booth and give each guest a snapshot of him- or herself as a takeaway.

How to get the word out: Once you've made the decision to have a second event, let people subtly know whenever they ask about your wedding plans (e.g., "We're having a small wedding in Jamaica in March but are planning a cocktail reception back home in April"). This will let people who aren't invited to the wedding know that they aren't being excluded. You need to be careful with the invitation wording so that it is clear the official wedding has already happened:

FORMAL WORDING

Barbara and Michael Swank

request the pleasure of your company
at a celebration to honor the recent marriage of
Elizabeth Justine
to
Sean Joseph Mack
the Tenth of July, 2010
at six o'clock
The Harvard Club
Boston, MA

INFORMAL WORDING

Please join us
to celebrate the recent marriage
of
Elizabeth Swank
to
Sean Mack
July 10, 2010
6 p.m.
The Harvard Club
Boston, MA

CASUAL WORDING

On April 15, 2010
In a sunset ceremony on St. John
Sean Mack and Elizabeth Swank
became husband and wife
Please join them in celebration
July 10, 2010
6 p.m.
The Harvard Club
Boston, MA

the guest list

TIMELINE

Write initial guest list	10+ months ahead
Reserve hotel rooms	8+ months ahead
Send save-the-date cards	6 to 8 months ahead
Finalize guest list	6 months ahead
Order invitations	6 months ahead
Give final names to calligrapher	4 months ahead
Mail invitations	3 months ahead
Plan itinerary for out-of-towners	2 months ahead
Send prewedding info packet	3 to 6 weeks ahead
Follow up on missing RSVPs	6 weeks ahead
Deliver final head count	2 weeks ahead
Draw up reception seating chart	1 week ahead
Drop off welcome gifts	2 days ahead

INFO TO TRACK

Name

Address

Telephone

E-mail

O Shower guest

O Bachelor/ette night guest

O Rehearsal dinner guest

O Postwedding brunch guest

in party _____

Save-the-date sent _____

Invite sent _____

RSVP received _____

Arrival time + date _____

Table # _____

Gift received _____

Thank-you sent _____

AMY & MARK · LOS CABOS, MEXICO

Hometown: Los Angeles, CA
Guests: 115

The Destination Decision: It was all about bonding at the beach. The California couple wanted an intimate spot where they could have all their wedding guests together under the same roof. Because Amy and Mark love to take weekend getaways to Los Cabos, a resort in Mexico was the obvious answer.

Planning Pointer: Take time to meet with your local vendors. Besides their wedding photographer, a family member, Amy and Mark used all Mexican vendors, which added local charm to a lavish celebration. Their wedding site, the One&Only Palmilla, had plenty of vendor suggestions, but the bride stayed actively involved, visiting the resort three more times to confirm all the style details of the day.

The Definitive Detail: Every event, from the Thursday-night Mariachis and Margaritas welcome party to the Saturday-night reception, was decorated in the wedding's signature color: orange. Centerpieces bursted with orange tulips and roses; orange place cards were calligraphed in white; orange ribbons hung from ceremony chairs; and even the bride switched up the white sash on her Monique Lhuillier gown for an orange one at the reception.

Ch. 5

playing cruise director: organizing the weekend activities

Although the wedding is the centerpiece of the weekend, it is hardly the only event you have to orchestrate: There are no less than five additional events—from a spa party for the bridesmaids to welcome cocktails for the guests—that you have the option of hosting.

Your guests will also look to you for meal ideas, transportation tips, and recommendations on what to do with their downtime. It's your job to make sure your nearest and dearest have a stress-free and fun-filled time from the moment they touch down until they head home. But while you want to make your guests' stay as memorable as possible, it's not your job to play full-time concierge. Don't take on the task of booking individual spa appointments or tee times or making dinner reservations for your guests—it will only stress you out. Just include all the info they'll need on your wedding website and in the prewedding info packet.

hello there: orchestrating the arrivals

You'll have a million things on your mind the day your guests begin arriving, but they'll have only one: finding you. How to smoothly get friends from the airport and checked into their hotels, with an understanding of what they're supposed to do next, is a project you'll need to plan, but hopefully not handle, yourself.

Your guests should know beforehand how they'll be getting from the airport to their hotels—landing in a strange city or country can be disorienting. If the hotels or resorts where guests are staying offer airport shuttles, be sure the appropriate person is aware of each guest's arrival time. If not, hire vans to pick up groups of guests who arrive on the same flights or at the same time. However, if arranging transportation for every guest who wanders in at a random time is too tricky and expensive, just give such stragglers the contact info for a reliable cab or car service and let them take care of it themselves.

Even if you sent a prewedding packet and provide a welcome kit and goody bag, there will still be guests who get nervous upon arrival and worry that they're missing something. To answer their number one question—What now?—highlight or create an event for people who will need direction: For example, "On Thursday guests will be lounging by the south pool, so upon arrival please come join us in the sun. Our first *official* activity will be welcome drinks at the Palm Bar at 6 p.m." This way, unsure guests won't feel they need to track you down to ask questions.

good stuff: it's in the welcome bag

Since you won't be able to greet all your guests personally upon arrival, a welcome bag (or basket) is a great way to touch base with them right away. Here are a few suggestions on what to include:

A WELCOME LETTER. Tell your guests how happy you are that they've made the trip with a short and sweet note. For simplicity's sake, use your computer to type and print the letters, but sign each one in ink for a personal touch.

A DETAILED SCHEDULE. List all of the weekend's events, including any optional ones. Include the time, location, dress code, and any other important details for each. Be sure to mention any extra costs for activities such as tours, lessons, sports activities, and so on.

KEY CONTACT INFO. Tell your guests how to reach the people you've designated as go-to contacts (family members, wedding attendants, and/or your wedding planner). Include both their cell phone numbers (be sure to get ones that work locally, even if you have to rent) and the landline number for their hotel rooms. Don't include *your* contact info—most people won't feel comfortable bothering you, and you'll have enough on your mind already.

A MAP OF THE AREA. Ask the hotel to give you a reliable one—don't trust something you find on the Internet unless it's posted by an authority like the chamber of commerce or visitors' bureau.

INFO ON LOCAL TRANSPORTATION. Bus schedules and the phone numbers of local taxi companies and car services will help your guests get around when they're on their own.

A LIST OF LOCAL RESTAURANTS. Include descriptions, locations, phone numbers, and price info, along with a selection of menus from places that deliver.

A LOCAL ENTERTAINMENT GUIDE. Check to see if the hotel or the local chamber of commerce publishes a brochure, or include the latest issue of a local magazine with listings.

THEMATIC SNACKS. A taste of locally made food and drink will introduce your guests to the destination's delicacies and help them avoid raiding the minibar. Try to include both savory and sweet things to satisfy different cravings: plantain chips in Puerto Rico, Jamaican Blue Mountain Coffee in Jamaica, macadamia nuts in Hawaii, Key lime cookies in Key West. Since your guests are on vacation, too, it's nice to greet them with a celebratory drink—a bottle of wine if you're in a region known for it, locally brewed beer, a mini bottle of the area's signature liquor, or a beautifully labeled bottle of lemonade. To take it a step further, give each guest the ingredients for the area's most popular cocktail, along with a recipe card.

DESTINATION ESSENTIALS. Anticipate little things your guests would appreciate having at the destination: sunscreen and a pair of flip-flops or a visor at the beach; a sweet-smelling bug repellent in the country; a subway card or bus tokens in the city. And no matter where you are, disposable cameras and bottled water are always welcome.

HOW TO PACK YOUR BAGS. The most cost-effective way to get all this gear to your destination is to gather all the welcome bag components back home and ask family and members of the wedding party to pack them for you with their luggage. Then you can assemble the bags when you arrive.

A more convenient—but also more expensive (especially if you're headed to a foreign country with duty taxes)—way is to ship all the ingredients for your welcome bags ahead to your destination. Just call shippers well in advance to find out how long it will take to get the gear to your destination.

PRECHECK YOUR PRODUCTS. Don't order items online and have them shipped directly from the manufacturer sight-unseen, because you won't have a chance to replace them if you're not satisfied (for example, if the bags that appeared to be the perfect shade of pale lilac online turn out to be more of an Easter egg lavender in person). If you must have products sent directly to your destination, always request to have at least one sent to your home, so if the color doesn't work or your names are spelled wrong you will have time to get it fixed.

quality time: an outing with your attendants

WHAT IT IS. A chance for you and your honey to chill out with your attendants and thank them for their support.

WHO'S INVITED. All bridesmaids and groomsmen and any other wedding participants you want to include: flower girls/ring bearers, mothers/fathers, readers, ushers/usherettes, and so on.

WHO PAYS. You pay for the food and drink, but if there's an extravagant outing involved (let's say you're in Scotland and all the groomsmen are hitting a legendary golf course), you're not expected to cover everyone's costs. However, you can make the event your gift to your groomsmen or bridesmaids.

WHAT HAPPENS. You share a meal with your wedding party (usually lunch) and/or bond over a fun group activity. Feel free to get creative: Go on a fishing trip at the beach, saddle up for a group ride in horse country, or sample Earl Grey, tea sandwiches, and scones at a high tea with your bridesmaids.

the preview: a rousing rehearsal dinner

WHAT IT IS. This traditional dinner that immediately follows the wedding rehearsal is a chance for your family, your wedding participants, and other invitees to bond before the wedding and toast you on the eve of your walk down the aisle.

WHO'S INVITED. At a minimum, anybody involved in the wedding ceremony (your wedding party, readers, ushers) and your immediate families should attend. You should also invite the officiant and his or her spouse. Often couples invite all "out of town guests" to the rehearsal dinner. Since at a DW most or all of your guests will be from out of town, you're not obligated, but it is a nice gesture.

If you want to keep it intimate, though, consider holding the rehearsal dinner two nights before the wedding so you can invite everybody to a welcome party on the night before the wedding.

WHO PAYS. The groom's family traditionally pays for the rehearsal dinner, but whatever arrangement works for you is acceptable.

WHAT HAPPENS. This event is less tradition-bound than the wedding reception, so let it take whatever form strikes your fancy—from a beach barbecue or a family-style meal at an Italian restaurant to a five-course French menu to hearty hors d'oeuvres. It's the perfect time to reflect on special memories of your childhoods and your courtship. You may want to screen a slide show, play a specially edited DVD that highlights your history together, or place photo albums on the tables. There'll be a lot of toasting. The best man and maid of honor usually speak, as well as one or both of the groom's parents, and whoever else is inspired to clink fork to glass. And since this may be your first chance to greet many of your guests, one or both of you should stand up and thank them for making the trip.

TIP

The rehearsal dinner is the perfect time to pass out gifts for your bridesmaids and groomsmen. If you give them something to wear—ties or cuff links for the guys, jewelry or wraps for the girls—be clear on whether or not you want the items worn at the wedding.

TIP

To find venues for these extra events, first check with the hotels where you and your guests are staying. At least one will likely have spaces you can rent (or just take over) for your events. If your wedding reception is at a hotel or a resort, try to cut a deal with them on other events you'd like to host there. And don't forget to talk to all of the locals you meet with on your first visit to the destination, from the vendors you interview to the taxi drivers. They'll likely be able to suggest little-known places you wouldn't stumble across on the Internet.

getting your guests around

In any setting other than a city where taxis are abundant, you should take it upon yourselves to help guests get around.

Unless your ceremony and reception will both take place at the resort where the majority of guests are staying, you should hire a bus or van service on your wedding day to ferry guests to and from the festivities. It will spare them the hassle of having to call cabs or, if they drive themselves, dealing with directions and picking a designated driver.

The itineraries you include in the welcome bag should clearly state when shuttles will depart from the various hotels to go to the wedding, and when they'll take people back. Plan on at least two (and possibly more) departure times from the wedding so some guests (especially elderly ones) can leave on the early side and others can dance until the venue turns off the lights. And no matter what transit you devise for the bulk of your guests, you definitely need to arrange day-of transportation for the wedding party. Hire vans to get them where they need to be.

It's not required that you arrange for your guests to get from their hotel to the airport for departure, since during the course of their stay they'll have ample time to book a cab or a car service through their hotels. But find out from the concierges how much time it takes to get from their hotels to the airport, and include this info in your itinerary.

Finally, there are other transportation issues to consider. Use this checklist to make sure you cover all of your bases.

O Bride and groom arrival at ceremony

O Bride and groom transportation to reception

O Bride and groom departure from reception

O Wedding party transportation to ceremony

O Wedding party transportation to/from reception

O Bride and groom home to airport

O Bride and groom airport to hotel

O Bride and groom hotel to airport

O Bride and groom airport to home

O Special on-site shuttles or other transportation

O Transportation to any special activities

come together now: where's the welcome party?

WHAT IT IS. This party is held on the night most of your guests arrive, so you can greet them and they can meet and mingle with one another.

WHO'S INVITED. Include all out-of-town guests and local wedding guests, too, if you wish.

WHO PAYS. You should factor the welcome party into your wedding budget. A welcome party doesn't have to be costly, and this is one instance where it's perfectly okay to have a cash bar if that's all your budget allows. To keep costs down, offer only wine and beer, or negotiate with the bar to get a special rate on a signature cocktail. If this party is doubling as the rehearsal dinner, the groom's parents may offer to pay.

WHAT HAPPENS. Invite guests to a convenient location, like a bar or a lounge in the hotel where most of them are staying. Hold the party either before or after dinner, and serve "cocktail hour" type food (pigs in a blanket, mini quiche, cheese puffs, etc.). If you can swing it, a casual dinner for all is a nice option.

Have your wedding party organize a "getting to know you" game to encourage guests to break up their cliques and get them talking to people they've never met before. One idea: Before the wedding weekend, ask each guest to send you a "little-known fact" about him- or herself ("I speak Swahili" or "I made out with George Clooney"). Print each up on a small piece of paper. When the guests arrive at the welcome party, each receives a slip of paper, and they spend the party trying to find the guest who goes along with that fact.

> **TIP**
>
> The welcome party is a great chance to showcase the local food. In the Caribbean have a fish fry; in New York City serve hot dogs for dinner and cheesecake for dessert; in Italy serve thin-crust pizzas alongside jugs of Chianti; in France serve cheese and chocolate fondue. For a summertime wedding in Aspen, place sunflowers in cowboy boots for a centerpiece; and in Mexico, skip the formal bar in favor of buckets of icy local beers like Tecate, Corona, or Pacifico.

Playing Cruise Director

keep it going: after-party principles

WHAT IT IS. Beginning immediately when the reception ends, this party provides a chance for the night owls in your group to keep the festivities going into the wee hours. You can host it at the bar back at your hotel or at a nearby club or lounge (though if the spot is too far away you'll need to factor in another round of shuttle buses for transportation—cabs will likely be hard to come by late at night, and you don't want anybody to drive).

WHO'S INVITED. Everyone from the wedding is invited, though it's likely to be the younger crowd who attends. You don't need any formal invitations; just give the after-party's location on the wedding schedule, and have the DJ or bandleader at the reception announce it toward the end of the evening.

WHO PAYS. The expense can come out of the wedding budget, or a friend or a family member may offer to throw it for you. It doesn't have to cost much: Instead of a DJ use an iPod to play tunes, and you can skip bartenders—just put beer, water, sodas, and Red Bull in mini refrigerators or ice-filled buckets and let guests help themselves.

WHAT HAPPENS. Make it an all-out dance party, or create a mellow, lounge-type atmosphere with mood music. Either way, provide beverages and some light munchies, since dinner will be long over and your guests will have stoked their appetites on the dance floor. Comfort food—mini burgers, tiny grilled cheese sandwiches, fries, and sweets such as Devil Dogs, Ring Dings, and Twinkies—is perfect.

TIP

Low sofas and comfy floor pillows for guests to unwind on plus tons of votive candles scattered around the room create a swanky late-night atmosphere.

wake-up call: morning-after munchies

WHAT IT IS. This casual breakfast or brunch gives you a chance to say good-bye to all your guests before you head off on the honeymoon. It's a great chance for everybody to recap the fun happenings of the preceding days.

WHO'S INVITED. Include all out-of-town guests and local wedding guests, too, if you wish.

WHO PAYS. A friend or a relative may offer to host this for you, or you or your parents can pick up the tab. If your wedding is being held in a hotel or a resort that also serves brunch, try to negotiate a deal when you first talk to the staff about the wedding. Eager to get your business for the reception, they may be quite flexible in regard to their brunch rates. If breakfast is already included in the price of your guests' rooms, try to haggle so that you end up paying little, if anything, for a group brunch. (You'll still have to shell out for guests not staying at the hotel and any extras like champagne.)

WHAT HAPPENS. Usually this is a laid-back affair since everyone will be pretty exhausted from the previous nights' parties. Plan on a buffet-style meal, and give guests a fairly wide window for their arrival (say, between eleven and one) rather than enforce a strict start time. Although you or your parents can stand up and briefly thank everyone again for making the trip, no grand speeches are necessary (you'll all be a little toast-weary by this point). The best approach is to stop by each table for a chat.

TIP

Encourage guests to double-check their flights both coming and going, as airlines tend to change or cancel flights without notice (this is especially true in Europe). Send this reminder via e-mail a few days before the wedding.

TIP

As a parting memento, give each guest a snapshot of him- or herself from the wedding or wedding weekend. Put a friend or a wedding party member in charge of taking photos for this purpose (Polaroids, digital printouts, or even regular film, if there's a one-hour developing shop you can access that morning). Don't worry if the photos are more wacky than flattering—the point is to capture the fun of the event on film.

How do we maintain some privacy with all those guests around, especially if our honeymoon will be at the same facility?

The best way to ensure time alone together is to arrive a couple of days earlier than everyone else and/or stay a bit longer after your guests depart. Make the postwedding breakfast or brunch the last item on your official itinerary, signaling the end of the festivities and the commencement of time for the two of you to enjoy being a couple *alone*. Or plan to honeymoon at a different resort in the same area.

the more the merrier: group activities

Your guests will have some free time when they're not at official wedding events, so plan group activities not only to keep them entertained but also to help your assorted family members and friends from various walks of life bond. One of the most satisfying experiences of hosting a DW is watching some of your favorite people start out as strangers and become friends over the course of your wedding weekend.

WHAT TO OFFER. Your destination will determine which group activities you organize. Beach destinations offer a wealth of fun water sports, while lots of cultural activities are available to your guests in urban locales. Take into account the style of your crowd. Only you know whether your friends and family are more likely to enjoy spending the afternoon in a rowdy game of touch football or on a walking tour of historical sites. If you've got a large, diverse guest list, plan both for the same chunk of time and let guests make the choice. You can arrange four main categories of recreation:

* Outdoor: sailing, hiking, snorkeling, horseback riding, biking, etc.

* Educational: wine tastings, surf lessons, cooking classes, or lectures about the local culture, history, or habitat. Some classes will have size restrictions, so you may have to break guests up into small groups and go at different times.

* Sightseeing: tours of the area or group visits to local attractions like museums and historic sites.

* Games/athletics: softball, touch football, golf, tennis or volleyball tournaments, any other organized competitions (don't focus solely on athletic contests—consider a sand castle–building challenge or a scavenger hunt for your guests who are more creative than sporty).

Check out these sources for fun ideas for group activities:

* Local chambers of commerce and tourism bureaus

* Your hotel or resort's website; also ask the concierge for popular choices among your guests' demographics (extreme-sports fans, older sightseers, history buffs, artsy types, etc.)

* Travel guides

* Friends who've visited the area

DOS AND DON'TS

Don't take up the whole day. Your guests will be happiest with activities that last no longer than three hours. They'll want enough downtime to relax and do their own thing.

Assign guests to teams. A little friendly competition via a scavenger hunt or a softball game will help guests bond. Craft the teams carefully: Break up cliques and mix guests from different parts of your lives so they'll have a chance to meet.

Don't make the competitions too serious. The tone should be lighthearted, not cutthroat.

don't neglect your parents

When you're the center of everybody's attention *and* wrapped up in making sure everything goes off without a hitch, it can be all too easy to forget about the people who are most important to you: your parents. Your wedding is as big a deal for them as it is for you, and they want to share it with you.

Make sure the weekend doesn't fly by before you have a chance to spend some quality time together: Build it into your schedule.

Write a letter. Last-minute preparations and excitement are overwhelming, so a week or so before the wedding (when you can still focus), sit down and write to your parents, thanking them for their help, patience, and support during the planning process. Let them know how you feel and deliver this heartfelt, handwritten note on your wedding day. They'll treasure it forever and always remember your graciousness.

Meet in the morning. One of the easiest ways is to have breakfast with them on the morning of your wedding (or, if time is too tight, the day before). You may want to split up, so that the groom eats with his parents and the bride with hers. This way, each set of parents gets a moment of private time with their daughter or son before their children become a permanent twosome. Take this opportunity to thank them for everything they've done (financially and otherwise) to pull off the wedding, and give them special thank-you gifts from both of you.

it's in the details

Get the following information for all activities you investigate:

○ Activity

○ Company

○ Phone number

○ Cost (per person/lump fee)

○ Days/times available

○ Minimum number of participants _____

○ Maximum number of participants _____

○ Must book by _____

○ Transportation required

○ Guests who may want to participate

Track RSVPs. To plan properly, you'll need to know well in advance who is going to participate in each activity, so ask guests to RSVP on postcards you include in the prewedding info packet.

DON'T BE INFLEXIBLE. Inevitably, some guests who didn't sign up for certain activities will want to join at the last minute, and others who said they would participate will be no-shows. Roll with whatever happens—after all, this isn't supposed to be stressful!

HOW TO ORGANIZE THEM. Work with the hotel concierge or your wedding planner to find and reserve the facilities for your group activities, and to hire any professional help you'll need, such as instructors or tour guides. For simple group activities, such as softball games and outings to local sites, designate one or two members of your wedding party as the person/people in charge.

WHO PAYS? You're not expected to subsidize the optional activities you arrange for your guests. Clearly state the cost of each activity on your wedding website and in the prewedding info packet, along with information on how guests can pay. Most tour guides and instructors will agree to a set per-person fee for activities like surf classes and wine tastings, as long as you guarantee them a certain number of attendees.

STEPHANIE & MATT · MONTEGO BAY, JAMAICA

Hometown: Milton, MA
Guests: 58

The Destination Decision: "I thought it was a great place to bring family—laid-back and easy to travel to," says Stephanie. After touring four possible hotels, she and Matt chose a villa-style resort where guests were grouped according to interests. "One of the best parts about planning this was all of the scouting trips!" adds Matt.

Planning Pointer: Make it as easy—and attractive—as possible for guests to plan for the trip. First, Stephanie and Matt sent save-the-date cards that featured an arty, alluring shot of a tropical ocean along with a brief itinerary: cocktails, a reggae concert, the wedding, and a farewell brunch. "These cards gave a real feeling of being someplace tropical," says Stephanie. "They were designed to *lure* guests!" They also gave the address of the couple's web page, which Stephanie updated with things like resort details, directions to the island, and registry info. Later, a three-page monogrammed, orchid-themed invitation went out with more details about the group activities and other fun options in Jamaica.

The Definitive Detail: When the guests arrived on Thursday, the couple hosted a kick-off cocktail party with Jamaican dancers and a calypso band.

Ch. **6**

destination "i do": designing your ceremony

The list of things to plan for a destination wedding seems so many miles long that you can somehow forget that the actual wedding ceremony is the reason for all of it. Don't let one of the most moving, memorable moments of your lives be an afterthought—start planning early.

The good news is that the gorgeous environment and rich cultural traditions of the destination you chose will help to make your ceremony feel inspired. Music will be an important factor in setting the right mood and marking key moments in the proceedings. Ultimately, however, it is the words you speak and rituals you perform that have the most impact. Here's everything you need to do to set up a ceremony that feels every bit as special as your relationship.

making it legal

It may be tempting to invite a bunch of friends to your stateside ceremony, but resist the impulse or risk making your second wedding feel anticlimactic. Keep it on the down low and invite just a couple of witnesses (siblings or another couple you're close to) to attend. Celebrate with a bottle of champagne and an indulgent lunch or dinner; the real party is still to come.

We already raised some of the legal issues in chapter 2. When planning your DW, you need to make sure your marriage will be recognized by law both in your destination *and* back home. Don't forget to consider religious requirements as well.

GO THROUGH OFFICIAL CHANNELS. As soon as you've decided on a destination, contact the local city hall as well as the American embassy (if you're getting married abroad) to find out what documents and procedures are required to get married there. Do this early in the planning process, but call and check again closer to your wedding date, in case any of the laws of the land have changed.

GET YOUR PAPERWORK IN ORDER. Depending on the location you choose for your DW, you need to present a variety of documents to get a marriage license: birth certificates, passports, proof of divorce or the death of a previous spouse (if either of you has been married before), and other site-specific forms. If your destination is a foreign country, you may need to send certified copies ahead of time so that they can be translated into the local language. Many places also require blood tests or other medical tests. Do your homework and get what you'll need early so you're not scrambling around at the last minute.

CONSULT WITH YOUR OFFICIANT. A local officiant should be able to walk you through the process of getting your marriage license and certificate. If you're flying in your officiant from your hometown, check with the local authorities to make sure a wedding that he or she conducts will be recognized.

MAKE SURE YOUR MARRIAGE WILL BE RECOGNIZED AS LEGAL BACK HOME. In the vast majority of cases, any marriage that is legally recognized in the country where it is performed will be considered legal by the U.S. government, but check with the attorney general's office of your state of residence to be sure. They can tell you about their country-specific policies and let you know what you need to do, if anything, upon your return to the United States.

TALK TO YOUR RELIGIOUS LEADERS. If sanction of your marriage by a particular religion is important to you, check with the authorities of your local church, synagogue, or other place of worship to find out what's required. If your destination ceremony doesn't pass official muster, arrange a second, religious wedding or just a blessing of your marriage upon your return.

CONSIDER A CIVIL SERVICE STATESIDE. If the procedures required to get married legally at your destination seem too daunting, you may want to get hitched at city hall right before you leave. While your destination ceremony will technically be a renewal of your vows, trust us, you'll still feel plenty of butterflies walking down the aisle—and your vows won't be any less heartfelt.

CALL YOUR LOCAL CITY HALL to find out how far in advance you'll need to get married before you take off for your destination. If your DW is a religious one, the officiant may want to see written proof that you're legally married before he or she will perform the ceremony, so make sure there's time for any paperwork to be processed before you depart.

choosing a ceremony style

Not having as much control over your ceremony as you would at home is one challenge of a destination wedding, especially if you're getting married in a foreign country where your religion isn't widely practiced. Knowing which of the three basic ceremony types—religious, interfaith, and civil—works best for you will determine the rest of your ceremony-planning to-do list.

Religious Ceremony

WHAT IT IS/WHO CONDUCTS IT. This type of wedding is conducted by an official clergyperson of your religion

the legal aspect

Be sure to make it official! Use this list to keep track of office locations and costs for the formal aspect of your wedding.

O Marriage license bureau in city or town where you will marry: _____

O Marriage license bureau in city or town where you live (if different): _____

O Blood tests required? Y_____ N_____

O Documents required: _____

O Fee for license: _____

O License valid for: _____

Do you need to find out the marriage requirements in your destination? Log on to theknot.com/destination wedding, or check out the Destination Directory on page 151.

(or by two officiants if you are from different faiths), either in a church, a synagogue, or another place of worship, or in a secular space.

THE ADVANTAGES. Knowing that a celebrant of your faith is blessing your marriage can make it extraspecial. Since religious officiants have defined ideas about what the ceremony can and can't include, they may be able to offer you planning guidance.

TIP

You cannot have a Catholic service outside the confines of a church.

THE DISADVANTAGES. You won't have total freedom to design your ceremony, although how much flexibility you have will depend on the rules of your religion, your officiant, the country where you choose to wed, and whether or not you get married inside a church or other house of worship. Don't expect the church at your destination to be as liberal as your own back home. There may be restrictions on what music you can play, or you may have to stick to an officially sanctioned script—which will cramp your style if you've dreamed of writing your own vows and walking down the aisle to the strains of U2.

Interfaith Ceremony

WHAT IT IS/WHO CONDUCTS IT. An interfaith minister will preside over a ceremony that has a religious bent without enforcing the customs of any one religion. Depending on what you want, the ceremony can combine two different religious traditions or work within the conventions of one. You can also skip the influence of an organized religion and opt for a ceremony that's simply spiritual in nature.

THE ADVANTAGES. Interfaith ceremonies are a great option for couples who come from different religious backgrounds, as well as those who consider themselves people of faith but aren't strongly affiliated with an organized religion. Interfaith officiants are usually pretty flexible and should work with you to find creative ways to incorporate both of your faiths into the ceremony. If you can't find a clergyperson of your religion in the country or region where you're marrying, an interfaith officiant will conduct a ceremony according to the guidelines of your religion.

THE DISADVANTAGES. Interfaith officiants are hard to find overseas and in some countries interfaith marriages aren't recognized as legit. For instance, in Greece, religious ceremonies are allowed only for Christians marrying Christians and Jews marrying Jews.

Civil Ceremony

WHAT IT IS/WHO CONDUCTS IT. A civil ceremony has no official religious element and can be conducted by anyone legally authorized to perform marriages in the country or region where your wedding takes place. Judges, magistrates, justices of the peace, county or court clerks, mayors, or notary publics are some of the options, though, of course, you'll need to confer with the legal authorities at your destination.

THE ADVANTAGES. Without a religious authority presiding over your ceremony, you're free to design it to suit yourselves. But you don't have to settle for a dry, city hall–style ceremony. You can still incorporate spiritual or religious elements; you just can't count on your officiant to do it for you. To give the event a more spiritual feel, ask friends to read favorite poems, prayers, or even Bible passages, and the musicians can play favorite hymns. Or you can make it short and sweet—a quick swapping of vows and declaration of marriage, sealed with a kiss—and you're off to your party!

THE DISADVANTAGES. If your religion is important to you, you may feel that something is missing without a clergyperson present to sanction your marriage. And it's possible that your congregation back home won't recognize you as officially married, though you can always have a religious ceremony, either before or after your destination wedding, to get their blessing.

Do we have to invite the officiant to the wedding reception and rehearsal dinner? I know it's customary, but it's a destination wedding and we're never going to see him or her again.

The tradition of inviting the officiant to both the rehearsal dinner and the wedding reception is a holdover from the days when the officiant was somebody you knew well, or at least a prominent member of the community. But since your relationship with your officiant is most likely going to end after the wedding weekend, it's understandable that you're reluctant to sacrifice seats at these events for him or her (and a spouse).

That said, you should keep in mind that the officiant is playing a very important role in your life, however briefly, so you should be as hospitable to this person as you can, and take the chance to get to know him or her a little bit better during the limited time you have. You never know—a brief conversation over drinks at your rehearsal or while table hopping at your reception could enhance your wedding experience in ways you didn't anticipate. So suck it up and invite your officiant to both events (and know that he or she may decline anyway—in which case it's a nonissue but you still come off as polite).

TIP

If you want a traditional
Jewish ceremony, you may
have difficulty finding a
rabbi in some parts of the
world, such as predomi-
nantly Christian countries
like Italy or small Caribbean
islands.

finding your officiant

How flexible you can be when choosing an officiant has everything
to do with where your ceremony will take place. If you're exchanging vows on the beach or your hotel terrace, you can shop around,
but if you have your heart set on being married in a historic
Catholic church, you'll probably need to work with a priest assigned
by the church. Likewise, if your religion isn't widely practiced in
your destination, your selection of officiants may be limited.

If you want a religious ceremony, your first step is to contact
local houses of worship. You may be asked to provide a letter of
referral from your hometown priest. If a local officiant isn't willing to perform a
nonparishioner's wedding, you may have to consider flying in a celebrant. (Asking a hometown minister, priest, rabbi, or other religious leader with whom one
or both of you has a strong connection to to perform your ceremony will no
doubt make it even more meaningful.)

The easiest approach is to find a local nondenominational officiant or a
Christian minister who will marry you regardless of whether you share his or her
faith—or each other's. If you find one who is very experienced with weddings
and has done DWs before, then he or she is likely to be versatile and willing to
let you two have control over the ceremony. Once you've found a good candidate,
sit down and ask him or her the following questions (keep in mind, overseas officiants may not speak English and you may need an interpreter):

WHAT DOES YOUR TYPICAL CEREMONY CONSIST OF?

POINTER: If the officiant works at a local church or synagogue, try to attend a service so that you can get a sense of his or her style. If that isn't an option, ask the
officiant if you can read the text of a ceremony. Even if it's just notes and a list
of what the readings were, it will give you a general idea of what to expect.

CAN WE MODIFY THE CEREMONY? IS IT OKAY IF SOME OF OUR READINGS ARE NONRELIGIOUS POEMS? IF OUR RECESSIONAL IS A BEATLES TUNE?

POINTER: Depending on the denomination of your officiant, you may need to
compromise when it comes to personalizing your ceremony. Restrictions vary
among churches and religions, so if you really want to marry in a certain spot,
you may have to forgo secular music or readings. If you feel strongly about

taking a less conventional route, you may need to wed outside of a church and/or find a nondenominational officiant who will help you build your ceremony your way.

DO WE NEED TO PRESENT BAPTISMAL CERTIFICATES OR SOME OTHER PROOF OF RELIGION?

POINTER: Do your homework beforehand to make sure you have copies of all the documents you need. If you are not sure what to bring, ask your officiant. Be sure to pack multiple photocopies and stash them in different suitcases.

CAN YOU MAKE SURE OUR MARRIAGE WILL BE LEGAL IN THE EYES OF THE LAW? THE EYES OF OUR RELIGION?

POINTER: A local officiant should be able to guide you through the process of having your marriage legally certified in the state or country you're in, though if you're flying in an officiant from home, you may need to do most of the legwork yourself. If the officiant is part of the recognized clergy of your religion, you should be all set on that front, but if you're getting married by a nondenominational celebrant or a justice of the peace, you'll need to talk to your place of worship to find out whether the wedding will be valid.

DOES THE SPACE/SITE HAVE ANY RESTRICTIONS?

POINTER: If the wedding will take place at a church or other religious venue, there may be some rules about what you can and can't do. Be sure to cover all of the following:

* Can we bring in outside musicians? Are any instruments forbidden?

outline of the standard ceremony

Before you and your officiant discuss adding personal touches to the ceremony, review this list of the key elements that go into a classic American wedding:

O Procession

O Opening remarks from the officiant

O Exchange of vows

O Reading of poems or religious or spiritual passages

O Sermon or some other remarks from the officiant

O Ring exchange and possibly other unity gestures, such as the lighting of a unity candle

O Pronouncement of marriage and kiss

O Closing remarks

O Recession

* Can we have a photographer and videographer at the ceremony? Is flash photography permitted?

* Are there any rules about how we can decorate the church or ceremony site?

* Are there any restrictions on tossing items (rice, petals, birdseed) at the end of the ceremony?

* Is there a dress code?

working with your officiant

TIP

If you're getting married on a breezy beach or any outdoor location where it may be hard for your guests to hear your officiant or your vows, consider setting up a microphone and a sound system. Either the event planner at your site or your musicians should be able to arrange it.

Ideally you'll have at least two face-to-face meetings with the person who will preside over your wedding: an initial interview to evaluate whether this is the person you want to perform your ceremony (ask questions and try to sense his or her vibe) and a second planning meeting once the officiant has signed on, to hammer out the details of what passages will be read, what music will be played, and how the ceremony will flow.

Although a lot can be communicated via phone and/or e-mail, these in-person meetings are essential for the officiant to get a sense of who you are and to plan the ceremony. Cover the following issues at the important second meeting:

DISCUSS ALL PROCEDURAL DETAILS. Presiding over a special spiritual ritual for the two of you isn't your officiant's only job—he or she will also be legally marrying you and, possibly, performing a religious sacrament. Go over specific logistics:

* When will you sign your marriage license—at the rehearsal, at the ceremony, or before the wedding?

* What will the rehearsal entail—when can it be held, who should attend?

* If the site is the officiant's church or synagogue or another house of worship, what does it provide and what must you provide yourselves (pew ribbons, aisle runner, flowers, candles)?

OPEN UP ABOUT YOURSELVES. Unless you're flying in an officiant you've known for years, the person conducting your DW will start out as a stranger. So reveal as much personal information about yourselves as you can—how you met, your favorite things to do together, your shared goals for married life, even the little quirks each of you finds endearing about the other. This will allow him or her to make the ceremony more personal. And ask questions about your officiant's life, too, so you'll feel you all know one another pretty well by the time your wedding day rolls around.

SHARE YOUR GOALS FOR YOUR DREAM CEREMONY. Is it superimportant to include your family? Is having lots of beautiful music one of your highest priorities? Maybe you want it to be engaging for your guests, and have the officiant share a bit of your love story with them, or maybe you don't even care if the guests can hear your vows, since your focus is on creating a romantic moment between the two of you.

ASK ABOUT YOUR OFFICIANT'S FAVORITE CUSTOMS. A great way to get ideas on how to make your ceremony more meaningful is to ask the officiant about rituals and special touches other couples have used, especially if he or she knows about unique local customs you can incorporate. You may find some of them inspiring, and you'll know that your officiant is comfortable with them.

TIP

Visit sunrisesunset.com to research what time the sun sets in your exact location on your wedding date. You don't want to book a sunset ceremony at 6:00 if the sun said good-bye at 4:47.

a world of ceremony ideas

Your goal is to make your ceremony feel special, and a destination wedding offers abundant ways to do that. Hold it in a visually arresting setting that's unlike anywhere back home or draw on your destination's culture to make the moment totally personal and unforgettable. Infuse your ceremony with local traditions from these popular destinations:

HAWAII: Play the beautiful local wedding classic "Hawaiian Wedding Song," made famous by Elvis in the movie *Blue Hawaii.* The bride can wear a woven garland of island flowers, called *haku lei,* instead of a veil. In addition to exchanging rings, exchange leis during the ceremony—they're a symbol of love—or have your officiant bind your hands together with a lei to represent your commitment.

PUERTO RICO: Have the officiant bless a plate of coins and give them to the groom, who then gives them to the bride after the exchange of vows. Local tradition dictates that the bride keeps the coins—which represent good luck and prosperity —as a gift from her husband.

IRELAND: End the ceremony with the blessing of a Celtic cross, which you can hang in your newlywed home.

MEXICO: After the vow exchange, have the officiant or your attendants place a large loop of rosary beads or a lasso in a figure-eight shape around your necks or wrists to symbolize unity and the idea that you two are bound together by love for the rest of your lives. If you're Catholic, follow the tradition of having the rosary blessed with holy water three times in honor of the trinity.

BERMUDA: After a wedding in Bermuda, newlyweds walk under one of the island's Moongates, a very round archway made of limestone and coral, for good luck.

JAMAICA: Follow the romantic tradition of the bride veiling her face until the groom lifts her veil when they're pronounced man and wife.

JAPAN: You can add a traditional touch to a wedding in Japan, or a Japanese garden anywhere in the world, by decorating your reception with white origami cranes, which are meant to bring good luck to newlyweds.

Aside from the native culture, you can design your ceremony based on your destination's climate and general vibe.

BEACH: Line the aisle with scattered seashells, or surround the ceremony space with tiki torches decorated with streamers in the wedding colors. Since lighting a unity candle may not work in the ocean breeze, try a "sand ceremony" instead. This is when the bride and groom combine sand of two different colors (you can use your wedding colors, or blue to represent the sky and natural for the earth) and pour both into one container, symbolizing their unity.

COUNTRY: Use tall wooden vases of sunflowers as the backdrop and line the aisle with bunches of wildflowers. Create a runner out of eyelet or embroidered burlap, and have fiddlers play at the ceremony.

CASTLES AND ROMANTIC SETTINGS: Line the aisle with a bright red carpet and tall, wrought-iron candlesticks adorned with red amaranth. Trumpeters can welcome the arriving guests.

MOUNTAIN/COLD CLIMATE: Greet arriving guests with mulled cider and hot chocolate; hang fake snowflakes and ice crystals from the rafters and the chuppah or a trellis set over the bride and groom. If the ceremony is outdoors, arrive in a sleigh, position fire pits strategically around the site, and give guests blankets to huddle under.

setting your service to music

At any wedding, music is an essential ingredient of a great ceremony—nothing pulls on the heartstrings and makes a moment moving like the right song.

Why not let the destination influence your ceremony's music? Either choose traditional songs from your destination and have them played by your regular wedding musicians or use local musicians who play native instruments—mariachis in Mexico, a steel drum band in the Caribbean, a mandolin player in Italy, a ukulele player in Hawaii.

If there is no specific music native to your locale, simply take direction from the feel of your immediate surroundings. A Gothic cathedral in France calls for thundering organ music, and a bluegrass band would provide the perfect sound track to a ceremony set in a country field. Here are a few more things to keep in mind:

* Schedule an appointment with the site's music director (if there is one) or event planner. If you're having your ceremony at a resort, there may be staff musicians, or even a DJ, you can use. He or she can tell you about the venue's acoustics and give input on what type of instruments and music sound best in that location.

* Investigate the available outlets—they may need to run an extension cord for the sound system.

* Delicate sounds—like string instruments—generally aren't the best choice for a beach ceremony, because the sounds of the sea may drown out your violinist.

* Investigate noise restrictions if you're holding your ceremony in a public place.

put it in the program

A well-done program will allow your guests to both follow along with the ceremony and understand any local traditions, meaningful readings, or unique music that are part of your wedding.

TIP

In any destination, have a flower girl scatter petals from local flowers down the aisle before you proceed in.

TIP

If your ceremony will be outdoors, make sure your musicians can take shelter if there's even the slightest hint of rain. Many instruments are fragile, so even a momentary drizzle could ruin the performance. Consider setting up a small tent for them to play under.

Destination "I Do"

here comes the bride ...

The following elements of the ceremony are traditionally set to music:

O PRELUDE: fifteen to thirty minutes' worth of music played as the guests are being seated and waiting for the ceremony to begin

_____

_____

_____

O PROCESSIONAL: music playing as you and your wedding party make your grand entrance

_____

O INTERLUDES: songs used during key moments of the ceremony, like the ring exchange or the lighting of the unity candle

_____

_____

_____

O RECESSIONAL: the music that accompanies your joyful exit from the ceremony

_____

O POSTLUDE: ten or so minutes of filler music to be played after the recessional as your guests file out of the church or ceremony area

_____

_____

_____

Find ideas online at TheKnot.com/music.

INCLUDE THE BASICS. No matter what form it takes, a wedding program should begin with the full names of the bride and groom, the wedding date, and the city and state (or country) where you're marrying. After this, spell out the elements of the ceremony, including the reading titles, authors, and readers, and the names of the musical selections, composers, and performers. If you'd like the crowd to sing along to certain songs or hymns, specify that in the program and include the lyrics. At the end of the program, list the names of the officiant, the wedding party, and, if you'd like, your parents and grandparents.

HIGHLIGHT THE SETTING. Since you've gathered people at this special place, be sure they know exactly why you chose both the destination and the specific ceremony location. If appropriate, include a short paragraph or two explaining why the site is meaningful to you.

HONOR THE ABSENT. Since some of your loved ones may not have been able to make the trip (elderly relatives, your cousin with the newborn twins), mention in the program that you know they are there in spirit. If you wish to honor deceased loved ones, include a memorial on the back page with a photograph or quote, a fond memory, or a poem.

EXPLAIN LOCAL TOUCHES. Give a few details on any local customs or rituals you're incorporating into the ceremony, and identify any exotic songs and musical instruments being played that your guests may not be familiar with.

SHOW YOUR THANKS. Many couples choose to end the program with a thank-you to both sets of parents and one to all the guests for attending. This is an especially nice touch when everyone has traveled to be there.

Here are ten ways to tie your program to the location

O Pick a symbol that relates to the setting (a bunch of grapes in wine country, a fleur-de-lis in France) and print it on the top or the cover of the programs, or repeat it on each page. Use the same motif on your save-the-dates, reception menus, and other printed materials.

O For an old-world European setting, print programs on marbled parchment paper rolled into scrolls and tied with a sage green ribbon and a sprig of eucalyptus.

O For a mountain or country destination, a small booklet with a cocoa- or mocha-colored cover can be bound with twine and finished with a tiny gold-glittered pinecone.

O If you're getting married in a snowy setting like Aspen, pin a silver-studded snowflake to the top of your wedding program.

O At the beach, bind a small program booklet with a string of seashells.

O A handmade paper cover and band with natural raffia will also be fitting for a seaside setting.

O In hot climates, print your program on paper fans that guests can use to cool themselves as they wait for the ceremony to start.

O Incorporate ethnic symbols and motifs. If your wedding is taking place overseas, use the symbols often associated with the region— shamrocks in Ireland, thistle in Scotland, fleur-de-lis in France, an Egyptian ankh—to continue the theme.

O For Southwest or desert-themed weddings, craft programs in the same muted colors found in the landscape, and bind together pages with twine or small twigs.

O Look to local nature for inspiration, too. Are magnolia blossoms everywhere you look? Are you saying "I do" in the evergreen forests of the Pacific Northwest? If so, think about using those elements as motifs on the pages of your programs.

Destination "I Do"

KATHRYN & CHAD · NANTUCKET, MA

Hometown: Boston, MA
Guests: 200

The Destination Decision: Water babies Kathryn and Chad had both spent summers on Cape Cod, Nantucket, and Martha's Vineyard, so offering guests a mini-vacation to Nantucket was an easy decision. "We rented a large house on the water with a tent outside for the wedding," says Kathryn. "Our entire wedding party got to stay with us in the house."

Planning Pointer: Don't be afraid to go for alternatives. The Catholic church on Nantucket was booked the weekend of the couple's wedding, but rather than reschedule, they adapted. "The First Congregational Church welcomed us—and our Catholic priest—with open arms," says Kathryn. The classic New England church contributed to guests' destination experience even during the religious part of the weekend. "The spectacular white church featured floor-to-ceiling windows, and it was on a hill that overlooked a gorgeous lawn and trees," says Kathryn.

The Definitive Detail: Kathryn gave her bridesmaids, who were dressed in lilac, bracelets made with pale purple stones that looked like sea glass. Groomsmen received silver cuff links engraved with "ACK"—the airport code for Nantucket.

Ch. 7

party on:
planning your reception

Since your wedding weekend will be packed with multiple gatherings, you need to find ways to make the reception *the* main event. The ingredients that guarantee it? Plenty of delicious food and drink, a great dance band, a dramatic atmosphere, and details that draw upon the style of your destination—and set your reception apart as truly unique.

But the main secret to a successful reception is ultimately invisible to anyone attending the wedding: good timing. A carefully thought-out schedule (when will the toasting begin? who will go first?), clear assignments of responsibility (who will invite guests from cocktails into the reception?), and good communication of this information to all involved (from the caterer to the band to the bridal party) are all essential to ensure the event appears and feels effortless.

the defining moments of a reception

Aside from being the first party you throw as husband and wife, the reception is set apart from the other wedding soirees by the flow of events—from the bridal party's entrance to the newlyweds' getaway.

COCKTAIL HOUR. Once guests leave the ceremony, they'll need somewhere to go and something to eat and drink. To set the mood, unveil a signature cocktail, or pass lemonade or punch in the warmer months and hot cocoa or flavored coffees in the winter. Hors d'oeuvres can be either presented buffet-style or passed by waiters, but go for one-bite options that guests can easily pop into their mouths as they stand and mingle. While they are reveling in your hospitality, you'll be touching up your makeup, taking pictures, and, hopefully, stealing a few quick minutes of alone time with your new spouse.

RECEIVING LINE. This isn't as crucial at a destination wedding as it is at a local event since you've probably already spent ample time thanking your guests for making the trip. If so, you can skip the line—though a short one (just you two and the parents) is still a good way to let everyone feel like they've had a chance to wish you well on your actual wedding day.

ENTRY INTO THE RECEPTION. After the guests have been brought into the main room, you'll need to kick things off somehow. Many couples do this by introducing the bridal party as they walk to their seats. Of course, the newlyweds are the last people to enter—pick out an upbeat song (Beyonce's "Crazy in Love" or Madonna's "Ray of Light") to make your "first appearance" as husband and wife a memorable one. If you've attended the cocktail hour, you can skip this "introduction."

FIRST DANCE. Even if you shun the spotlight and your new husband's got two left feet, it's best to embrace tradition and take a twirl. You can follow immediately with the special dances—father/daughter, mother/son, and wedding party—in fact. All three of these can be done over the course of one or two songs, if everyone involved is okay about sharing part of their time in the spotlight. Otherwise the special dances can be announced by the bandleader at the start of the general dancing period postdinner.

HOST AND WEDDING PARTY TOASTS. Keep these to a minimum at the reception. Only the father of the bride (he's the ceremonial, if not financial, host in most cases) and the best man are required to speak, but often the maid of honor says a few words at this time as well. All of the toasts should be short and sweet. Your dad can thank everyone for coming, offer words of love and advice (he's *still* a parent, after all), and wish the guests a good time. The best man can speak about his close friendship with the groom and, of course, say something glowing about the bride and how she made the groom a better man. Longer speeches, stunts, and anything involving props should be reserved for the rehearsal dinner.

DINNER SERVICE. Often the first course is already on the tables when guests enter the dining room, or is served while the toasts are being made—about twenty minutes into the reception.

DANCING. Let the party begin! At some receptions, guests will want to dance between courses or whenever they hear a favorite song. At others, dancing will commence after dinner but before dessert. Think about which kind of event you want, and what kind of crowd you've gathered, and make sure your musicians play appropriate music.

COUPLE'S TOAST. All of these people have gathered to celebrate you, so you've got a duty to thank them. This is the time when the couple takes the floor in order to express their love and happiness, and to thank everyone who's come out to celebrate with them. Some less-energetic guests will want to leave just after the cake cutting, so you'll want to work these public sentiments in before then.

CAKE CUTTING. One thing's for sure: Whether you've got four or four hundred people watching, the cake-

your turn to toast

Don't forget to toast your guests for coming to celebrate with you! It doesn't have to be anything elaborate or profound, just make it sincere.

Start off with an engaging or humorous story about your new spouse or about the wedding-planning process.

Then segue into how happy you are that the day has finally arrived, and how much it means to you that those gathered can share it with you.

Be sure to thank your parents, in-laws, and any other key players. And it's especially important to thank the crowd for making the trip.

Finally toast your new husband or wife. One person should start and the other should finish, or if this seems too awkward—or one of you is not the toasting type—it is okay for someone to stand silently, just remember to look out at the crowd and raise your glass and toast your parents and guests on cue.

in-the-face move is a bad one. Cut into the bottom tier, pull out a slice, smile for the camera, and feed each other a piece. The caterer will take care of slicing, plating, and serving the rest. It's important to make this moment somewhat obvious because traditionally it's in poor taste to leave before the cake cutting.

BOUQUET/GARTER TOSS. Go the traditional route by gathering all single women for the bouquet toss and all single men for the garter, and then having the lucky catchers share a dance. Or tweak tradition and make the ritual more location specific. Toss a lei to the single ladies at a Hawaiian wedding, or throw out heart- or snowman-shaped hand warmers at slopeside nuptials.

LAST DANCE. This signals that the reception is coming to an end. Make sure the bandleader or DJ announces it so everyone knows the night is winding down.

GETAWAY. A getaway may feel a little strange if you know you're going to an after-party or to brunch the next day, but a lot of people will linger at the reception confused if you don't have one. Light sparklers, ring bells, blow bubbles— do something to mark the moment, especially if you really are saying good night!

create a mood

Since you're getting married in a distinct environment, design elements and motifs will practically present themselves. That said, you don't want your reception to strike a one-note "theme" based solely on the location. Here are five sure-fire approaches to crafting a reception that reflects your destination *and* suits your unique style:

GET INSPIRED BY THE LANDSCAPE. If natural beauty is one of your location's signature features, look for ways to play it up at your reception. You can bring elements of the outside in by using local foliage (palms, fall leaves, holly berries, or whatever defines the surrounding terrain) in the centerpieces, in your bouquets, or to decorate the cocktail tables and bar. Or use one of the region's signature flowers or plants as a recurring motif at the reception (printed on the menus, place cards, favor tags, etc.).

CELEBRATE THE DESTINATION'S REPUTATION. If your setting is especially famous for one thing, use that as a starting point for reception ideas (Newport lends itself to a yachting motif, Napa to a wine and artisanal food theme). If it feels too expected to play up this signature, simply use it as a starting place. For instance, if images of surfboards and hula dancers seem too trite for Hawaii, design your reception around the classic Elvis flick *Blue Hawaii* with retro, Hawaii-in-the-fifties touches and songs by the King playing at cocktail hour.

PLAY OFF THE NATIVE CULTURE. International destinations offer a wealth of ideas for reception themes and design since you can emphasize unique aspects of another culture. Think of the reception as an opportunity to immerse your guests in the style and customs of the country so they get a strong sense of why you decided to host your wedding there. Serve regional cuisine, play the native music, and work national colors and symbols into the table decor.

WORK THE STYLE OF THE SPACE. Whether you've traveled to the tropics or the European countryside, it's absolutely an option to disregard the customs of the land and have the same style of wedding you'd have had at home. In that case, take your cues from the look of the reception space. A ballroom is the perfect place for elegant black-tie style (even if that ballroom is in Hawaii), and you can give an afternoon garden party a preppy all-American feel (even if that garden is in France). It's your wedding, after all!

MIX IT UP. To create a feel that's elegant but casual, avoid perfectly matching tables. Centerpieces should be closely coordinated but not clones. Mix several shades of linens, or use banquet-style seating to create an intimate environment.

FLOWERS. Nothing brings a space to life like a profusion of beautiful blooms, though if your reception site is already visually interesting, you won't need a lot of elaborate floral arrangements. Choose your flowers with an eye toward what works with the surrounding landscape. For urban settings—where there's little natural foliage—you can choose virtually any floral style. Some pointers:

* Pick flowers that are similar in color or feel to the local foliage.

* If your reception is being held al fresco, or even in a room with lots of views to the outdoors, it's especially important that you choose flowers that complement, and don't clash with, what's outside.

TIP

Lighting can completely transform the feel of a space. Consider dimming the lights and relying heavily on candles, or investigate using a custom lighting design, such as colored gels, patterns, or pin spotting, that can add drama to your decor.

TIP

Get creative by labeling your tables using names rather than numbers. This is particularly appropriate at a destination wedding, where it can help underscore your theme. If you're getting married at the peak of fall foliage season, name the tables after vibrantly colored trees like oak, maple, poplar, aspen, and so on. Headed for the Caribbean? Make your mark with tropical flowers or fish.

* If you're surrounded by fields or mountains carpeted in wildflowers, then tightly sculpted modern centerpieces may look totally out of place.

* No matter where you are, you can use flowers to create subtly different moods for the ceremony, cocktail hour, and dinner spaces. Try using three different flowers in one color scheme (white lilies at the ceremony, white roses for cocktail hour, and white peonies for dinner), or use the same flower in three different colors (white roses for the ceremony, pink ones for cocktail hour, red ones for dinner).

* Don't forget to consider the climate. If it's hot and humid, delicate flowers (like gardenias, lilies of the valley, tulips, and wildflowers) might wilt midway through the event. Pick sturdy flowers instead. Tropical flowers, sunflowers, zinnias, dahlias, lilies, and hydrangeas are all great options.

PLACE SETTINGS. Carefully chosen glassware, dishes, and table linens can subtly inject your reception site with a big dose of style. Make sure these elements reflect the overall tone of your reception and look for ways to make them bring out the vibe of your destination.

* Colored glass and unique china will bring your room alive. Look for richly hued water goblets and glass chargers (aka presentation plates). If you're at a beach destination, pick green or blue sea-glass hues; at a mountain location, look for glass in the colors of fall foliage; and no matter where you are, vibrant reds and pinks will make the space pop with passion and romance. For a trendy, very modern look (perfect for an urban setting) pair dramatic black glass and crystal with silver-trimmed white china.

* Choose linens that reflect your region. In the tropics, use bold hues like turquoise, lime, or tangerine. Tablecloths rich in texture like a heavy linen or a raw silk suit an American country setting. In a castle, a beaded or embroidered organza overlay will lend an appropriately royal air.

a world of flowers

Greece: Work ivy into your centerpieces, and string it along the bar. In ancient times, Greek brides often carried ivy as a symbol of undying love for their grooms.

Italy: Add herbs such as rosemary to the flower arrangements—brides in ancient Rome carried herbs to symbolize fidelity and fertility (plus, they'll smell delicious). Decorate the front grill of your "getaway car" (if you have one) with flowers, an Italian custom meant to pave the road to a happy life together.

England: Go traditional and focus on roses. The Victorians popularized the rose as *the* wedding flower, because in their culture it represented true love.

Spain: Use lots of sweet-smelling orange blossoms, which are abundant in Spain and considered to be a symbol of true love.

Hawaii: Cover your reception space in dendrobium orchids, which come in white, yellow, or shades of purple and are one of the islands' traditional wedding flowers.

* The containers used to create your floral arrangements can add to the decor. Instead of the standard clear-glass vases, put your flowers in local pottery. At an intimate reception in England, use an eclectic collection of antique tea services as the foundation for the centerpieces. Consider a wrought-iron candelabra in a castle in Europe. In a beachy setting, bamboo containers create the right casual feel.

* Scent is another way to create mood. At each table, replace one votive candle with one infused with your destination's signature flower, fruit, or herb (don't use all scented votives or the smell could be overpowering).

* Napkin rings emblazoned with your monogram or wedding motif are a tiny personal touch with lots of impact. Tying each napkin with a ribbon and stem of a flower with significance to the season or region—lavender in the South of France, rosemary in Italy, a sprig of grape hyacinth in springtime—makes a simple but strong visual statement.

TIP

If you are using your venue's in-house caterer, they might not have as many tabletop options as you'd like—but ask for what you want anyway: They may go out of their way to try to accommodate you. Or see if you can find a florist who does elements of reception design beyond the blooms. Many florists now will coordinate the selection and rental of tableware and other decorative elements for a party.

ideas for beach destinations

Since so many destination weddings take place on or near water, here's a roundup of beach-themed decorating ideas:

○ Line the walkways to and from the reception with large cotainers filled with sand and seashells, or position potted palms along the aisle.

○ Use seashells and flowing ribbons to cover a trellis for guests to walk through as they enter the reception.

○ Place large blue and green pillows on the sand to create an outdoor lounge where guests can sit during cocktail hour or retreat after dinner to enjoy the music.

○ Paint names and table numbers on sand dollars and use them as escort cards.

○ Line the dance floor with baskets of flip-flops, so guests can ditch their wedding shoes for dancing or walks in the sand as the night wears on.

○ For centerpieces, arrange flowers in large conch shells or brightly painted beach pails.

○ Conjure up an underwater wonderland by combining blue and green flowers with sand-colored table linens and shell accents.

○ Scatter sea glass on the tables if you are using standard linens.

PAPERS. The paper products required for your wedding don't stop with the stationery—if you choose to use escort cards, place cards, menu cards, and the like, you'll need to pick a design that ties them together with the other elements of your reception.

* Use colored ink that matches or complements the colors of your bridesmaids' dresses, your centerpieces, or other decorative elements.

* Pick a typeface that reflects the mood you're trying to create—ornate script for a reception set in a historic mansion; spare sans serif if you're celebrating in a sleek hotel in South Beach.

* Print up cards for the bar listing any signature cocktails and the wines being served. This is especially important if you're serving drinks unique to your destination that your guests might be unfamiliar with.

* For foreign destinations, work touches of the native language into the place cards or menus. Swap "Monsieur and Madame" for "Mr. and Mrs." in a French-speaking country, or take it a step further and translate the entire menu (have an English version printed on the opposite side for the sake of guests unfamiliar with the native tongue).

* Print up notes to be attached to the favors, with a little message from the two of you thanking guests for making the trip.

focus on the food

At many venues, working with the in-house food service means you may have less control than if you could choose from a variety of outside caterers. The key to getting a meal that will be mouthwatering and memorable lies in the choices you make.

START WITH WHAT THE CHEF DOES BEST. Although the catering manager may claim the kitchen can tailor a menu to your specific requests, you're probably best off sticking with their classic dishes, at least for the entrées. You don't want the kitchen testing out new things for you since the results could be iffy (even if they can make it work for your tasting, it's another thing to pull off a dish for a large group). Ask which of their main courses are most popular, and try a variety of them at your tasting.

HAVE AS MANY TASTINGS AS YOU NEED. If you aren't wowed by the options at your first tasting, speak up. Tell them specifically how you'd like the food to be different or which dishes you'd like to replace. Then insist on having as many subsequent tastings as it takes for the kitchen to nail it (even offer to pay for them if you have to).

GO LOCAL. At a DW you're almost obligated to showcase some of the culinary creations the area is known for. That doesn't mean you must do a total theme meal, but if you're on an island awash in seafood, why fly in filet mignon from the mainland? Celebrate regional cuisine. Fresh, local food will probably taste better, and serving it will give your guests a sense of the surrounding culture via their taste buds. However, avoid anything *too* exotic. Only serve unfamiliar things if you're sure everyone will love them. Otherwise, it's probably safer to serve ethnic food as hors d'oeuvres and, at dinner, look for ways to tweak some classic dishes with regional spices and garnishes.

PICK A WEATHER-APPROPRIATE CAKE. If your destination has a tropical (or just hot) climate, steer clear of ingredients that won't hold up in heat and humidity. Custard will go rancid, so opt for ganache or fruit-based fillings instead. And, unfortunately, the ultrapopular buttercream frosting melts in tropical temps (as will whipped cream and cream cheese–based frosting), so stick with sturdy fondant. But if you have your heart set on a buttercream-frosted cake, ask your baker to do a layer of it underneath a topping of fondant.

> **TIP**
>
> Let your destination subtly influence a regular wedding cake. Work an ingredient the area is known for into a more traditional recipe: lemon-flavored cake on the Amalfi coast, coconut-dusted icing in Hawaii, and filling laced with rum at a Caribbean reception.

classic dishes from your destination

Mexico: Kick off your celebration with an *añejo* tequila tasting bar (fine tequilas that have been aged for twelve months). For the main meal, take culinary cues from the region: Feature an entrée showcasing mole sauce if you're in Puebla; tomato-based Veracruz sauce if you're in, you guessed it, Veracruz; and citrus-based sauces if you're in the Yucatán. Serve Mexican wedding cookies, a sampling of Mexican candies, or a *tres leches* cake in addition to wedding cake for dessert.

New England: Host a casual rehearsal dinner clambake, with clams, mussels, baked potatoes, and corn on the cob cooked right in the ground. For your cocktail hour, stock the bar with local artisanal beers such as Harpoon, Magic Hat, or Smuttynose. Do a cheese course that features selections from the fresh dairy farms in the area (Bayley Hazen Blue, Capri goat cheese, Hooligan cow's milk cheese), and consider serving lobster, scrod, or swordfish (all locally caught) as your main course.

Miami: Plan a Cuban-inspired menu: Begin your cocktail hour with a drink selection featuring variations on a mojito theme, everything from traditional and raspberry to mango and guava. Follow up with mini Cuban sandwiches and a *ceviche* bar, where guests can choose from different combinations of fresh fish salads. Hire a cigar roller to be the focus of attention during a *plein air* coffee course at the meal's end.

Bahamas: Work conch fritters, one of the island's most famous dishes, into a guise more appropriate for a formal setting by adding them to a microgreen and tropical fruit salad, or by preparing the conch in a different way—grilled and served alongside a main course. Grouper makes a traditional choice for a seafood entrée—serve it blackened, grilled, or with an elegant beurre blanc and herb sauce. For dessert, serve banana or coconut ice cream along with the traditional wedding cake.

Napa Valley: A wedding in Wine Country is the perfect excuse to try out as many of the local varieties of vino as possible. Build your meal around a selection of your favorite wines. For a wine-bar effect, arrange for rounds of heavy hors d'oeuvres and pair them with suggested wines. Some of the first (and best) organic and local restaurants got their start in Napa Valley, so incorporate local produce, savory herbs, and a healthy bent—think grilled, not fried—of great salads and plenty of sourdough bread and infused olive oil for dipping.

Hawaii: Plan a full-on luau complete with a pig roast and poi (a traditional Hawaiian dish traditionally made by cooking taro root in an underground oven, pounding it to a smooth paste, and sometimes storing it in banana leaves). Fresh fish like mahimahi or Pacific blue marlin caught in local waters is perfect paired with fruity rum cocktails. And, of course, a Hawaiian take on a pupu platter (or two) full of island-style hors d'oeuvres like fried shrimp, dumplings, and skewered beef.

Jamaica: Serve a sampling of traditional Jamaican appetizers in miniature sizes (which gives them a more elegant feel), including mini beef and chicken patties and fried plantains. Serve small tastes of a different rum drink with each course, to familiarize guests with the island's variety, then offer your entrée at three different levels of spiciness to introduce guests (gently) to the fiery Scotch Bonnet pepper. For dessert, serve individual portions of Jamaican rum cake.

Italy: Start the meal with aperitifs of limoncello or amaretto—or toast with Bellinis (champagne and peach juice), which originated at Harry's Bar in Venice. Serve a first course of pasta, being careful to select a sauce and ingredients typical of the region where you're getting married— up north, choose pesto; near Parma, feature prosciutto; near Naples, choose eggplant, anchovies, or olives; down south, serve a fish pasta (and leave off the cheese). After your entrée, plan a cheese course featuring regional Italian varieties and then draw upon the Italian penchant for not-too-sweet desserts by serving a wedding cake filled with fruit, alongside more traditional choices such as individual jam *crostatas* and homemade gelati. End the meal with an espresso bar, offering guests an array of different kinds of liquors to splash into their drinks.

France: Plan for wine to be an integral part of your reception meal. Choose a different varietal for each course and include the reason for selecting it on your written menu. Begin your meal with a simple mussel dish in broth and use your entrée to showcase some of the country's contributions to the world of sauces. Serve a sirloin steak (as one entrée choice) and offer Choron, béarnaise, and whole-grain mustard as toppings. End with a cheese course. Wrap up the seated portion of your meal with a tower of petit fours and get guests moving by welcoming them to sample a diverse dessert buffet full of individual tarts, cakes, and cookies.

get serious about seating

Unless you're serving a very casual meal, and your guest list is under fifty people, you probably want to give people specific seating assignments. Although it might sound stuffy to you, people actually *prefer* to be told where to sit. It spares them the confusion and awkwardness of trying to figure out where and with whom to sit, and shows that you cared enough to handpick a seat for them. Heed these guidelines when plotting your seating chart:

DO YOUR SEATING PLAN EARLY. Get it done at least a week before you depart for your destination so you're not stressing out about it the night before your flight. You may have to make a couple of last-minute changes, but you'll be glad you've got the basic plan in place.

DON'T LEAVE ANYBODY WITHOUT A SEAT. Double-, triple-, and quadruple-check that you have a seat assignment for every single person who will be in attendance, including the local officiant and his or her guest.

BE FLEXIBLE. It's likely that you'll have a no-show or two (one guest gets snowed in at his hometown airport, another gets sabotaged by work at the last minute), so pack a few blank escort cards; that way, you can change seating arrangements at the last minute.

ASK YOUR PARENTS WHAT THEY PREFER. It's traditional for both sets of parents to sit at the same table, along with the officiant and his or her partner, but this probably makes sense only if your wedding is on the small side. Otherwise, your parents will probably want to "host" their own tables so they can spend time with friends and family who have traveled so far to be there.

SEPARATE SWORN ENEMIES. If certain friends or family members get along like cats and dogs, try to seat them outside of each other's line of sight. You don't want any dirty looks or bad vibes to sully your reception.

PLAY MATCHMAKER. Place single guys and girls together, and mix up different groups of friends. Everyone feels flirtatious at weddings, so you never know what sort of sparks might fly! Don't worry that they'd rather be seated with people they know well; since yours is a multiday affair, they'll have plenty of time to hang out with their old buddies.

Do we need to give favors and welcome bags to each guest, or is it okay to just give one per couple?

There's nothing wrong with giving one favor and one welcome bag per couple. If you have any single guests, of course, each should get his or her own. Tell the resort to hand out one welcome bag per hotel room. It's a little trickier for your favors, since you can't put up a sign saying "one per couple" or anything like that. Instead, put the favors at the place settings. For couples, place the favor between the two place cards or very near them so that they understand it's meant for both. For single guests, favors can go directly behind the place cards or on top of the plates. That way, no one gets left out.

Any ideas for favors that our guests will make a point to pack? Here are some of our favorite destination favor ideas:

O Leather luggage tags personalized with each guest's name and address

O Local delicacies like maple syrup, candies, honey, or anything sweet

O Small stacks of postcards from the destination (prestamped, so guests can write their friends back home)

O A CD by a great local musician, whether an icon (Jimmy Buffett in Key West, Bob Marley in Jamaica) or a little-known but killer band you've discovered

O Mini photo albums they can fill later with photos from the event

reception music

Make certain to choose specific songs for at least these key events:

First dance

_____

_____

Father/daughter dance

_____

_____

Mother/son dance

_____

_____

Special guest dances

_____

_____

_____

Ethnic dances

_____

_____

_____

Cake cutting

_____

_____

Special requests

_____

_____

_____

Announcements and toasts

_____

_____

Last dance

_____

_____

let's dance: mastering your music

A surefire way to ensure that everyone has a good time is to play crowd-pleasing music. If you're going to have a dance floor, your goal is to get your guests onto it as much as possible.

PLAY SONGS THAT SPAN THE DECADES. Getting your preteen cousins, hard-partying college pals, and pacemaker-equipped great-grandparents to boogie down together can be a challenge. The secret lies in choosing a sound track with lots of variety. Ask your band or DJ to play songs from different eras, from big band standards to the Beatles to U2. Try to focus on classic songs from each time frame so that guests in each age group will be familiar with them (that strategy will work best for your destination band or DJ, too, since they may not be familiar with more obscure American tunes). As a general rule, play more of the parent- and grandparent-friendly songs at the beginning of the night, and switch over to the current hits once the older crowd begins to put their feet up or head back to their rooms.

PICK THE SOUND TRACK FOR SPECIFIC MOMENTS. You obviously need to specify which song you want for your first dance, as well as the father/daughter and mother/son songs. But you should also hand-pick tunes for the event's other big moments: the cake cutting, the bouquet toss, and the last dance. If the band you've hired can't play all the songs you've chosen, bring along CDs, making sure in advance that the venue has a CD player hooked up to the sound system.

GUARD AGAINST GHASTLY TUNES. Probably more important than your play list is your "do not play" list, those songs you find so trite or annoying that hearing them makes you want to retch. You may also want to disuss how to handle requests with your band or DJ. Fueled by flowing cocktails, many guests will ask to have *their* favorite songs played, with no regard to your preferences. Tell the band to ignore all requests but yours.

GIVE CLEAR INSTRUCTIONS to your DJ or bandleader about when to play emcee. If you want him or her to announce the wedding party, then write down people's names (with pronunciations), wedding roles, and their relationship to you (maid of honor, bride's parents, and so on). But if you don't want to hear a peep (other than music) from your entertainment, make sure they know that their sole duty is turning out tunes.

PLAY UP THE VIBE OF YOUR DESTINATION by hiring local musicians to perform the region's traditional tunes. (If you don't want to commit to that theme for the entire reception, have them play just during the cocktail hour.) Some location-specific ideas to celebrate multicultural musical traditions:

Bermuda: junkaroo players
Jamaica: reggae or ska musicians
Miami: a Cuban big band, or a DJ who evokes the clubs of South Beach
Caribbean islands: a steel drum band
Mexico: mariachis or a salsa band
Italy: mandolin or accordion players
India: sitar player
Ireland: a pipe band

TIP

Ace your first dance by having a pro teach you how to match smooth moves to your chosen song. Even if your reception has a defined theme or a cultural influence related to your destination, this is one moment when you should ignore all that and pick a tune that means the most to you. For great ideas for first dance songs in every style from romantic to hip, check out theknot.com/firstdance.

enjoy every minute

This is a party! It's a gigantic party to celebrate a gigantic moment. As any new-lyweds will tell you, the reception goes by in a blink, so you'll want to make sure to get the most out of every moment. Before the reception really gets under way, touch base with your wedding planner and banquet manager. Let them know it's their show from that point on, and that you trust them to make it fabulous but you'll want them to check in every so often as the celebration unfolds. That way if you do have any needs, you won't have to spend your precious time tracking them down.

BE A GUEST Once you've checked in with your point people, start acting like the man and woman of the hour—you're the guests of honor after all. This means that if you see flowers in a slightly different spot than you expected, or if your guests switch their place cards, you'll let it go. A cranky or uptight bride will be remembered for ages, but no one will hold slightly askew table bunting against you.

EAT The hardest part of playing the guest will be making sure to eat in between all of the greeting, meeting, dancing, and smiling, but you should make sure to enjoy the menu you worked so hard to plan. If you simply can't sit down, or feel like you haven't had enough, ask the banquet manager to pack a bride-and-groom doggie bag so you can indulge later that evening.

MAKE THE ROUNDS Even though you may have seen many of your guests at the welcome dinner or on the golf course, you'll still want to take time to stop by every table. This is particularly important if you are skipping the receiving line. Don't get into deep conversation, but do say hello and thank everyone for coming.

ESCAPE Sitting down for a second to eat is one good way to get in some chill time in the midst of everything, but it's not going to be enough. It's important for you and your groom to take a moment to step outside—alone—and soak it all in. If you think you're going to have a hard time getting away, enlist an ally. Ask someone—your mom, wedding planner, a bridesmaid, or groomsman—to tell you at a certain time that so-and-so needs you outside. Politely disengage from your conversation, thank your conspirator, and sneak away. You'll be glad you did. Then you can go back into the reception with a little perspective, ready to relish every minute.

TERESA & PRESTON · CABO SAN LUCAS, MEXICO

Hometown: Asheville, NC
Guests: 70

The Destination Decision: Teresa and Preston had both always wanted an oceanside wedding. They chose Cabo because neither had been there before; it would incorporate Teresa's Mexican heritage, and the world-class golf courses would lure their links-loving families.

Planning Pointer: "Flexibility is key when planning a destination wedding. You never know what you might get," says Teresa. When her dream of bouquets of lilies, tulips, roses, orchids, and alstroemeria turned out to be different because many of those flowers aren't easily available in Mexico, she opted for locally grown substitutes. When the couple learned that the wine they'd ordered wouldn't be available after all at the last minute—they took a gamble on a different wine they'd never tried. (It turned out to be delicious.) When the cake arrived, it bore little resemblance to the one that Teresa had designed. "We laughed it off," she says. "You just can't control everything."

The Definitive Detail: After the sunset ceremony, guests moved to a warmly lit terrace overlooking the ocean where they enjoyed margaritas and sangria and danced to the sounds of a mariachi band. Appetizers like tropical fruit kebabs and seafood ceviche were served before the main course of locally inspired dishes like grouper with Veracruz sauce and mango flan.

the destination directory

Ready to dig in and start booking your getaway? (One more thing to cross off your to-do list!) To make your life easier, we've scoured the globe for the most beautiful, most romantic, most perfect wedding day destinations and come up with this list of our favorites. Keep in mind, fabulous resorts are opening up all the time all over the world, so this list is by no means exhaustive.

CARIBBEAN AND BERMUDA 154

Anguilla 154
Antigua 155
The Bahamas 156
Bermuda 157
Jamaica 158
Nevis 159
Puerto Rico 160
St. Thomas and St. John 161
Turks and Caicos 162
Caribbean Island Details 163

HAWAII 165

Oahu 165
The Big Island 166
Maui 166
Kauai 167
Lanai 167

MAINLAND UNITED STATES 168

Aspen, Colorado 168
Florida 169
Las Vegas, Nevada 171
Maine 172
Massachusetts 173
Napa Valley, California 174
Newport, Rhode Island 175
New York City 176
Tucson, Arizona 177

LATIN AMERICA 178

Mexico 178
Costa Rica 180

EUROPE 181

Italy 181
France 183
United Kingdom 184

PACIFIC RIM 186

Australia 186
Fiji 186
Indonesia 186
New Zealand 187
Tahiti 187
Thailand 187

NOTE: Although The Knot strives to provide valid information, we assume no responsibility for accuracy or changes and strongly suggest that you confirm all information personally before making your final decision (but you knew that).

For more information and a constantly updated resources list, visit **TheKnot.com/destinationweddings**

$ We've used this icon to identify resorts that will be a bit easier on the wallet.

The Destination Directory

153

CARIBBEAN AND BERMUDA

anguilla

ONLINE INFO: www.anguilla-vacation.com

WHY ANGUILLA: Tiny Anguilla, just sixteen miles long and three miles wide, is one of the most exclusive spots in the Caribbean, and it is peppered with upscale resorts, four-star restaurants, unspoiled scenery, and pristine white beaches (no cruise ships, high-rises, or casinos allowed). You won't get a direct flight from the States (you'll have to take a boat from St. Martin), but you and your guests will consider the destination well worth the extra travel time. As a bonus, native Anguillans are known for their hospitality, and the island is virtually crime-free.

WHEN TO GO: While you should be aware of hurricane season, which runs from June through November, temperatures are perfectly pleasant (highs in the low 80s and lows in the low 70s) year-round.

GUEST MUST-DOS: Any Anguillan agenda should include swimming, snorkeling, and savoring the chance to wear shoes as infrequently as possible. Guests who are less beach-focused will enjoy exploring the island's archaeological and cultural sites, such as the Heritage Collection Museum in East End, and taking a guided bird-watching tour. The island is known for its delicious food (some of the best in the Caribbean) at both beach shacks and elegant restaurants such as Blanchard's, which may be its most famous. For first-rate nightlife, send guests to Elio's, a small but stylish Valley bar that offers a selection of high-end sipping rums and two hundred brands of cigars.

STYLE IDEA: Carry a bouquet of oleander, hibiscus, and cedar, all flowers found on Anguilla.

HOT PROPERTIES

O Cap Juluca, www.capjuluca.com
With eighteen stark white, Moorish-style villas set against the bright blue sea, this resort looks like no other in the Caribbean. Its long list of celebrity guests guarantees it doesn't feel like anything else either. Choose from intimate villa ceremonies or beautiful vow exchanges right on the beach.

O $ Carimar Beach Club, www.carimar.com
These seaside villas are each outfitted with outdoor grills and fully equipped kitchens, making Carimar an excellent choice for couples inviting guests on a variety of budgets. The resort can accommodate weddings of all types, from casual lawn lunches to formal beach ceremonies.

O CuisinArt Resort and Spa, www.cuisinartresort.com
Couples looking for four-star reception food will appreciate a wedding at the CuisinArt Resort and Spa (yes, of kitchen appliance fame). Both the restaurants (including a hydroponic garden) and the property itself (on a stretch of pearl white beach) are among the most stellar on the island.

O Kú, www.ku-anguilla.com
Meaning "sacred place" in the Arawak Indian language, this beautiful and intimate Anguilla resort boasts the same charms—white sand beaches and beautifully appointed suites—as some of the more expensive locales on the island. All of the rooms have some kind of ocean view, and each suite includes a kitchen for the convenience of you and your guests.

O Covecastles, www.covecastles.com

O Malliouhana Hotel and Spa, www.malliouhana.com

MARRIAGE REQUIREMENTS

Legal Age: 18
Residency Requirement: None, but the license you need takes two working days to process.
Necessary Documents: Proof of citizenship from resident country is required, such as a valid passport or birth certificate, accompanied by a photo ID. All documents must be in English; if not, they must be translated and notarized. An application can be obtained from the Judicial Department and takes 48 hours to

process. Divorce or death certificate required (if applicable). Two witnesses are required for the ceremony.

Note: Special requirements apply for Catholic marriages. Couples seeking a Catholic marriage have to give three to six months' advance notice, take part in a Pre-Cana course, and submit a baptismal certificate, confirmation papers, and freedom-to-marry papers.

Fee: If one partner resides in Anguilla for at least fifteen days before the date of marriage, the cost of the license is U.S. $40. If the stay is shorter, then the cost of the license is U.S. $284.

For More Info: www.anguilla-vacation.com

antigua

ONLINE INFO: www.antigua-barbuda.org

WHY ANTIGUA: This island idyll not only has a whopping 365 beautiful beaches but also is steeped in nautical history. In the eighteenth and nineteenth centuries, Antigua was home to a huge British naval base and its harbor is still a popular yachting destination for the international jet-set. If you want to host your nuptials at a high-end all-inclusive resort, look no further— many of the world's swankiest are here.

WHEN TO GO: The high season runs from mid-December through April. After April, rates go down as much as 40 percent, but some places do close down between August and October. The humidity and rainfall are low year-round, and hurricane season runs from June through November.

GUEST MUST-DOS: History buffs can tour Nelson's Dockyard National Park at historic English Harbor. Those up for some exercise can hike to the Megaliths of Greencastle Hill, with mysterious six-hundred-foot-high rock formations said to have been created by early inhabitants for better worshipping of the sun and moon. The uninhibited might want to hit the clothing-optional beach at Hawksbill. Even if you're camped at an all-inclusive, try to steal away for a few meals off-property. Try some of the traditional West Indian dishes at the Home Restaurant in Gambles Terrace.

HOT PROPERTIES

○ Jumby Bay, www.jumbybayresort.com
Situated on a private three-hundred-acre island two miles off the coast of Antigua, this elegant resort focuses on enhancing its lush natural surroundings and on fostering serene seclusion. Say your vows on one of three sandy beaches or take the opportunity to reserve the entire resort for your celebration.

○ Ⓢ Jolly Beach Resort, www.jollybeachresort.com
Antigua's largest resort is a great way to stretch your dollar, offering all-inclusive stays on the beach. Huge pools and a wide range of activities keep guests busy day and night. The more guests you bring, the more the resort throws in for free.

○ Hawksbill, www.hawksbill.com
This thirty-seven-acre all-inclusive resort is set right on the ocean and features four secluded beaches—including Antigua's only "clothing optional" setting. Stay in one of the detached cottages with an ocean view, or opt for the Great House villa on the tip of the peninsula, complete with three bedrooms and panoramic vistas.

○ Galley Bay, www.eliteislandresorts.com

○ Carlisle Bay, www.carlisle-bay.com

MARRIAGE REQUIREMENTS
Legal Age: 15
Residency Requirement: None
Necessary Documents: Valid passports as proof of citizenship; divorce decree or death certificate (original or certified copies); original marriage certificate when presenting death certificate of former spouse(s), if applicable. Need at least two witnesses (not including marriage officer).
Fee: U.S. $240
For More Info: www.antigua-barbuda.org

NOTE: As of January 1, 2007, you must have a passport or other document that establishes identity and nationality in order to enter Bermuda, the Caribbean, Central and South America, and Mexico.

the bahamas

ONLINE INFO: www.bahamas.com

WHY THE BAHAMAS: This collection of 700 islands has something for every taste—enjoy complete privacy by renting your own island, or host hundreds of your favorite people at a megaresort. Nassau and Paradise Island are two of the most visited and activity-packed destinations, while more remote areas such as Harbor Island and the Exumas tend to feel more laid-back. And since the Bahamas are just a thirty-five-minute plane trip from Florida, it's an easy journey for guests.

WHEN TO GO: The high season lasts from mid-December to mid-April, while summers are sleepier. Although hurricanes are infrequent, they can occur, so it's best to avoid the area June through November.

GUEST MUST-DOS: Scuba dive around Andros Island (the third largest barrier reef in the world), stroll the white-sand beaches, tour the historic homes of Nassau, and sip Goombay Smashes while snacking on conch fritters.

HOT PROPERTIES

○ One and Only Ocean Club, Paradise Island, www.oneandonlyoceanclub.com
Without equal in the Bahamas for luxury and elegance (and host to many celebrity unions), this seaside resort's Versailles-inspired terraced garden is a unique ceremony location that accommodates up to 120 guests. Villas perched above the beach feature private infinity pools, and villa guests are offered iPods for use during their stay. Most rooms on the property have sweeping views of the ocean.

○ Atlantis, Paradise Island, www.atlantis.com
Part amusement park, part Vegas-style hotel, this enormous Paradise Island resort features six aquariums (some with live sharks), a casino, and the largest ballroom in the Caribbean. A top-notch audiovisual team will make your wedding video more spectacular than you ever dreamed, and on-property excursion centers ensure that guests never have a dull moment. A great choice for wedding parties with lots of children.

○ Ⓢ Pelican Bay at Lucaya, Grand Bahama Island, www.pelicanbayhotel.com
A beautiful boutique setting on Grand Bahama Island, this resort can accommodate wedding parties with up to eighty guests. Host your ceremony on the beach and head to the Ferry House nearby for your reception dinner.

○ Old Bahama Bay Resort and Yacht Harbor, Grand Bahama Island, www.oldbahamabay.com

○ Kamalame Cay, Andros, www.kamalame.com

○ Bluff House Beach Hotel and Yacht Club, Abaco Beach www.bluffhouse.com

MARRIAGE REQUIREMENTS
Legal Age: 18
Residency Requirement: 24 hours
Necessary Documents: Passports; birth certificates; proof of divorce or death certificate of former spouse(s), if applicable; declaration certifying both parties are unmarried U.S. citizens, sworn before a U.S. consul at the American embassy in Nassau; a marriage license from the Commissioner's Office on other islands (if you're marrying on an island other than Paradise Island); evidence of date of arrival in the Bahamas.
Note: Both parties must apply in person.
Fee: U.S. $100 payable to the Registrar General.
For More Info: www.bahamas.com

bermuda

ONLINE INFO: www.bermudatourism.com

WHY BERMUDA: Though geographically removed from the Caribbean, Bermuda shares many of the traits of those beachy, beautiful islands. If you love the idea of a Caribbean destination wedding but also want something formal and elegant, consider Bermuda. Famous for its tranquil pink-sand beaches and proper British history, the island has no casinos and few fast-food restaurants. But perhaps its biggest selling point is that it takes just a couple of hours to fly there from the East Coast, and flights are often cheaper than those to Caribbean destinations.

WHEN TO GO: May through early September. Bermuda is only 850 miles off the coast of North Carolina, so its weather resembles the coastal U.S.'s more than it does the Caribbean islands' to the south. Typical temperatures hover around 85 degrees in the summer and climb to only around 70 in the winter. Although hurricanes are infrequent, they can occur, so be aware of any warnings from June through November.

GUEST MUST-DOS: Spend days teeing off on one of the country's eight golf courses (this island is a links-lover's paradise), visiting the botanical garden, or scuba diving among reefs and shipwrecks. Rent a scooter (lots of fun but also a practical necessity, as visitors aren't allowed to rent cars) to tour around the island's iconic pastel-hued houses.

HOT PROPERTIES

○ Horizons and Cottages
www.horizonscottages.com
This Relais & Châteaux property sits on a hilltop overlooking the dramatic vistas of the island's south shore. The main building, which was originally part of an eighteenth-century plantation, includes various oceanview verandas—perfect settings for sunset cocktail hours and plein-air receptions.

○ The Reefs
www.thereefs.com
An award-winning resort with one of the best spas in all of Bermuda, the Reefs is set on a beautiful stretch of private beach overlooking the Atlantic. Stay in an oceanview guest room (try to book the Point Suites), or reserve one of the cliff-hugging cottages spread out over the property.

○ Cambridge Beaches
www.cambridgebeaches.com
A gorgeous beachfront property made up of a series of tastefully decorated cottages, Cambridge Beaches offers destination couples a variety of robust wedding and honeymoon packages.

○ Pink Beach Club, www.pinkbeachclub.com

○ Elbow Beach, www.mandarinoriental.com/bermuda

○ Ⓢ Waterloo House, www.waterloohouse.com

MARRIAGE REQUIREMENTS

Legal Age: 21. All minors under the age of 21 must have the written consent of both parents, the surviving parent, or a legal guardian.
Residency Requirement: None
Necessary Documents: Passports and a "Notice of Intended Marriage" form from Bermuda's Registrar General's Office, which must be filed two weeks before the wedding. The form is available at www.bermudatourism.com. Fill it out and mail it back to the Registrar General, along with the fee (see below). Your license will be valid for three months and can be picked up at the registrar's office by you or a designated person.
Fee: U.S. $120 (cashier's check or bank draft payable to Accountant General, Hamilton, Bermuda)
For More Info: www.bermudatourism.com

jamaica

ONLINE INFO: www.visitjamaica.com

WHY JAMAICA: Jamaica offers much more than just beaches and palm trees—it's steeped in world-class culture: reggae, Rastafarianism, and indigenous spices and glamorous globetrotters all call it home (Ian Fleming wrote the first James Bond book, *Casino Royale,* from his seaside abode here). The site of many all-inclusive resorts, Jamaica can be one of the most affordable of the Caribbean islands, but it has superposh options, too, including private villas that come with their own chefs, housekeeping staffs, and security.

WHEN TO GO: Avoid March, aka spring break season, as well as the hurricane season, June through November.

GUEST MUST-DOS: See a live reggae performance, indulge in a spa treatment featuring indigenous ingredients and techniques, and absorb the local culinary culture by dining on jerk chicken, munching plantain chips, having an ackee and saltfish breakfast, or by sipping Jamaican rum.

STYLE IDEA: Thank guests for coming with packets of Blue Mountain Coffee—or with the seasonings to make jerk chicken once they get back home.

HOT PROPERTIES

O Half Moon, www.halfmoon.com
Rent out one or two of the royal villas (with up to seven bedrooms each) or put guests up in the many rooms and suites with ocean views at this Montego Bay beachfront resort. Couples can choose from beautiful beach, gazebo, or terrace settings for their ceremony location.

O Strawberry Hill, www.islandoutpost.com/strawberry_hill/
Nestled in the lush Blue Mountains overlooking the bustling capital city of Kingston, this tranquil spot with jaw-dropping views is a destination for spa lovers and their guests alike (it's the only full-service Aveda Concept Spa in the Caribbean). Highlights include an amazing infinity pool,

superb New Jamaican cuisine, and romantic four-poster mahogany wooden beds.

O Round Hill Hotel and Villas, Montego Bay, Jamaica, www.roundhilljamaica.com
With oceanfront hotel rooms and hillside private villas to chose from, the resort hosts just 30 weddings a year (ranging from 2 to 120 guests), ensuring that each couple gets the kind of detailed attention they deserve. Have your ceremony seaside, poolside, or in a private villa overlooking the Caribbean.

O Sandals Whitehouse European Village and Spa, www.sandals.com
With acres of beachfront ceremony locations to choose from, Sandals is an expert in the world of Caribbean destination weddings, and their new Whitehouse location along Jamaica's southern shore is one of the most secluded and elegant. Choose from one of celebrity stylist Preston Bailey's signature wedding packages or work with the on-site planners to create a custom celebration.

O $ Sandals Dunn's River Villaggio, www.sandals.com

O Jamaica Inn, www.jamaicainn.com

O The Ritz-Carlton Golf and Spa Resort, Rose Hall, www.ritzcarlton.com

O Bluff House Beach Hotel and Yacht Club, www.bluffhouse.com

MARRIAGE REQUIREMENTS
Legal Age: 18
Residency Requirement: 24 hours (provided you've already applied for a marriage license)
Necessary Documents: Passports; certified copies of birth certificates that include father's name; proof of divorce or death certificate of former spouse(s), if applicable.
Note: Application must be made 48 hours in advance of trip by calling the Ministry of National Security at (876) 906-4908.
Fee: U.S. $75 to $80
For More Info: Jamaica Tourist Board, (800) 233-4582, or www.visitjamaica.com

nevis

WHY NEVIS: Nature lovers, this is your island. Known as the Queen of the Caribbees, Nevis has a high-end, posh pedigree and is home to some of the Caribbean's best-preserved beaches, rain forests, and reefs.

WHEN TO GO: Nevis maintains temperatures averaging between 72 and 87 degrees year-round. Be aware of hurricane season, though, which lasts from June through November.

GUEST MUST-DOS: Experience the sights and sounds of exotic animals as you explore the rain forest—or climb to the top of Nevis Peak (3,232 feet). Saddle-savvy guests will enjoy an equestrian outing (horseback riding is very popular here) along the pristine beaches, trails, and mountain slopes. For an educational tour, take a walk on the beach alongside a biologist and learn about sea turtle nesting—or check out night beach-walking tours where naturalists help guide as you observe and study the faraway stars.

HOT PROPERTIES

O Four Seasons Resort Nevis, West Indies, www.fourseasons.com/nevis
Palm trees flank the large glass doors, which open onto white sand and the Caribbean Sea beyond at this resort's ballroom entrance. Couples looking for an equally evocative but less formal setting can opt to exchange vows at the historic Sugar Mill Ruin or in the barefoot comfort of a ceremony in the sand.

O Golden Rock Plantation Inn, www.golden-rock.com
Originally designed as a sugar plantation, the family-owned Golden Rock has all the luxury of a modern resort while still retaining the flavor of the property's colonial past. Couples who wed here experience the best of both worlds: West Indian hospitality and European standards of service.

O Montpelier Plantation Inn, www.montpeliernevis.com
With thirty acres of beautiful gardens and tropical forests, the scenic Montpelier Plantation Inn offers one perfect photo spot after another. During breaks in your wedding weekend, guests can join island ecologists for hikes through the rain forest and nearby sugar plantations.

MARRIAGE REQUIREMENTS

Legal Age: 18

Residency Requirement: Two weekdays on either St. Kitts or Nevis

Necessary Documents: Valid passports or birth certificates; an affidavit from a notary public for those who have never been married; proof of divorce or death certificate of former spouse(s), if applicable; if a minister is performing the ceremony, a letter from the couple's resident minister stating that the couple is known and unmarried.

Fee: If the couple is residing or staying on St. Kitts or Nevis for the minimum period of two weekdays, the license fee is U.S. $80; if the couple is residing here for fifteen days prior to the marriage, the fee is only U.S. $20.

For More Info: www.nevisisland.com

puerto rico

ONLINE INFO: www.gotopuertorico.com

WHY PUERTO RICO: Puerto Rico's got all the assets of the other Caribbean islands—gorgeous beaches, friendly locals, plush resorts—plus one big one that sets it apart: It's a U.S. territory. That means you and your guests will have few if any of the hassles associated with travel abroad: No passports are required, you won't need to go through customs, phone service is excellent, and most people speak English.

WHEN TO GO: As with the rest of the region, beware of hurricane season, which lasts from June through November.

GUEST MUST-DOS: Puerto Rico offers a blend of both traditional beachy relaxation and unique cultural and historic sights (your non-beach-going guests will appreciate the options). Consider suggesting this perfect day: Begin by sipping some of the country's famous locally grown coffee, move on to a beach outing (if you're staying in busy San Juan, it's worth the drive to Luquillo beach, a white-sand stretch with a coral reef), and cap off the afternoon with some sightseeing through the streets of Old San Juan, which look much as they did during the colonial era. Although American-style restaurants are everywhere, suggest that guests try dining at one of the many restaurants serving Criolla cuisine, which is a blend of Taíno, Spanish, and African influences. *Tostones* (fried green plantains) are a staple.

STYLE IDEA: Hire a salsa instructor for your reception so guests can master the moves of this sexy Latin dance.

HOT PROPERTIES

O Horned Dorset Primavera, www.horneddorset.com
This Spanish-style property, perfect for small weddings, sits on a stone retaining wall over the ocean on Puerto Rico's secluded west coast. Choose from open-air dining options or the more formal second-floor dining room. Duplex suites have private plunge pools.

O El Conquistador Resort & Golden Door Spa, www.elconresort.com
For beautiful oceanside ceremonies with all the benefits of a big hotel wedding, El Conquistador, with its on-property Golden Door Spa, makes a great location choice. Choose from outdoor settings such as the Trellises and Mirador Terrace, or grand indoor spaces like the Magnolia or Grand Caribbean Ballroom.

O Hix Island House, Vieques, www.hixislandhouse.com
It doesn't get hipper than this—a property so stylish it seems plucked from the pages of *Architectural Digest,* situated on one of the Caribbean's chic islands. Have your cocktail reception around the pool and gaze out at the view to the water.

O The San Juan Water and Beach Club Hotel, www.waterclubsanjuan.com

O The Westin Rio Mar Beach Golf Resort and Spa, www.westinriomar.com

O Las Casitas Village and Golden Door Spa www.lascasitasvillage.com

MARRIAGE REQUIREMENTS

Legal Age: 18. If younger, you will need your parents' authorization.
Residency Requirement: None
Necessary Documents: Valid photo ID or passports; proof of divorce or death certificate. Marriage license has to be acquired in advance from the Puerto Rico Demographic Department up to ten days before the wedding.
Note: Blood tests are required from a federally certified laboratory (in the U.S. or Puerto Rico) within ten days of the wedding date. Doctor will need to sign and certify marriage certificate after examination of the bride and groom in Puerto Rico.
Fee: None for a Judicial Center ceremony; U.S. $150 to $200 if holding a private ceremony.
For More Info: www.gotopuertorico.com

st. thomas and st. john

ONLINE INFO: www.usvitourism.vi

WHY THE VIRGIN ISLANDS: Along with Puerto Rico, the U.S. Virgin Islands may be one of the most hassle-free places to have a Caribbean destination wedding. There are lots of direct flights to St. Thomas (and St. John is a *short* ferry ride away), airfare is usually competitive, the U.S. dollar is the official currency, and you should have great cell phone service. St. Thomas can sometimes feel a bit crowded, since it's a main stop on the itineraries of many cruise lines, and it's quite developed for the Caribbean. But it's nonetheless brimming over with natural beauty. St. John, while a bit harder to reach, is more rugged, unspoiled, and higher-end, with fewer big resorts.

WHEN TO GO: Tourist season is at a high from mid-December through mid-April. Highs are in the mid-80s and lows are in the 70s year-round, though hurricane season runs from June through November.

GUEST MUST-DOS: In St. Thomas, visit the capital city of Charlotte Amalie to see historical sites such as Fort Christian, built in 1672, and for tons and tons of duty-free shopping. St. John is known for its plentiful and easily accessible snorkeling sites—especially Trunk Bay, which has underwater signs that identify the fish—as well as its national parks, which can be explored via one of the many hiking trails or by renting a jeep and driving through.

HOT PROPERTIES

O Caneel Bay, St. John, www.caneelbay.com

Although this luxurious property includes seven beaches, don't limit your festivities to the water's edge when there are so many diverse settings to choose from. Plan an intimate rehearsal dinner in the romantic, candlelit Sugar Mill Ruins and then host a postwedding brunch on the grassy knoll at Turtle Bay Point.

O The Ritz-Carlton, St. Thomas, www.ritzcarlton.com/resorts/st_thomas

With tropical gardens named among the ten most beautiful hotel gardens in the world, the Ritz-Carlton is situated on a thirty-acre peninsula on the eastern tip of St. Thomas. Choose from ceremonies in the Italian palazzo-style Courtyard, amid the weathered sea grape trees on Great Bay Beach, or on the Great Bay Terrace, with sweeping views of the ocean and St. John beyond.

O $ Wyndham Sugar Bay Resort and Spa, St. Thomas, www.wyndhamhotels.com

Carved into the mountainside and overlooking the beach, this all-inclusive resort has a good range of activities for guests of all ages and interests. A kids' program and on-site child care keeps little ones busy and supervised, while the Journeys Spa and Ocean Club Gaming Center (casino) attends to their parents.

O $ Frenchman's Reef & Morning Star Marriott Beach Resort, St. Thomas, www.marriott.com

O The Westin Resort, St. John, www.westinresortstjohn.com

MARRIAGE REQUIREMENTS

Legal Age: 18

Residency Requirement: Eight-day waiting period

Necessary Documents: Driver's licenses or passports; proof of divorce or death certificate of former spouse(s), if applicable; letter accompanying application for marriage stating date of visit, length of stay, and date you plan to pick up your license. Note: Application must be received two weeks prior to wedding.

Fee: U.S. $100

For More Info: Virgin Islands Department of Tourism at (800) 372-USVI

turks and caicos

ONLINE INFO: www.turksandcaicostourism.com

WHY TURKS AND CAICOS: Less developed and more upscale than much of the Caribbean, this collection of forty islands, eight of which are inhabited, has an intimate feel. Many of the islands are surrounded by a natural reef, making the turquoise waters just offshore clean, calm, and full of sea life. The islands are also relatively easy to reach, since you can fly direct from a number of U.S. cities to Providenciales, the main island.

WHEN TO GO: The climate is sunny and dry, with highs between 80 and 84 degrees from November to May. However, during the summer and early fall, daytime highs range from 85 to 90 degrees, sometimes reaching the mid-90s in late summer. Hurricane season also runs from June through November.

GUEST MUST-DOS: Snorkeling and scuba diving are great takes, since Turks and Caicos has some of the best underwater sightseeing around. Historic Cockburn Town on Grand Turk is also worth a visit for history buffs—some say it's the spot where Columbus first landed in 1492. Whale- and bird-watching are two other popular activities, and sunsets over Grace Bay are unforgettable.

HOT PROPERTIES

O Grace Bay Club, www.gracebayclub.com
   Small and elegant, this resort has adopted a Spanish architectural style with all suites leading out to oceanview terraces. The suites and penthouses have four-star amenities, including full kitchens, Egyptian cotton linens, and flat-screen TVs. New villas on the property welcome children, and the resort has developed a comprehensive kids' program.

O The Palms, www.thepalmstc.com
   This chic property on Grace Bay beach features a spectacular infinity pool, a first-class restaurant, and one of the most serious spas in the Caribbean. Host your ceremony right on the beach (one of the most jaw-dropping stretches of white sand and azure water you've ever seen) or in the beautiful private function room above the resort lobby.

O The Meridian Club, www.meridianclub.com

O Villa Renaissance, www.villarenaissance.com

O Parrot Cay, www.parrotcay.como.bz

O Le Vele, www.levele.tc

MARRIAGE REQUIREMENTS

Legal Age: 21
Residency Requirement: Must be on the island for twenty-four hours before applying for the license, to establish residency; license takes two to three days to process.
Necessary Documents: You must present a passport, an original birth certificate, and proof of single status. You also need to show a letter that states both of your occupations, marital status, ages at your last birthdays, present addresses, and the full names of your fathers. The required documents must be in English and originals; translations into English must be notarized by your consulate. Bring photocopies of all the original documents when you go to apply for your marriage license. If previously married, you will need to present either an original or a notarized copy of your divorce decree with a seal of the clerk of the court, or a copy of the death certificate of your former spouse.
Fee: U.S. $50

MORE CARIBBEAN PROPERTIES

O Grand Cayman Marriott Beach Resort, www.marriott.com

O The Sugar Mill, Tortola, www.sugarmillhotel.com

O Anse Chastanet, St. Lucia, www.ansechastanet.com

caribbean island details

ISLAND	GEOGRAPHY/ AFFILIATION	LANGUAGE	CURRENCY	FLIGHT TIME IN HOURS	FEATURES	TOURIST BOARD	TIE THE KNOT
ANGUILLA	Lesser Antilles/ British	English	Eastern Caribbean dollar (EC), U.S. dollar	7/NYC, 7/Chicago, 7.5/Dallas, 13.5/LA		(800) 553-4939 Anguilla-Vacation.com	Yes
ANTIGUA & BARBUDA	Lesser Antilles/ British	English	Eastern Caribbean dollar (EC), U.S. dollar	4/NYC, 8/Chicago, 7/Dallas, 10/LA		(888) 268-4227 Antigua-Barbuda.org	Yes
ARUBA	Netherlands Antilles/Dutch	Dutch, English, Spanish, Papiamento*	Aruban Florin (AFl), U.S. dollar	4/NYC, 9/Chicago, 8/Dallas, 11/LA		(800) TO-ARUBA Aruba.com	Yes
BAHAMAS	British	English	Bahamian dollar (BSD), U.S. dollar	5.5/NYC, 5.5/Chicago, 5.5/Dallas, 8/LA		(800) BAHAMAS Bahamas.com	Yes
BARBADOS	Lesser Antilles/ British	English	Barbados dollar ($BD), U.S. dollar	4.5/NYC, 8/Chicago, 7/Dallas, 9.5/LA		(800) 744-6244 VisitBarbados.org	Yes
BONAIRE	Netherlands Antilles/Dutch	Dutch, English, Spanish, Papiamento*	Netherlands Antilles guilder (NAFl), U.S. dollar	7/NYC, 9/Chicago, 10/Dallas, 15/LA		(800) BONAIRE InfoBonaire.com	Yes
CAYMAN ISLANDS	British	English	Cayman Island dollar (CI), U.S. dollar	6/NYC, 7/Chicago, 6/Dallas, 8/LA		(212) 889-9009 CaymanIslands.ky	Yes
CURAÇAO	Netherlands Antilles/Dutch	Dutch, English, Spanish, Papiamento*	Netherlands Antilles guilder (NAFl), U.S. dollar	7/NYC, 9/Chicago, 8/Dallas, 11/LA		(800) 328-7222 Curacao.com	Yes
DOMINICA	Lesser Antilles/ French-British	English, Local Patois**	Eastern Caribbean dollar (EC), U.S. dollar	7/NYC, 12/LA		(888) 645-5637 Dominica.dm	Yes
DOMINICAN REPUBLIC	Greater Antilles/ Spanish	Spanish, English	Dominican peso (RD$)	4/NYC, 7/Chicago, 9/Dallas, 11/LA		(800) 723-6138 Dominicana.com.do	Yes
GRENADA	Lesser Antilles/ British	English	Eastern Caribbean dollar (EC)	4/NYC, 9/Chicago, 12/Dallas, 17.5/LA		(800) 927-9554 GrenadaGrenadines.com	Yes
GUADELOUPE	Lesser Antilles/ French	French, English, Creole	Euro	7/NYC, 8/Chicago, 8/Dallas, 12/LA		(011) 590-590-82-0930 Antilles-Info-Tourisme.com/guadeloupe	No
JAMAICA	Greater Antilles/ British	English, Local Patois**	Jamaican dollar (J$)	4/NYC, 6/Chicago, 7.5/LA		(800) 233-4582 VisitJamaica.com	Yes
MARTINIQUE	Lesser Antilles/ French	Creole, French, English	Euro	11/NYC, 13/LA		(011) 0596-61-61-77 Martinique.org	No
MONTSERRAT	Lesser Antilles/ British	English	Eastern Caribbean dollar (EC), U.S. dollar	5/NYC, 9/Chicago, 8/Dallas, 11/LA		(664) 491-2230 VisitMontserrat.com	Yes
NEVIS & ST. KITTS	Lesser Antilles/ British	English	Eastern Caribbean dollar (EC), U.S. dollar	6/NYC, 6/Chicago, 10/LA		(800) 582-6208 & (866) 556-3847 StKittsTourism.kn & NevisIsland.com	Yes
PUERTO RICO	Greater Antilles/ U.S.	Spanish, English	U.S. dollar	4/NYC, 5/Chicago, 7/Dallas, 10/LA		(800) 866-7827 GoToPuertoRico.com	Yes
SABA & ST. EUSTATIUS	Lesser Antilles/ Dutch	Dutch, English Papiamento*	Netherlands Antilles guilder (NAFl), U.S. dollar	7/NYC, 8/Chicago		(011) 599-416-2231 & (011) 599-318-2433 SabaTourism.com & StatiaTourism.com	Yes (Saba) No (St. Eustatius)
ST. BARTHELEMY	Lesser Antilles/ French	French English	Euro, U.S. dollar	6/NYC, 10/Chicago		(011) 590-590-27-8727 St-Barths.com	No
ST. CROIX	Lesser Antilles, U.S.V.I./ U.S.	English	U.S. dollar	5/NYC, 7/Chicago, 6/Dallas, 10/LA		(800) 372-USVI USVITourism.vi	Yes
ST. JOHN	Lesser Antilles, U.S.V.I./ U.S.	English	U.S. dollar	4/NYC, 8/Chicago, 7/Dallas, 11/LA		(800) 372-USVI USVITourism.vi	Yes

CONTINUES

KEY

- ✓ ALL-INCLUSIVE
- BEACHES
- $ BUDGET TRAVEL
- CASINOS
- ECOTOURISM
- GOLF
- HIKING
- HURRICANE SAFE
- ✳ LOTS TO DO
- LUSH FLORA
- ♪ MUSIC
- Y NIGHTLIFE
- PACKAGES
- PEACE & QUIET
- ⇒ QUICK ESCAPE
- RAIN FORESTS
- SAILING
- SHOPPING
- TENNIS
- WATER SPORTS

caribbean island details continued...

ISLAND	GEOGRAPHY/ AFFILIATION	LANGUAGE	CURRENCY	FLIGHT TIME IN HOURS	FEATURES	TOURIST BOARD	TIE THE KNOT
ST. LUCIA	Lesser Antilles/ British	English, Creole Patois	Eastern Caribbean dollar (EC), U.S. dollar	7/NYC, 10/Chicago, 6/Dallas, 12/LA		(888) 4-STLUCIA StLucia.org	Yes
ST. MAARTEN	Lesser Antilles/ Dutch	Dutch Papiamento*, English	Netherlands Antilles guilder (NAFI), U.S. dollar	6/NYC, 7/Chicago, 7/Dallas, 12/LA		(800) 786-2278 St-Maarten.com	Yes
ST. MARTIN	Lesser Antilles/ French	French, English	Euro, U.S. dollar	6/NYC, 7/Chicago, 7/Dallas, 12/LA		(877) 956-1234 St-Martin.org	No
ST. THOMAS	Lesser Antilles, U.S.V.I./U.S.	English	U.S. dollar	3.5/NYC, 8/Chicago, 7/Dallas, 11/LA		(800) 372-USVI USVITourism.vi	Yes
ST. VINCENT & THE GRENADINES	Lesser Antilles/ French-British	English	Eastern Caribbean dollar (EC), U.S. dollar	8/NYC, 10/Chicago, 14/LA		(800) 729-1726 SVGTourism.com	Yes
TORTOLA & VIRGIN GORDA	Lesser Antilles, B.V.I./British	English	U.S. dollar	4.75/NYC, 7.5/Chicago, 6/Dallas, 10/LA		(800) 835-8530 BVITourism.com	Yes
TRINIDAD & TOBAGO	British	English, French, Spanish, Hindi	Trinidad and Tobago dollar (TT), U.S. dollar	8/NYC, 9/Chicago, 11/Dallas, 12/LA		(888) 535-5617 VisitTNT.com	Yes
TURKS & CAICOS	British	English, Creole	U.S. dollar	4/NYC, 7/Chicago, 6/Dallas, 13/LA		(800) 241-0824 TurksandCaicosTourism.com	Yes

KEY

✓ ALL-INCLUSIVE	$ BUDGET TRAVEL	⚲ GOLF	✳ LOTS TO DO
🏖 BEACHES	♤ CASINOS	⛰ HIKING	❀ LUSH FLORA
	🌐 ECOTOURISM	🌀 HURRICANE SAFE	♪ MUSIC

♈ NIGHTLIFE	⇨ QUICK ESCAPE	🛍 SHOPPING
🎁 PACKAGES	🌲 RAIN FORESTS	TENNIS
☮ PEACE & QUIET	◺ SAILING	⊘ WATER SPORTS

HAWAII

WHY HAWAII: Year-round gorgeous weather, world-class beaches, dramatic mountains, a famously friendly, laid-back vibe, and some of the most dramatic sunsets on the planet make it hard to beat the fiftieth state for romance.

WHEN TO GO: There's really no bad time to go to Hawaii weatherwise. Temperatures year-round are in the high 70s and 80s during the day. It's a bit warmer and drier from April through October than in the winter months, but it's never uncomfortably hot. Although it rains frequently during the winter, the short and mild showers are usually followed by one (or more) of those famous Hawaiian rainbows. Typically, the southwestern parts of each island are driest, with most of the rain falling in the mountains and northeastern exposures. As for most tropical getaways, demand and prices are highest in winter and early spring. Although they're universally gorgeous, each of the Hawaiian islands is unique. To understand the individual assets of the primary ones, read on.

TIP: Having trouble deciding between the islands? Choose one to get married on, and then spend your honeymoon exploring the others.

MARRIAGE REQUIREMENTS

Legal Age: 18

Residency Requirement: None

Necessary Documents: Birth certificate (if under 18) and a valid photo ID; both bride and groom must be present when applying for license; there is no waiting period and license is valid for thirty days; no divorce decree or death certificate required if previously married.

Fee: $50 (cash only)

For More Info: www.hawaii.gov

oahu

WHY OAHU: The liveliest of the Hawaiian islands, Oahu is more densely populated than the others—and is the one most widely visited by tourists. Honolulu, the island's most famous city, is located here, as is Waikiki, home of the island's main entertainment district and a hopping nightlife scene. But Oahu is still packed with lots of natural beauty and native culture, and is the most convenient island for a destination wedding because it has the biggest airport and the most frequent direct flights from the mainland.

GUEST MUST-DOS: Anyone who's ever dreamed of learning to surf should take a lesson, since Oahu's North Shore is home to the world's most storied waves—at Sunset Beach, Banzai Beach, the Pipeline, and Waimea Bay.

HOT PROPERTIES

O Turtle Bay Resort, www.turtlebayresort.com
Just forty-five minutes from the hustle and bustle of Honolulu is Turtle Bay, a large lush resort encompassing over five miles of beach. Each room and cottage has views of the ocean, and two championship golf courses ensure that your link-loving guests will be well entertained.

O Halekulani, www.halekulani.com
Host your wedding at one of the biggest and best on Oahu, where the A-listers stay. Spend your wedding night (or longer) in the new Vera Wang Suite, created by the eponymous bridal designer, complete with a selection of signature beauty products, favorite movies, and butler service.

O ⑤ Waikiki Beach Marriott Resort and Spa, www.marriottwaikiki.com

O Sheraton Moana Surfrider, www.moana-surfrider.com

the big island

WHY THE BIG ISLAND: The island of Hawaii is called the Big Island to avoid confusion. It is (you may have guessed) the largest in the chain and offers incredibly diverse topography. In fact, eleven of the world's thirteen climatic zones can be found on the island (there's even snow on top of the highest mountains!). The landscape varies dramatically as you travel around the perimeter. The Kona coast to the west has a lunarlike landscape, while the north and east coasts are wet and superlush.

GUEST MUST-DOS: Check out the lava oozing from the Kilauea volcano on a hiking tour of Hawaii Volcanoes National Park—or, for a better view, take a helicopter tour. Additionally, explore the rain forest region of the island, go horseback riding, strap on snorkel gear and get to know the reefs, or just laze on the beach sipping tropical drinks.

HOT PROPERTIES

O Hapuna Beach Prince Hotel,
   www.princeresortshawaii.com
   Serious golfers and beach lovers alike will appreciate the Hapuna's location—surrounded by an Arnold Palmer–designed eighteen-hole golf course and asserting a prominent presence over one of the nicest beaches on the Big Island. Choose from poolside venues, perfect for cocktail hours, to rugged grassy lava bluffs overlooking the Pacific.

O Kona Village Resort, www.konavillage.com
   This no-TV, no-telephone property prides itself on giving guests an authentic, yet luxurious, old-Hawaiian experience. Couples stay in individual *hales,* or thatched roof cottages, interconnected by walkways.

O $ Royal Kona Resort, www.royalkona.com

O The Palms Cliff House, www.palmscliffhouse.com

maui

WHY MAUI: Many visitors think of Maui as the most romantic Hawaiian island, perhaps because it's filled with waterfalls and rainbows. Its beaches are considered to be among the best in the world.

GUEST MUST-DOS: Active visitors will want to head for the west coast, known fondly to some as the "Golf Coast," and surfers (or aspiring ones) will find some of the world's most famous waves here. Drive along the amazing Road to Hana, a jaw-dropping route hugging cliffs that overlook beaches and lush jungle. Of course, snorkeling, kayaking, whale-watching, and all the activities you'd expect from a tropical paradise should be on the agenda, too.

HOT PROPERTIES

O The Fairmont Kea Lani, www.fairmont.com/kealani
   A few of Kea Lani's many lures: a privileged position on Maui's Polo Beach, where you can snorkel, sail, and windsurf; a swank group of signature suites with dreamy views of the shoreline; and the Honi Honi Romance Package (highlights include a private dinner and sunset cruise).

O Ho'oilo House, www.hooilohouse.com
   A beautiful Balinese-inspired bed-and-breakfast with a total of five rooms, this is a great option for couples wishing to take over an entire property. This intimate, secluded location offers sweeping views of the ocean.

O Hotel Hana-Maui, www.hotelhanamaui.com

O $ Sheraton Maui Resort, www.starwoodhawaii.com

kauai

WHY KAUAI: Kauai is known as the "Garden Island" for its incredibly lush tropical landscape. It remains the least developed of the four main islands, and life here tends to move at a slower pace. Although Kauai's Mount Waialeale is considered the wettest spot on earth (it receives an average of more than four hundred inches of rainfall per year), the island's southern coast is perpetually sunny.

GUEST MUST-DOS: Take a surf lesson, get an aerial view of the island's beauty during a helicopter tour, and hike the Kalalau Trail, a rigorous trek through some of the island's most breathtaking terrain. For a bit of history, tour the Gay and Robinson sugar plantation, one of Hawaii's few remaining operating sugar mills.

HOT PROPERTIES

O Grand Hyatt Kauai Resort and Spa, www.kauai.hyatt.com
Lush gardens, gorgeous ocean views, a Robert Trent Jones–designed golf course, and amazing ANARA Spa treatments are a few of the draws of this Kauai resort. Exchange vows on the Regency Club lawn in the beautiful white wedding gazebo, where your ceremony will be framed by the placid ocean beyond.

O ⑤ Hanalei Bay Resort
www.hanaleibayresort.com/weddings
With the same view as some of the ritzier resorts up the beach, the Hanalei Bay Resort on the north shore is a perfect choice for couples seeking luxury on a budget. Host your reception at the Bali Hai Restaurant at sunset—you won't believe your eyes.

O Princeville Resort, www.princeville.com

O The Ritz-Carlton, Kapalua
www.ritzcarlton.com/resorts/kapalua

lanai

WHY LANAI: What other island can lay claim to being home to both a Garden of the Gods and a croquet lawn? As one of the smallest of Hawaii's islands, Lanai is a quiet tropical paradise that has retained much of its native culture but doesn't shortchange visitors in search of luxe. Thanks to the Dole company setting up shop here at the turn of the last century, Lanai is nicknamed "Pineapple Island." High-end resorts and local hotels coexist alongside the central highlands that tumble into the blue Pacific.

GUEST MUST-DOS: There's a lot of activity packed into a tiny space. Duffers should hit the links on one of the two challenging courses. Water bugs can check out sea life on a snorkeling trip—look out for the Rectangular Trigger, Hawaii's state fish. And active landlubbers can go off-roading on guided 4x4 tours. There are plenty of scenic spots and serene lanais for lounging and simply soaking up paradise.

HOT PROPERTIES

O Four Seasons Resort Lana'i at Manele Bay,
www.fourseasons.com/lanai
The Four Seasons' legendary service lives on at the Four Seasons Resort Lana'i at Manele Bay and at the Four Seasons Resort Lana'i, The Lodge at Koele. The lodge offers the charm of a country manor, while couples at Manele Bay can exchange vows cliffside, in gardens, or on Hulopoe Beach.

O Hotel Lanai, www.hotellanai.com
Also located in the central highlands, the oldest hotel on the island, Hotel Lanai retains the laid-back spirit it's had since its inception as a retreat for executives of the Dole (as in Dole pineapples) Company. Its small scale—10 rooms and a cottage—allows your guests to get to know each other well.

MAINLAND UNITED STATES

aspen, colorado

ONLINE INFO: www.colorado.com

WHY ASPEN: This Rocky Mountain town possesses the perfect mix of natural beauty, rustic charm, and posh amenities. Its gorgeous mountains and valleys will thrill any outdoors enthusiast, while its ample selection of high-end shops and swank restaurants can keep indoorsy types more than entertained.

WHEN TO GO: While many couples book their event sometime in November through early March to create the winter wonderland wedding of their dreams, keep in mind that the summer and fall are also gorgeous times of year here.

GUEST MUST-DOS: The main focus of the winter and early spring months in Aspen is skiing and snowboarding, though the daring can try more extreme activities, like paragliding and even dogsledding (and everyone can enjoy toasty après-ski drinks at the famous Ajax Tavern). But the less-crowded summer season actually offers a broader range of options—cycling, horseback riding, hiking, fly-fishing, white-water rafting, and just about any other al fresco activity you can think of. At any time of year your guests will love Aspen's nightlife options, especially the J-Bar, a Western-style saloon at the Hotel Jerome.

HOT PROPERTIES

O Hotel Jerome, www.hoteljerome.com
Located right on Main Street in the heart of town, this is Aspen's ultimate old-school hotel. The ballroom accommodates 250 for dinner, and the adjacent garden terrace makes the perfect spot for your cocktail reception (it can be tented and heated during the winter months).

O The Little Nell, www.thelittlenell.com
This posh Relais & Châteaux property is situated right at the base of Aspen Mountain, but its biggest attraction for brides and grooms may be that it offers you the chance to say your vows at 11,200 feet.

O St. Regis Resort, Aspen, www.stregisaspen.com

O Hotel Aspen, www.hotelaspen.com

MARRIAGE REQUIREMENTS

Legal Age: 18
Residency Requirements: None
Necessary Documents: One current form of ID that indicates date of birth—birth certificate or passport may be acceptable. If previously married, know the dates of divorce or death; no documents required, unless marriage ended within thirty days prior.
Note: Both bride and groom must be present when applying for the marriage license, which is valid within the state for thirty days.
Fee: Varies from county to county
For More Info: www.colorado.com

MORE ROCKY MOUNTAIN PROPERTIES

O Big Sky Resort, Big Sky, MT, www.bigskyresort.com

O Sun Valley Resort, Sun Valley, ID, www.sunvalley.com

O Spring Creek Ranch, Jackson Hole, WY, www.springcreekranch.com

O Snow King Resort, Jackson Hole, WY, www.snowking.com

florida

WHY FLORIDA: With its sunny weather and beautiful beaches, Florida competes with the Caribbean and Mexico in beach appeal and is likely to be cheaper and easier for your guests to travel to. In addition to sand and surf, it boasts world-famous amusement parks and great access to golf and other outdoor sports. Each Florida location is a unique experience: head to Palm Beach for a preppy, country club–style affair, Miami for an event with international flavor, and the Keys to soak up a laid-back island vibe.

WHEN TO GO: North Florida's high season runs from Memorial Day through Labor Day, while southern Florida's high season is December through April. The summer months are also beautiful and may be less expensive (although it can be very hot). Be sure to keep hurricane season in mind (officially June through November). And you may want to avoid spring break destinations such as Miami and Fort Lauderdale during February and March, when those cities tend to be overrun with partying college kids.

GUESTS MUST-DOS: Coastal Florida is all about the beach, so guests can lie on it lazily or head into the water for waterskiing, fishing, sailing, and parasailing. Golf addicts will have plenty of greens to choose from, and the area surrounding Orlando is theme-park central, perfect if you have lots of little kids in your family and circle of friends. With its big-city sophistication and lengthy beaches, Miami has it all. The tropical setting is lush and the sunsets are romantic. From shopping to snorkeling, this famous honeymoon destination has you covered.

STYLE IDEA: Celebrate south Florida's Cuban influence by hiring a cigar roller for the reception.

HOT PROPERTIES

O Delano Hotel, Miami, www.delano-hotel.com
For seekers of hip, chic surroundings, it doesn't get more South Beach Miami than the Ian Schrager–designed Hotel Delano. Case in point: the underwater music piped into the pool, the all-white decor (how bridal), and the state-of-the-art David Barton gym.

O Hotel Victor, Miami, www.hotelvictorsouthbeach.com
An ultra-luxurious, modern hotel set in the heart of the Art Deco district of South Beach, this ninety-one-room property caters to couples that want a glam setting. Infinity soak tubs, outdoor rain showers, and 350-thread-count Egyptian cotton sheets are some of the amenities that await.

O Fontainebleau Suites Miami Beach, www.fontainebleau.com
It's an all-suite skyscraper of a hotel with great views of the ocean from most rooms. Upcoming renovations will include the creation of six on-site restaurants and 45,000 square feet of ballroom space.

O Hawk's Cay Resort, Duck Key, www.hawkscay.com
Experience a Caribbean vibe without crossing the U.S. border. In addition to all the standard water sports, guests can learn to scuba dive, sail, and—one of the resort's major attractions—frolic with the dolphins that live on the premises.

O Little Palm Island Resort & Spa, Little Torch Key, www.littlepalmisland.com
Arrive by boat to this beautiful, secluded island, which can accommodate weddings with up to forty guests. After an afternoon on the beach or in the Indonesian-theme spa, retire to your private bungalow suite to witness breathtaking views of the setting sun.

O Disney's Grand Floridian Resort & Spa, Orlando, www.disneyworld.disney.go.com
The crown jewel of the Disney hotel empire, this beautiful hotel is the most elegant of the on-property accommodations. Have your ceremony at the Wedding Pavilion and spend the days leading up to your festivities riding the monorail back and forth between theme parks.

- O Hyatt Regency Grand Cypress, Orlando, www.grandcypress.hyatt.com

  Just outside the Disney compound, this hotel offers easy access to the parks and tons of activities on property, such as tennis, golf, and horseback riding. Choose from outdoor and indoor ceremony locations.

- O ⑤ Hyatt Regency Coconut Point Resort & Spa, Bonita Springs, www.coconutpoint.hyatt.com

  Gourmet menus, full-service wedding coordinators, and on-site activities like fly-fishing, golf, and eco-tours are all part of the weekend wedding picture at this top-drawer resort.

- O The Breakers, Palm Beach, www.thebreakers.com

  This 560-room, Italian Renaissance–style hotel is a Palm Beach landmark. Although the town, once considered stuffy, is undergoing a bit of a style renaissance, your guests may never leave the grounds of the Breakers, since it offers two championship golf courses, ten tennis courts, a massive spa, and a bevy of shops and restaurants.

- O The Don CeSar Beach Resort, St. Pete Beach, www.doncesar.com

  This flamingo-pink Mediterranean castle on the Gulf Coast specializes in weddings and offers lots of flexibility—events can be big or small, barefoot on the beach, or black-tie in the ballroom, and you can use the resort's recommended vendors or choose to go with outside ones. Whatever your wedding fantasy (a hot-air balloon departure?), they're committed to making it a reality.

- O Casa Morada, Islamorada, www.casamorada.com

- O ⑤ Azul del Mar Resort, Key Largo, www.azulkeylargo.com

- O Sanibel Harbour Resort & Spa, Fort Myers, www.sanibel-resort.com

- O Marco Beach Ocean Resort, Marco Island, www.marcoresort.com

MARRIAGE REQUIREMENTS

Legal Age: 18

Residency Requirements: None

Necessary Documents: Valid photo ID that shows date of birth and a social security card; if previously married, there is no official documentation needed unless marriage ended sixty days or less prior to the ceremony.

Note: Both bride and groom must be present when applying for the marriage license, which is valid within the state for sixty days; there is a three-day waiting period for Florida residents; there is no waiting period for nonresidents.

Fee: $93.50, or $61 and no waiting period upon certificate of completion of a premarital course from a certified provider.

For More Info: www.visitflorida.com

MORE ATLANTIC COAST PROPERTIES

- O China Grove Plantation, Arapahoe, NC, www.chinagrove.com

- O The Sanctuary at Kiawah, Kiawah Island, SC, www.thesanctuary.com

- O Kehoe House, Savannah, GA, www.kehoehouse.com

las vegas, nevada

ONLINE INFO: www.visitlasvegas.com

WHY LAS VEGAS: Drive-through chapels, Elvis impersonators as officiants, your first wedded moments spent at a blackjack table—Las Vegas offers all of that, but there's a whole other side to Sin City. You'll also find elegant ballrooms, a destination your guests will love, and sophisticated, traditional receptions, too.

WHEN TO GO: You and your guests can have a ball just about any time, but try to avoid the hottest summer months (June, July, and August); spring and fall, however, are gorgeous. Prices spike and availability plummets on holiday weekends, big-deal sports weekends (like the Super Bowl and NCAA Final Four), and times when there are giant conventions or events scheduled.

GUESTS MUST-DOS: Hit the Strip. (New York-New York, Paris Las Vegas, the Bellagio, and Caesars Palace are all centrally located resorts.) Casino buffets are a staple, so dig in before you head out for a show (Bally's is the only one with the old-school feather girls), and on your way out, sacrifice some small change to the one-armed bandits. Beyond the casinos are the Elvis and Liberace museums and the roller coasters at the Stratosphere Tower. Vegas's version of laid-back is found poolside.

HOT PROPERTIES

○ Bellagio, www.bellagio.com

Bellagio was one of the first hotel casinos to understand that Las Vegas needed more wedding options than the Little Church of the West and "Can't Help Falling in Love" on a boom box. The amenities are vast, and the accommodations luxe. This is a place for a very grown-up Vegas wedding.

○ The Mirage, www.mirage.com

The exotic South Seas, complete with a regularly exploding volcano, have found a stateside home in Las Vegas. The hotel and casino are top-notch, the location is convenient for guests, and there's an entire company within the resort devoted to event planning—they sweat the details so you don't have to.

○ The Ritz-Carlton, Lake Las Vegas, www.ritzcarlton.com
Located off of the Strip, the Ritz-Carlton's European architecture brings Old World elegance to the Nevada desert. Though it's not in the midst of the hurly-burly of central Vegas, guests will have no shortage of activities. They can enjoy golf, world-class meals, and an unbelievable spa. And it's the Ritz-Carlton, so brides can feel confident that every detail will be taken care of, and every wish granted.

○ Mandalay Bay Resort and Casino, www.mandalaybay.com

○ Monte Carlo Resort & Casino, www.montecarlo.com

○ Wynn Las Vegas, www.wynnlasvegas.com

maine

ONLINE INFO: www.visitmaine.com

WHY MAINE: The East Coast's northernmost state is bursting with natural beauty—a rugged, winding coastline complete with sheltered coves and wildlife-packed state and national parks. It also boasts lots of charming New England towns filled with antique stores, classic roadside diners, and an impressive selection of art museums and galleries. If you dream of swapping vows in an old-fashioned country church, you're certain to be able to find one here.

WHEN TO GO: Summer is when the state attracts the most visitors, especially in July and August, when the weather is warmest (average highs are in the high 70s, average lows in the high 50s), but you should consider having your wedding in September instead, when it's less crowded and the crisp fall weather (highs around 67, nighttime lows in the 50s) lights up the foliage.

GUEST MUST-DOS: In the summer, the state offers the perfect chance to enjoy water sports such as sailing, canoeing, and kayaking. Nature lovers will want to hit the hiking trails in one of Maine's many parks and nature preserves, such as Acadia National Park, a 35,000-acre spread of mountains, woodlands, lakes, and oceanfront that contains 120 miles of hiking trails. Culture vultures will want to check out local art landmarks, such as Winslow Homer's studio in Prout's Neck, the Farnsworth Art Museum in Rockland (which is chock-full of work by the Wyeth family), and Portland's Museum of Art. Everyone should dine on lobster rolls and blueberry pie, two of Maine's scrumptious signature dishes.

STYLE IDEA: Maine is famous for blueberries, so place blueberry jam in your guests' welcome bags, or serve mini blueberry cobblers alongside your wedding cake.

HOT PROPERTIES

O White Barn Inn, www.whitebarninn.com
New England charm at its most quaint and elegant, both the individually decorated rooms in the inn and the waterfront cottages two-tenths of a mile away from the main property are charming. The kitchen here is also a real foodie mecca in Maine.

O Ⓢ Spruce Point Inn, www.sprucepointinn.com
Sitting on fifty-seven acres of green lawns and gardens overlooking Boothbay Harbor, this lodge offers accommodations for more than one hundred couples. Whatever outdoor venue you choose as your ceremony location, the breathtaking Atlantic Ocean serves as your backdrop.

O The Claremont Hotel, www.theclaremonthotel.com
Located on Mount Desert Island, the site is surrounded on all sides by stunning views of the water, mountains, and forests. Make sure your guests' plans include some time at nearby Acadia National Park.

O Asticou Inn, www.asticou.com

O The Inns at Ullikana, www.ullikana.com

MARRIAGE REQUIREMENTS

Legal Age: 18
Residency Requirements: Maine residents must obtain license from town in which they reside.
Necessary Documents: Photo ID, such as a driver's license; if previously married, divorce decree or death certificate may be required.
Note: Either bride or groom must be present with all the relevant information (though this varies among municipalities); there is no waiting period; the license is valid for ninety days within the state.
Fee: Varies by county
For More Info: www.visitmaine.com

. . . .
DID YOU KNOW? Maine has more beachfront than any other state in the nation. Even though it's smaller overall, Maine's winding coastline boasts more coastal mileage than California.
. . . .

massachusetts

ONLINE INFO: www.mass-vacation.com

WHY MASSACHUSETTS: Due to its popularity and prime location, Cape Cod in Massachusetts offers a plethora of resources, from elegant catering to yacht clubs, clambakes, resorts, and gardens. This region can easily play host to small private gatherings, large elegant affairs, and everything in between. The Berkshires is home to several sophisticated, low-key mountain towns and some of the best regional music and theater that the country has to offer.

GUEST MUST-DOS: In coastal towns, sampling a little authentic clam chowder and lobster is a must. Each of the Cape's islands and towns has its own attractions, from the art scene in Provincetown to the Salty Dog Oceanfront Cottages near Martha's Vineyard and Nantucket ferries. The Freedom Trail in Boston is a walk through both history and the city. Inland hiking and biking and other outdoor activities take priority, and there's almost always something worth seeing at the Tanglewood Music Center in Lenox.

HOT PROPERTIES

O Wheatleigh, Lenox, www.wheatleigh.com
   With a grand stair, lit by Tiffany windows and out-of-this-world service, the architecture of this mountain getaway was inspired by a French country château. Between the setting and the service, you'll feel like a worldly princess.

O Winnetu Oceanside Resort, Edgartown, www.winnetu.com
   This new (for Martha's Vineyard) hotel opened in 2000 and has been gaining rave reviews ever since. The charming seaside location and a staff that's ready and able to create a custom reception will make for a headache-free wedding weekend.

MARRIAGE REQUIREMENTS

Legal Age: 18 without parental consent
Residency Requirements: None statewide, but individual cities and towns may have requirements.
Necessary Documents: Birth certificates may be required to show proof of age; a medical certificate stating both members of the couples are in good health and free of syphilis and other STDs; if either of you has been previously married, a divorce decree or death certificate is not necessary.
Note: Both bride and groom must be present to apply for a license. While there is no residency requirement, there is a three-day waiting period after you apply for your marriage license. Once the license has been issued, you may marry immediately. The license expires in sixty days.
Fee: $5 to $50
For More Info: www.mass.gov

MORE NEW ENGLAND IDEAS

O Beach Plum Inn, Menemsha, www.beachpluminn.com

O The Gateways Inn, Lenox, www.gatewaysinn.com

O The Wauwinet, Nantucket, www.wauwinet.com

napa valley, california

ONLINE INFO: www.visitcalifornia.com

WHY NAPA VALLEY: The Napa region is filled with stunning landscapes—rolling hills, lush valleys, and acre upon acre of vineyards. Of course, the main thing that draws pleasure seekers to the area is the abundance of delicious wine produced here, and the world-class restaurants that make food worthy of accompanying it. In the rare moments when you and your wedding guests aren't savoring all that food and wine, explore the charming towns in Napa Valley (filled with chic boutiques, galleries, and gourmet stores), indulge in spa treatments, play golf, or even take a hot-air balloon ride.

WHEN TO GO: Summer and October are the best times to visit the region. September can be beautiful, but you may have problems with availability, and rates will be at their peak because it's harvest season. Even though you're in California, temperatures can drop at night (mid-50s in the summer—good for grape growth), so be sure your guests know to bring sweaters and wraps for the evenings.

GUEST MUST-DOS: You can't visit Napa without touring vineyards, sampling their products, and, more than likely, ordering a case or two to be shipped back home. The sheer number of vineyards in the area is totally overwhelming, so give guests an info packet filled with suggestions. One of the most popular wineries to visit is Rubicon Estate (owned by Francis Ford Coppola), which contains memorabilia from the famous director's movies as well as a store selling gourmet goodies and stylish home accessories.

HOT PROPERTIES

O Meadowood, www.meadowood.com

Hidden on 250 private acres, this resort has eighty-five rooms in a variety of sizes, including freestanding cottages. And the hotel takes pride in their top-quality food, much of which (including the heirloom tomatoes, olives, and honey) is grown or produced on the premises.

O Mayacamas Ranch, www.mayacamasranch.com

Have your ceremony in a grassy meadow with Mount St. Helena in the background, then follow a path flanked by lavender fields to a cocktail hour by the hilltop pool.

O $ Applewood Inn, www.applewoodinn.com

Lush gardens and sunny terraces abound at this historic bed-and-breakfast. Many couples opt to get married at the site's beautiful gazebo, tucked away in an enchanted "fairy circle," surrounded by whimsical statues and flowing fountains.

O Honor Mansion, www.honormansion.com

This resort offers everything you and your guests can possibly want, from outdoor massages and a pool to a championship putting green and a boccie-ball court. The colorful rose garden is a popular place for wedding day photos.

O Gaige House Inn, www.gaige.com

O The Carneros Inn, www.thecarnerosinn.com

O Bacara Resort and Spa, www.bacararesort.com

MARRIAGE REQUIREMENTS

Legal Age: 18

Residency Requirements: None

Necessary Documents: Valid, government-issued photo ID; if previously married, a divorce decree or death certificate is required in some counties.

Note: Both bride and groom must be present when applying for the marriage license, which is valid within the state for ninety days.

Fee: Varies by location

MORE CALIFORNIA PROPERTIES

O Hotel del Coronado, San Diego, www.hoteldel.com

O The Inn at Spanish Bay, Pebble Beach, www.pebblebeach.com

O Ventana Inn & Spa, Big Sur, www.ventanainn.com

O Figueroa Hotel, Los Angeles, www.figueroahotel.com

newport, rhode island

ONLINE INFO: www.gonewport.com

WHY NEWPORT: Newport offers the perfect mix of New England charm and old-fashioned glamour. This seaside community was the playground of the fabulously wealthy at the turn of the last century, when captains of industry from Boston and New York built huge mansions meant to rival the castles of Europe on Newport's cliffs. Today, Newport is still a favorite summer destination of the well-heeled, and it offers a plethora of activities—from sailing to high-end shopping—for wedding guests young and old.

WHEN TO GO: As with Maine and most of the Atlantic coast, it's warmest, and busiest, during the summer months, when the highs average near 80. But the shoulder season months of May and September are beautiful times to visit as well. (In May the average high is 63 and the average low is 48; in September the high is 71 and the low is 58.) For a few days each August, the Newport Jazz Festival fills the town with musicians and music lovers—which means you and your guests will have lots of great music to listen to, but the town will be more crowded than usual.

GUEST MUST-DOS: History and architecture buffs will want to tour some of Newport's historic mansions, such as the Breakers and the Astors' Beechwood. Outdoorsy types can take to the water in a sailboat or a motor yacht, or arrange to go fishing, sea kayaking, or windsurfing. And all of your friends and family will love Newport's evening scene, which involves sipping sunset cocktails while watching boats return to the harbor, dining on lobster and other seafood taken from the water just hours before it reaches your plate, and listening to live blues, jazz, or rock at one of Newport's many music-centered bars and lounges.

HOT PROPERTIES

O The Chanler at Cliff Walk, www.thechanler.com
Built in 1865 as the first mansion on the famed Cliff Walk, the hotel offers an oceanfront ceremony and a tented reception in its Japanese gardens, with catering by the highly rated Spiced Pear restaurant.

O Vanderbilt Hall Hotel, www.vanderbilthall.com
This building—a 1908 Georgian Revival mansion donated to the city by the Vanderbilt family—features rooms decorated with antiques, armoires, and fabrics with period patterns. Your reception dinner at the hotel's restaurant is served on Wedgwood china, but this place is anything but stuffy—the menu includes chicken potpie and macaroni and cheese.

O The Preservation Society of Newport County, www.newportmansions.org
With a mix of old-school elegance and glamour, the Rose-cliff mansion is modeled after the Grand Trianon at Versailles. It is home to the largest ballroom in Newport, and features a heart-shaped staircase—perfect for the bride's grand entrance.

O Hotel Viking, www.hotelviking.com

O The Atlantic Inn, www.altlanticinn.com

O The Weekapaug Inn, www.weekapauginn.com

O ⑤ Newport Marriott, www.marriott.com

MARRIAGE REQUIREMENTS
Legal Age: 18
Residency Requirements: If neither bride nor groom is from Rhode Island, the couple must get a license in the town in which they will marry. If one (but not both) lives in the state, the couple must get a license in the Rhode Island town in which the resident lives.
Necessary Documents: Valid photo ID and certified copy of birth certificate; if previously married, divorce decree or death certificate required.
Note: Both bride and groom must be present to apply for the marriage license, which is valid for ninety days; the couple can only marry in the town in which the marriage license was granted.
Fee: $24
For More Info: www.gonewport.com

DID YOU KNOW? John F. Kennedy and Jacqueline Bouvier were married in Newport in 1953, before more than eight hundred guests at St. Mary's Church.

new york city

ONLINE INFO: www.nycvisit.com

WHY NYC: New York offers something to get every one of your guests giddy with anticipation—Broadway shows, museums and galleries, four-star restaurants, crazy-fun nightlife, block after block of tiny boutiques, as well as classic tourist attractions such as the Empire State Building, the Statue of Liberty, and Times Square. When it comes to wedding-planning resources, too, there's no shortage: You'll have innumerable caterers, florists, photographers, and bands to choose from. Another of the city's assets is that it's supereasy for your guests to get around: With taxis on every block, there's no need for them to rent a car, wrestle with maps, or designate drivers.

WHEN TO GO: Any month can be a good time for a New York wedding. Most of the city's main attractions are indoors, so it doesn't matter much what the weather is like. That said, summers in New York, especially during July and August, can be uncomfortably hot and humid. The city gets extremely crowded during the holiday season, but your guests may love the chance to catch the Christmas show at Radio City Music Hall, ice-skate in Central Park, and browse the decked-out posh department stores.

GUEST MUST-DOS: Shopaholics will want to hit "the three B's" (Barneys, Henri Bendel, and Bergdorf Goodman, high-end department stores all within a few blocks of each other on Fifth and Madison Avenues), as well as the hip boutiques of the SoHo and NoLita neighborhoods. The newly renovated Museum of Modern Art is a must-see, though those more interested in ancient history will want to visit the Temple of Dendur's Egyptian ruins in the Metropolitan Museum of Art. For a bracing dose of the city's after-dark energy, you and your guests should visit the Meatpacking District, where dozens of clubs, lounges, and sidewalk cafés keep the streets crawling with partiers until 4:00 a.m. or later!

STYLE IDEA: Celebrate the cultural and culinary diversity of New York at your rehearsal dinner or reception with different comfort food stations: a Lower East Side station serving pastrami sandwiches, pickles, and knishes; a hot dog cart with Coney Island hot dogs, French fries, and old-fashioned lemonade; a Chinese station serving up dim sum; and a Little Italy station offering pizza and cannolis.

HOT PROPERTIES

O The St. Regis Hotel, www.starwoodhotels.com/stregis
One of the city's most-established and swankest hotels, the St. Regis has a variety of banquet rooms that can accommodate wedding receptions from 50 to 350. Feel totally spoiled by treating guests to afternoon tea in the Astor Court, or by hosting an old-school cocktail party in the King Cole Bar, a classic New York watering hole.

O Mandarin Oriental, www.mandarinoriental.com
One of New York's nicest places to stay, eat, drink, and spa. The Ballroom seats up to five hundred and provides incomparable views of Central Park. An on-site spa offers a lengthy menu of tempting couple treatments.

O The Waldorf-Astoria, www.waldorf-astoria.com
From the Austrian crystal chandeliers to the elevated views of the city, the Waldorf, which hosted the engagement party of Princess Grace and Prince Rainier of Monaco, is the crème de la crème in New York City wedding venues. A peek at the flags hanging above the Park Avenue entrance gives onlookers a clue to the nationalities of the dignitaries currently in residence.

O New York Palace Hotel, www.newyorkpalace.com

O The Pierre, www.tajhotels.com

O Ritz Carlton New York, Battery Park, www.ritzcarlton.com

MARRIAGE REQUIREMENTS

Legal Age: 18

Residency Requirements: None

Necessary Documents: Valid photo ID; if previously married, divorce decree or death certificate required.

Note: Both bride and groom must be present to apply for the marriage license, which is valid only within the state for sixty days. There is a twenty-four-hour waiting period.

Fee: Varies among boroughs; in Manhattan the fee is $35, payable by money order only.

For More Info: www.nycvisit.com

TIP: Research any special events that may be occurring during your wedding weekend—they might tie up traffic and affect hotel availability. For example, the New York City Marathon (the first Sunday in November) draws more than eighty-five thousand applicants, and more than two million spectators.

tucson, arizona

ONLINE INFO: www.arizonaguide.com

WHY TUCSON: Retreat to the city of turquoise jewelry, saguaro cacti, and deep orange sunsets. Located in the southern region of Arizona between Phoenix and the Mexican border, Tucson offers a natural and rugged rendition of the Southwest landscape.

WHEN TO GO: Tucson's weather is generally mild year-round, and most days are bright and sunny.

GUEST MUST-DOS: Catch a glimpse of a roadrunner while hiking through Sabino Canyon, tour the historic Mission San Xavier del Bac, or peruse the photo and art galleries full of Native American and Mexican textiles and jewelry.

HOT PROPERTIES

O **$** Hacienda del Sol, www.haciendadelsol.com
This historic resort's amazing views of the Santa Catalina Mountains have attracted such famous guests as the late Spencer Tracy, Katharine Hepburn, and John Wayne. Recently redesigned, its Southwestern style includes hand-painted tiles, adobe walls, and original fireplaces, as well as three unique wedding ceremony sites.

O Casa Tierra, www.casatierratucson.com
The all-adobe inn features more than fifty arches, as well as entryways with vaulted brick ceilings and courtyards with fountains. Each guest receives a welcome basket of fruit and snacks, iced tea, and chocolates when he or she checks in.

O Arizona Inn, www.arizonainn.com
Get the best of both worlds at this historic hotel: Exchange vows with the sound of water flowing in the fountains and the scents of roses and orange blossoms in the air at the Sundown Fountain, then move on to an elegant ballroom reception at the Tucson Room.

MARRIAGE REQUIREMENTS

Legal Age: 18

Necessary Documents: Birth certificate or passport (if under 21) and valid photo ID; if previously married, divorce decree or death certificate requirements vary by location.

Note: Both bride and groom must be present when applying for the marriage license, which is valid within the state for one year.

Fee: $50 (method of payment varies by location)

MORE SOUTHWEST IDEAS

O L'Auberge de Sedona, Sedona, AZ, www.lauberge.com

O Arizona Biltmore Resort & Spa, Phoenix, AZ, www.arizonabiltmore.com

O Sanctuary on Camelback Mountain, Paradise Valley, AZ, www.sanctuaryoncamelback.com

O Hacienda Doña Andrea de Santa Fe, Cerrillos, NM, www.hdasantafe.com

LATIN AMERICA

mexico

ONLINE INFO: www.visitmexico.com

WHY MEXICO: While most Americans head to Mexico to lie on its gorgeous beaches and soak up the south of the border sun, the country has much more to offer than sand and surf. It boasts a staggering array of natural wonders and ancient archaeological sites such as the Maya ruins on the Yucatán Peninsula and the pyramid-lined Avenue of the Dead in Teotihuacán, just outside of Mexico City.

WHEN TO GO: The high season begins in mid-December and typically lasts through Easter, with the rainy season running from May through mid-October. Although temps may only top out at 90 degrees in June, July, and August, the humidity can make a trip to the Yucatán Peninsula (and most coastal areas) uncomfortably hot. Hurricane season affects the coastal areas, especially June through October, and beware of spring break crowds in March and April.

BAJA PENINSULA

WHY BAJA: Located at the southern tip of the Baja peninsula, Los Cabos is a vacationers' paradise, specifically the town of Cabo San Lucas, which is equipped with a wealth of lodging options, from lavish resorts to condominiums and low-key inns. You and your guests can throw yourselves into one or more of the many water sports available, or give yourselves permission to do nothing but curl up on the beach with a book and a steady supply of tequila-laced libations.

GUEST MUST-DOS: Boating is a quintessential Cabo activity, so charter a sailboat or try your hand at sport fishing—beneath the ocean's surface lies an abundance of sailfish, marlin, yellowtail, and other fish. Those who want to stay on land should explore the Sierra de la Laguna mountain range.

HOT PROPERTIES

O One and Only Palmilla, www.oneandonlyresorts.com
Built with a respectful nod to old Mexico, this resort boasts a vantage point on the tip of the peninsula from which you can spot gray whales in the distance as you sip your cocktail. Accommodations are first class with an emphasis on subdued luxury.

O Las Ventanas al Paraíso, www.lasventanas.com
Set right on the ocean, this ultraluxe property features suites with marble showers, limestone floors, and a telescope to better see the canopy of nighttime stars. Say your vows on the resort patio, with the shimmering Sea of Cortez as your backdrop.

O ⑤ Riu Palace, Cabo San Lucas, www.riu.com
Situated right on the beach, this enormous, all-inclusive property features interconnected pools, swim-up bars, and an array of dining options. At night, the resort comes alive with a jumping after-hours scene.

O Marquis Los Cabos, www.marquisloscabos.com

O Esperanza-An Auberge Resort,
www.esperanzaresort.com

TIP: One of Baja's most popular ceremony spots is the appropriately named Playa del Amor (Lover's Beach), a short boat ride from Cabo, which has breathtaking views of the Pacific.

THE YUCATÁN PENINSULA

WHY THE YUCATÁN: The beach towns on the Yucatán peninsula, which include Cancún, Playa del Carmen, Puerto Morelos, and Isla Mujeres, are situated between the idyllic Caribbean Sea and some of the Western hemisphere's most fascinating archaeological sites, the ruins of the ancient Maya empire.

GUEST MUST-DOS: You and your guests can dive, snorkel, and otherwise enjoy the beauties of the beach, but you'll want to spend some time inland, too—touring the awe-inspiring Maya ruins. By night you can enjoy chilled tequila and live mariachi bands at one of the region's plethora of welcoming nightspots.

STYLE IDEA: Decorate your reception by stringing brightly colored piñatas over the dance floor—then toward the end of the evening your guests can tear them open to find candy and other treats. Give each guest a bottle of Xtabentún liqueur (native to the Yucatán peninsula), or serve it up in small glasses at your reception during dessert.

HOT PROPERTIES

○ Presidente InterContinental Cancun Resort, www.ichotelsgroup.com

Although the area's beaches were severely eroded by Hurricane Wilma in 2005, the Presidente InterContinental was able to repair its amazing stretch of private beach, and also added more than fifteen feet to the area. The hotel is home to three restaurants and two bars featuring live music—perfect for entertaining your guests.

○ Ⓢ CasaMagna Marriott Cancun Resort, www.marriott.com

The CasaMagna has a catering and banquet staff ready to make your dream wedding day a reality. Hold your ceremony at the gazebo overlooking the crystal blue ocean, then move inside for your reception in the elegant Maya Ballroom, which can hold up to six hundred people. The resort also has a relaxing spa where you and your guests can unwind.

○ The Ritz-Carlton, Cancun, www.ritzcarlton.com

○ Hotel el Rey del Caribe, www.reycaribe.com

MARRIAGE REQUIREMENTS

Legal Age: 18

Residency Requirement: None

Necessary Documents: Certified copies of birth certificates previously "legalized" and translated by the Mexican consulate with jurisdiction over the place of filing; driver's licenses or passports valid for at least six months; certified proof of divorce or death certificate of former spouse(s), if applicable, previously "legalized" by the Mexican consulate with jurisdiction over the place of filing; judge's form; tourist cards; Mexican-performed blood test results and X-rays.

Note: The marriage requirements in Mexico vary from city to city and judge to judge. The Mexican Ministry of Tourism recommends that you budget two to four days to complete all requirements. It is recommended that you work with a wedding planner to help you fulfill all requirements properly.

Fee: Approximately U.S. $30 (varies by location)

costa rica

ONLINE INFO: www.visitcostarica.com

WHY COSTA RICA: If you crave an unspoiled tropical wilderness but don't want to sacrifice your modern urban tastes, Costa Rica could be the destination for you. Unlike some of its Central American neighbors, this nation has long been democratic and peaceful (the army was abolished in the 1940s) as well as devoted to protecting its natural wonders—even though the country only covers 0.03% of the planet's surface, it still makes up approximately 6% of the world's biodiversity.

WHEN TO GO: You'll want to schedule your wedding during the dry season, from late December through April, rather than the green or "wet" season (when you can kiss your chances of unfrizzed wedding hair good-bye!). The Pacific coast is drier than the Caribbean one.

GUEST MUST-DOS: Costa Rica is a paradise for adventure travelers and nature lovers, who can head inland to explore the land's rain forests, volcanoes, and waterfalls, or stay seaside to surf, kayak, or dive. Soak up the local culture by shopping for handmade ceramics and eating fresh tortillas at roadside stands.

HOT PROPERTIES

O ⑤ Almonds and Corals Lodge, www.almondsandcorals.com

If you love to camp but want a little more luxury for your DW, check out Almonds and Corals, situated in the Gandoca-Manzanillo Wildlife Refuge. Guests stay in raised and roofed tents, which are outfitted with electric lamps, a fan, and a bathroom. After exploring all that Mother Nature has to offer, relax in the resort's Jacuzzi, located right in the heart of the rain forest.

O Lapa Rios, www.laparios.com

Originally built as a private nature reserve, this luxe eco-resort overlooks the point where the Golfo Dulce meets the Pacific Ocean. Guests looking for a more active trip will enjoy kayaking, surfing, and hiking through the rain forest, while others can sip a cocktail by the pool, enjoy a massage, or watch the sunset from their bungalow.

O Sueño del Mar, www.tamarindo.com/sdmar

O Florblanca Resort, www.florblanca.com

O Hotel Punta Islita, www.hotelpuntaislita.com

O Peace Lodge at La Paz Waterfalls Gardens, www.waterfallgardens.com

MARRIAGE REQUIREMENTS

Legal Age: 18

Residency Requirement: None

Necessary Documents: Passport valid for at least six months; original birth certificates; certified copy of your police record; affidavit of single status; official copy of divorce decree or death certificate of former spouse(s) if one or both parties has been previously married; marriage certificate issued by the Costa Rican Civil Registry.

Note: Issuance of a Costa Rican marriage certificate normally takes four to six weeks. A Costa Rican marriage license must be authenticated and translated into English by an official translator of the Ministry of Foreign Relations. The certificate must also be notarized and signed by the U.S. Embassy Consular Section, and there is a $30 fee for this service. All of these steps may be performed by a Costa Rican attorney.

Fee: Contact embassy (see below) for cost.

For More Info: http://usembassy.or.cr/consfaq.html

MORE LATIN AMERICAN IDEAS

O Blue Reef Island Resort, Ambergris Caye, Belize, www.bluereefresort.com

O Jaguar Reef Lodge, Hopkins Village, Belize, www.jaguarreef.com

O Maruba Resort Jungle spa. Belize, www.aruba-spa.com

EUROPE

italy

ONLINE INFO: www.italiantourism.com

WHY ITALY: The question is not why you should go to Italy, the birthplace of the phrase *la dolce vita* (the sweet life), but where in this country of art, ancient history, ethereal vistas, top-notch cuisine, and abundant wine (Italy leads the world with more than four million acres of vineyards) is the ideal destination for you.

WHEN TO GO: April through June, September, and October are the best times to explore Italy, with mild temperatures and smaller crowds. August is uncomfortably hot, and it's the month when most Italians go on vacation, so many shops, hotels, and restaurants may be closed. Winters in the north are cold and rainy (you may even see snow), while the south stays on the warmer side, with temps averaging around 50 degrees.

NORTHERN ITALY

From the small villages lining the Lake Como region to the big cities packed with art, architecture, fine dining, and fashion, northern Italy offers old-world culture mixed with modern cities and historic attractions.

GUEST MUST-DOS: Shop 'til you drop in Milan (the epicenter of Italian design), and while there be sure to take a tour of the world's fourth largest cathedral. In Venice, hop on a gondola through the canals. In the lakes region, cruise around Lake Como and try to spot the celebrity-owned villas (George Clooney and Richard Gere both have homes there).

HOT PROPERTIES

O ⑤ Fonte de' Medici, www.fontedemedici.com
Fonte de' Medici is a cluster of farmhouses tucked away in the Tuscan vineyards between Florence and Sienna. The brightly colored walls and charm of the Chianti region will

suit the couple who wants a relaxed atmosphere, great food and wine, and an intimate setting where guests can all get to know one another.

O Hotel Principe di Savoia, www.hotelprincipedisavoia.com
A one-stop shop for couples looking to plan a sophisticated Italian weekend with a youthful edge. The staff here can help with everything: finding florists, booking spa treatments for the wedding party, planning the menu. All you have to do is arrive, enjoy, and say "I do."

O Villa d'Este, Cernobbia, www.villadeste.it
This amazingly regal lakeside property is a former sixteenth-century residence for European aristocrats, and weddings here take on that same old-world, lavish feel. Set on the shores of Lake Como, guest rooms are uniquely decorated with period furnishings, and some have balconies with a view of the lake. Have your ceremony and reception in one of the many banquet rooms, terraces, or gardens.

O Grand Hotel et de Milan, www.grandhoteletdemilan.it

O Hotel Cipriani, www.hotelcipriani.com

O Hotel Certosa di Maggiano, www.certosadimaggiano.it

O Villa La Massa, Florence, www.villamassa.com

SOUTHERN ITALY

When it comes to picturesque settings, it's hard to beat southern Italy, with its majestic peaks, gentle valleys, and miles of lovely coastline.

GUEST MUST-DOS: Tour the Catacombs of the Capuchins, which contain thousands of mummified bodies; shop for local fare at the Ballarò street market in Palermo; visit the cathedral at San Giorgio dei Genovesi, where Sicily's kings and queens are buried; be at the cathedral of Messina at noon to see the world's largest animated clock perform; take a drive to Piazza

Armerina, a town with a spectacular hilltop view and what's thought to be a hunting lodge with mosaics dating back to the fourth century A.D.; and gander at Mount Etna, the largest active volcano in Europe.

HOT PROPERTIES

O San Domenico Palace, Taormina, www.thi.it
Built on the site of a fifteenth-century monastery, the San Domenico Palace offers sweeping views of the water and Mount Etna. Hold your ceremony in the property's lush garden, then move inside for the reception in one of the hotel's four banquet rooms, which can accommodate anywhere from 90 to 350 people.

O Massimo Plaza Hotel, www.massimoplazahotel.com
The perfect setting for a princess bride, the palazzo has a striking outdoor staircase, which sets the tone for a weekend of royal treatment. The recent renovations (supported by the city of Palermo) retained the hotel's character while modernizing the amenities.

O Grand Hotel Ortigia, www.grandhotelsr.it

O Ⓢ Hotel Villa Athena, www.athenahotels.com

AMALFI COAST

When the backdrop for your wedding is a citrus grove that overlooks Italy's jaw-dropping Amalfi coast, "great wedding pictures" take care of themselves.

GUEST MUST-DOS: The Amalfi Drive is one of the most scenic stretches of Italian coastline, comprised of a winding clifftop road offering dramatic views of the sea. Pay a visit to the ruins of Pompeii; visit the thirteenth-century Black Madonna in Positano; take a boat trip through the Blue Grotto off Capri; visit the seaside village of Sorrento; and walk the ancient, narrow streets of Naples's "Old Spacca Quarter."

STYLE IDEA: Give espresso beans, a bottle of limoncello, or five Jordan almonds (which the Italians take to represent five wishes for the bride and groom: health, wealth, happiness, fertility, and longevity) as wedding favors.

HOT PROPERTIES

O Grand Hotel Ambasciatori, www.manniellohotels.it
This hotel was once the home of a well-known fortune-teller, which the town believes gives the property good luck. Close to the center of Sorrento, it offers a unique view of the Gulf of Naples and of Mount Vesuvius.

O Hotel Caesar Augustus, www.caesar-augustus.com
Situated on a cliff a thousand feet above the sea, the hotel has fifty-six rooms with private balconies and panoramic views of the Bay of Naples, Mount Vesuvius, and the island of Capri.

O Ⓢ Hotel dei Cavalieri, www.hoteldeicavalieri.it
This family-owned hotel has a view of the Gulf of Salerno and is only a ten-minute stroll to the center of Amalfi. Make sure to request a room with a balcony.

O Le Sirenuse, www.sirenuse.it

o Grand Hotel Cocumella, www.cocumella.com

O Palazzo Sasso Ravello, www.palazzasasso.com

MARRIAGE REQUIREMENTS

Legal Age: 18
Residency Requirements: None
Necessary Documents: Passports or armed forces ID cards; certified copies of birth certificates; proof of divorce or death certificate of former spouse(s), if applicable; a declaration sworn to by four citizens before an Italian consular officer stating that there are no obstacles to the marriage according to U.S. law; all documents issued outside of Italy must be translated into Italian and certified by an Italian consular officer with special "apostille" seals from the Secretary of State from the state where the documents originated.
Note: Working with a wedding planner is *highly* recommended to fulfill all requirements properly. A translator may be required to attend the wedding if neither the bride nor the groom speaks Italian.
Fee: Contact the Italian Government Tourist Board office at (212) 245-4822

france

ONLINE INFO: www.francetourism.com

WHY FRANCE: The country is home to one of the most romantic cities in the world—Paris. And just an hour outside the city is the château-rich and rolling Loire Valley, cherished for its fairy-tale castles, historic villages, charming people, wines, and food.

WHEN TO GO: April through June, and September through early November. While the weather is mild year-round, the rainy season varies by region and runs from mid-November through February; stay away during July and August unless you want to deal with huge crowds.

GUEST MUST-DOS: The City of Light boasts world-renowned boutiques, cozy streetside cafés, grand avenues, jazz clubs, galleries, and museums—and let's not forget the Eiffel Tower. Since the Loire Valley is so close, you and your guests can also enjoy the country life: take a wine-tasting tour, pay a visit to the Château d'Useé, said to be the setting of the French fairy tale "Sleeping Beauty," in the village of Rigny-Ussé, and take a taste (or two) of the beloved tarte tatin (upside-down apple tart).

HOT PROPERTIES

O Four Seasons Hotel George V, Paris, www.fourseasons.com/paris
Luxury is present here in spades (the event-planning staff knows who all the best vendors in the city are, while the concierges are there to help your guests). The hotel's central location (blocks from the Champs-Elysées, within eyesight of the Eiffel Tower) is perfect for an old-school city chic celebration with a *très Francais* flair.

O Le Meurice, Paris, www.lemeurice.com
Every floor of this five-star hotel—located across the street from the Tuileries Garden—is decorated in a style reminiscent of Louis XVIII. All rooms are soundproof, and the 3,200-square-foot private terrace of the Belle Étoile Suite offers a spectacular 360-degree, panoramic view of Paris.

Espace Bien-Être, the hotel's 3,000-square-foot spa, features specially trained masseuses from Les Sources de Caudalie, the world's first "vinothérapie" spa.

O Château de Marçay, Loire Valley, www.chateaudemarcay.com
This fifteenth-century fortress, surrounded by its own vineyard, is perched at the top of a slope overlooking the village. The rooms are done in a French provincial style, many under a network of rough wooden ceiling beams. And the restaurant is renowned for its gourmet cuisine, guaranteeing a sumptuous wedding day feast.

O Domaine des Hauts de Loire, Loire Valley, www.domainehautsloire.com
A fine ivy-covered faux château built in 1860 by a publishing magnate boasts a swimming pool, tennis courts, and flower gardens.

O Le Château de Gilly, www.grandes-etapes-francaises.fr

O Grand Hotel du Cap-Ferrat, France, www.grand-hotel-cap-ferrat.com

O Ⓢ La Ferme de La Huppe, www.lafermedelahuppe.com

MARRIAGE REQUIREMENTS

Legal Age: 18 for males; 15 for females.
Residency Requirements: Forty days (for at least one of you).
Necessary Documents: Most *mairies* (town halls) in France require some or all of the following documents, but check locally for specific requirements: a valid U.S. passport, or a French residence permit (*carte de séjour*); a birth certificate (*extrait d'acte de naissance*) less than three months old. Also need an affidavit of marital status, an affidavit of law, and a medical certificate no more than two months old.
Note: Most town halls require that you present a certified copy of your birth certificate with a certified translation. You must obtain the translation from a sworn translator (*traducteur assermenté*). You must also post marriage banns (intent to marry) at the local *mairie* no less than ten days prior to the wedding date. Sworn translators are listed at every mairie: france.usembassy.gov/consul/guideoas/translators.pdf
Fee: Contact below for cost
For More Info: http://france.usembassy.gov

united kingdom

ONLINE INFO: www.visitbritain.com

WHY THE UNITED KINGDOM: If the words *fairy tale* defines your idea of a dream wedding, get thee (and thine) to Great Britain. Amid the isles, heaths, and mist, not only does your chariot await, but so do your castles, gardens, and Royal Guard, too.

WHEN TO GO: May through October. The best weather is usually from May to September, with short showers common throughout the year (don't forget to pack an umbrella or a slicker).

GUEST MUST-DOS: In England, visit the incredible collection at the British Museum and get a history lesson at the Houses of Parliament (and see Big Ben). Hop on the Tube (subway) to Covent Garden and Soho for shopping and dining out, then take a stroll along the Thames before stopping at a pub for a pint. In Northern Ireland: Learn how whiskey is made and sample "the water of life" (as whiskey is known here) at the Old Jameson Distillery in Dublin; enjoy the greenery in Phoenix Park; pay a visit to the Rock of Cashel (St. Patrick allegedly picked a shamrock here to explain the Trinity) and the breathtaking Cliffs of Moher, a five-mile-long sea wall that soars up to nearly seven hundred feet. In Scotland: take a tour through Edinburgh Castle, the seat of Scottish power before its union with Great Britain; play a round of golf at one of Scotland's many unbelievable courses; try to spot the Loch Ness Monster!

HOT PROPERTIES

○ Hartwell House, England, www.hartwell-house.com

Set on ninety gorgeous acres, this castlelike property is a lush, regal choice for a wedding celebration. Reserve the Old Rectory (including four bedrooms, sleeping up to eight guests) with a private pool, tennis court, and staff, or take over the entire hotel.

○ Mandarin Oriental Hyde Park, England, www.mandarinoriental.com/london/

A great choice for couples looking for a swank London locale, the Mandarin Oriental offers all the pomp and circumstance of old London plus the conveniences of a modern hotel. Choose to have your ceremony in a place of worship or in the hotel itself, as they hold a license to conduct services in any of their banquet rooms.

○ Adare Manor Hotel and Golf Resort, Ireland, www.adaremanor.com

There is no greater golf destination than the Adare Manor in Ireland. Castlelike property, estate grounds, and opulent accommodations ensure that couples and their guests get the royal treatment.

○ Dalhousie Castle, Scotland, www.dalhousiecastle.co.uk

Dalhousie Castle is a thirteenth-century fortress set in vast, wooded parkland on the banks of the River Esk. And while each of the guest rooms is distinctive, the one to grab (after the bridal suite, where the property's original well is still located) is the Sir William Wallace room, which boasts doors leading out onto the castle battlements. To the delight of Harry Potter fans worldwide, a distinguishing characteristic of a Dalhousie wedding is the owl that delivers your wedding rings to the altar, if you so choose.

DID YOU KNOW? Though the origin of the word *honeymoon* is still unknown, some believe it originated in Ireland. It refers to a honey-based drink called mead that newlyweds would share for one full moon (a month) after their wedding to give them powers of virility and fertility.

MARRIAGE REQUIREMENTS

ENGLAND

Legal Age: 16. You'll need written parental consent if under 18.
Residency Requirements: seven days; fifteen-day waiting period
Necessary Documents: Passports or certified copies of birth certificates; proof of divorce or death certificate of former spouse(s), if applicable. Couples will also need a marriage visa to marry in the UK, which can be obtained through the British

Consulate General. Couples must also give "Notice of Intent to Marry" at the local Register Office.

Fee: £30 for the "Notice of Intent to Marry"

For more info: Visit Britain, (800) 462-2748; British Consulate General, (212) 745-0200; or www.britainusa.com

NORTHERN IRELAND

Legal Age: 16. You'll need written parental consent if under 18.

Residency Requirement: For marriage license, fifteen days with seven-day waiting period. For marriage certificate, seven days with twenty-one-day waiting period

Necessary Documents: Valid passports; birth certificates; certified copy of divorce or death certificate if one or both parties has been previously married.

Note: You must submit completed marriage license forms eight to ten weeks before marriage.

Fee: £100 for a civil marriage (payable to the Registrar of Civil Marriages)

For More Info: www.groireland.ie/getting_married.htm

SCOTLAND

Legal Age: 16. You'll need written parental consent if under 18.

Residency Requirements: None

Necessary Documents: Passports or certified copies of birth certificates; proof of divorce or death certificate of former spouse(s), if applicable; certificate of no impediment. Couples will also need a marriage visa to marry in the UK. These can be obtained through the British Consulate General.

Note: Notice must also be sent to the registrar at least four to six weeks in advance of the wedding. Either the bride or the groom must also meet with the registrar in advance.

Fee: About £103.50

For More Info: Visit Britain, (800) 462-2748; British Consulate General, (212) 745-0200; or www.britainusa.com

---

MORE EUROPEAN IDEAS

O Hotel Heliotopos, Santorini Island, Greece, hotel.heliotopos.net

O Suvretta House, St. Moritz, Switzerland, www.suvrettahouse.ch/en

O Hotel Monasterio San Miguel, Spain, www.jale.com/monasterio

PACIFIC RIM

WHY THE PACIFIC RIM: If your friends and relatives count themselves as intrepid travelers, or if you and your fiancé are looking for an intimate tropical escape, the Pacific Rim is hard to beat. Consisting of the islands and nations scattered throughout the vast Pacific Ocean, the area boasts some of the most amazing scenery (both above and below sea level) and romantic getaways on the planet.

WHEN TO GO: December through February is summer in Fiji, and there can be rain, depending on where you are on the island. The same is true of Tahiti from November through March, though the island still averages more sunshine during this time than other tropical destinations. Temperatures in Indonesia hover in the 80s on average, and May to October sees the lowest humidity, while New Zealand is at its best from February to May. June through September is the rainy season in Thailand.

australia

ONLINE INFO: www.australia.com

HOT PROPERTY
O Park Hyatt Melbourne, www.melbourne.park.hyatt.com

MARRIAGE REQUIREMENTS
Legal Age: 18
Residency Requirements: None
Necessary Documents: Passports and birth certificates; proof of divorce or death certificate of former spouse(s), if applicable; couples must also complete a Notice of Intended Marriage Form (available at any Australian Embassy or Consulate), to be signed by an Australian Diplomatic Officer or an Australian Consular Officer and filed with the officiant a minimum of thirty-one days before the ceremony.
Fee: None

fiji

ONLINE INFO: www.bulafiji.com

HOT PROPERTY
O Sonaisali Island Resort, Nadi, www.sonaisali.com

MARRIAGE REQUIREMENTS
Legal Age: 21. You'll need notarized letters of parental consent if younger.
Residency Requirement: None
Necessary Documents: Passports; birth certificates; proof of divorce or death certificate of former spouse(s), if applicable.
Note: Registration takes about fifteen minutes (you both must appear), but processing the paperwork takes one working day. Other requirements vary by church.
Fee: $16.50 (Fiji dollars)

indonesia

ONLINE INFO: www.indonesia-tourism.com

HOT PROPERTY
O Nusa Dua Beach Hotel and Spa, Bali, www.nusaduahotel.com

MARRIAGE REQUIREMENTS
Legal Age: 21. You'll need parental consent if younger.
Residency Requirement: None
Necessary Documents: Passports; birth certificates; details of religious faith (i.e., baptism certificates); occupations and residency information for both the bride and groom; divorce decree or death certificate of former spouse(s), if applicable;

eight photographs of the couple together (FYI: photos will be attached to your wedding certificate).

Note: Couples who are of one of the five religions recognized by the government (Protestant, Catholic, Muslim, Hindu, and Buddhist) may be legally married in Indonesia; Catholic couples must present additional paperwork; two witnesses must be present during ceremony.

Fee: Contact embassy

new zealand

ONLINE INFO: www.newzealand.com

HOT PROPERTY
O Villa Toscana, Whitianga, www.villatoscana.co.nz

MARRIAGE REQUIREMENTS
Legal Age: 16; if under 18, you'll need parental consent.
Residency Requirement: None
Necessary Documents: Passports; birth certificates; couples are required to submit a Notice of the Intended Marriage with their officiant or to the Registry Office at least three days before the marriage, as well as proof of divorce or death certificate of former spouse(s), if applicable.
Note: Marriage license is valid for only three months; you must have two witnesses during the ceremony.
Fee: $120 (New Zealand dollars) if conducted by a celebrant; $170 (New Zealand dollars) for a civil marriage

tahiti

ONLINE INFO: www.tahiti-tourisme.com

HOT PROPERTY
O Sheraton Moorea Resort and Spa, www.sheratonmoorea.com

MARRIAGE REQUIREMENTS
Legal Age: 18 for males; 15 for females. You'll need written parental consent if under 18.
Residency Requirement: At least one of you must live in French Polynesia for thirty days.
Necessary Documents: Birth certificates (issued within three months of your wedding and translated into French); medical certificates; one certificate of residency; one copy of notarized marriage contract; customary certificates; certificates of celibacy; and a certificate of publication of marriage bans in the nonresident's hometown.
Fee: Varies

thailand

ONLINE INFO: www.tourismthailand.org

HOT PROPERTY
O Banyan Tree Phuket, Phuket, www.banyantree.com/phuket

MARRIAGE REQUIREMENTS
Legal Age: 17; you'll need parental consent if under 20.
Residency Requirement: One working day
Necessary Documents: Passports; original birth certificates; proof of divorce or death certificate for former spouse(s), if applicable.
Note: Couples must go to their home embassy in Bangkok and sign statutory declaration forms stating that you're both free to marry; all documents must be translated into Thai and certified by the Ministry of Foreign Affairs in Bangkok; you then must register the marriage at the District Office in the town where the wedding will take place.
Fee: Varies

destination wedding worksheets

your wedding day timeline

A good timeline means you won't have to stress out and worry your way through this memorable day. Here's a sample timeline for a wedding day with a 5:00 p.m. ceremony. Stretch or shorten it to suit your needs.

___:___ (10:00) **BREAKFAST WITH YOUR PARENTS OR BRIDESMAIDS.**
You're going to have a full day. Fuel up!

___:___ (10:00) **VENDOR DELIVERIES AND SET UP.**
(Up to 12 hours before. See individual contracts for details.) Make sure your vendors check in with you or your planner. You want to know five hours, not five minutes, before the wedding if something is awry, or if you need to go with Plan B.

___:___ (12:00) **HAVE YOUR WEDDING GOWN STEAMED OR PRESSED.**
Gown and accessories need to be delivered to the location where the bride will be getting dressed.

___:___ (1:00) **HAVE HAIR AND MAKEUP DONE FOR YOU AND YOUR BRIDESMAIDS.**
Remind everyone to wear button-front shirts. This is a good time to grab a salad or a sandwich. Once people are in their dresses, you don't want to risk dripping salad dressing or spilling sodas.

Time ___:___ Bride _____

Time ___:___ Maid _____

Time ___:___ Maid _____

Time ___:___ Maid _____

Time ___:___ Maid _____

Time ___:___ Maid _____

___:___ (2:00) **BRIDESMAIDS GET DRESSED.**
If hair and makeup were done off-site or in a different place than yours, round everyone up now to finish getting ready.

___:___ (2:30) **PERSONAL FLOWERS ARE DELIVERED TO THE BRIDE'S ROOM.**
You, your planner, your mother, or a trusted bridesmaid should check the arrangements against the original order form to make sure everything has arrived. Someone should call to make sure the groomsmen have their boutonnieres, too.

___:___ (2:30) **GROOM AND GROOMSMEN GET DRESSED.**

___:___ (3:00) **PHOTOGRAPHER REPORTS TO BRIDAL AREA AS BRIDE GETS DRESSED.**
He'll need time to set lights, snag candid shots, and get your last-minute instructions. If you haven't given him a list of must-take shots (your great-aunt and -uncle dancing, all of the groom's cousins, etc.) or reviewed any sticky family situations (your divorced parents don't want to be in a picture together), do so now.

___:___ (3:30) **BRIDAL PARTY PHOTOS ARE TAKEN.**
Superstitious brides can take all of the shots that don't consist of both the bride and the groom. Couples who crave efficiency over tradition can go for the full set of posed shots with each other, the various bridal party permutations, and family photos.

_____:_____ (4:15) **USHERS REPORT TO CEREMONY AREA.**
The best man or planner will now give the guys last-minute seating instructions and make sure all boutonnieres are affixed and the various accessories (vests, ties, cummerbunds) are in place. Someone needs to check that the best man has the rings, that the groom has the marriage license, and that the groom's microphone has been attached. Now is also the time when the appointed people can put out the ceremony items like programs, the unity candle, accessories for a sand or water ceremony, a glass to break, or the chalice for wine.

_____:_____ (4:30) **CEREMONY MUSICIANS SET IN PLACE.**
They need a few seconds to assemble, tune up, and set sound levels.

_____:_____ (4:30) **BRIDE ARRIVES.**

_____:_____ (4:40) **PRELUDE BEGINS; GUESTS ARE SEATED.**
If guests have gathered near the ceremony area, the music and the presence of the ushers will let them know it's time to take their seats. The prelude should be something expectant that also fits the overall tone of your setting and event. The mother of the bride is traditionally the last person seated, and she is taken to her place by the head usher.

_____:_____ (5:00) **THE PROCESSIONAL BEGINS.**
As the processional music plays, the members of your wedding party take their places for the ceremony. Once everyone's assembled, there will be a pause before the music switches to the song you've chosen for your wedding march. You and your ceremony escort(s) then head down the aisle to join your groom and attendants.

_____:_____ (5:30) **THE CEREMONY CONCLUDES.**
You've been pronounced husband and wife and raced up the aisle with beaming smiles, timed to mark the moment with a dove release, fireworks, sparklers, rose petals, bells ringing, or some other sort of fanfare to kick off the celebration.

_____:_____ (5:45) **FORMAL PORTRAITS SESSION.**
While guests are starting the cocktail hour, the families and couple assemble to take the remaining photographs.

_____:_____ (6:00) **COCKTAILS.**
Your reception officially begins with the cocktail hour. This can be outside on a patio or a deck, in an anteroom outside the dining room, or in any other spot where a bar can be set up and hors d'oeuvres passed. The musicians should be in place ten minutes before guests are expected so that they are already playing when guests arrive.

CONTINUES

___:___ (7:00) **GUESTS ARE TOLD TO TAKE THEIR SEATS FOR DINNER.**

___:___ (7:15) **BRIDAL PARTY INTRODUCTIONS.**
If you didn't join guests at the cocktail hour, you can ask your bandleader or DJ to introduce you and the wedding party as you enter the dining area.

___:___ (7:20) **THE FIRST DANCE.**
With all eyes already on you, now is a good time for your first dance, father/daughter, mother/son, and wedding party dances. The floor isn't open to guests until you take these twirls, so get out there early! (Allow about three minutes for each.)

___:___ (7:30) **TOASTS.**
Before dinner is served, your father (and mother) as hosts should give a toast, which will be followed by words from the best man and sometimes the maid of honor.

___:___ (7:40) **MAIN COURSE IS SERVED.**
Allow 15 minutes for one entrée, 20 for two. This could be longer or shorter depending on the number of guests being served and the amount of available waitstaff.

___:___ (8:30) **DANCING.**
Have the band or DJ kick it up a notch to encourage dancing as guests are finishing their meals. Take this opportunity to relax and have a great time with your guests.

___:___ (9:30) **COUPLES TOAST/CAKE-CUTTING.**
It's time to cut the cake and serve dessert. You and your groom will want to get everyone's attention so that you can thank them for coming and share how much the day and their presence mean to you.

___:___ (9:45) **BOUQUET AND GARTER TOSS.**
While you still have everyone's attention as dessert is being served, grab your unmarried guests and head to the dance floor for the traditional bouquet and garter toss.

___:___ (10:00) **LAST DANCE AND SEND-OFF.**
Chances are you've reserved the reception space for a set block of time (usually four hours). The best way to send everyone off happy and convinced they won't miss anything is with a last dance and your departure marked with sparklers or the like.

___:___ (10:30) **AFTER-PARTY.**
Some guests will want to keep the party going, so make sure you've got some drinks and snacks ready to go in a hospitality suite in the hotel where most people are staying. For more ideas, see page 108.

your wedding budget

	Budget	Actual	Notes
RECEPTION 35%			
Food ($ per person x # of guests)			
Bar and beverages			
Cake/cutting fee			
Vendor meals ($ per person x # of vendors)			
Service fee/tip			
Reception venue fees			
Rentals (tent, tables, linens)			
SUBTOTAL			
RINGS 10%			
Bride's wedding band			
Groom's wedding band			
SUBTOTAL			
TRAVEL AND LODGING 10%			
Scouting trips			
Bride and groom travel			
Bride and groom hotel room			
Limo/wedding transportation			
Guest shuttles			
Tips			
SUBTOTAL			
PHOTO AND VIDEO 10–12%			
Photographer and assistant's fee			
Development/album fee			
Videographer's fee			
Photographer/videographer travel			
Photographer/videographer lodging			
SUBTOTAL			

Help make sense of your dollars by keeping track of your costs here (or by transferring this information to theknot.com/my budgeter).

	Budget	Actual	Notes
FLOWERS AND DECOR 8%			
Ceremony site decorations			
Reception flowers/decorations			
Bride's bouquet			
Bridal party bouquets			
Flower girl's bouquet			
Boutonnieres/corsages			
SUBTOTAL			
MUSIC 6%			
Ceremony musicians			
Cocktail-hour musicians			
Reception band/disc jockey			
After-party musicians			
Tips			
SUBTOTAL			
ATTIRE 8%			
Bride's dress and alterations			
Veil/headpiece			
Shoes/underpinnings			
Groom's tuxedo and accessories			
Hair and makeup			
Spa (manicure/pedicure)			
SUBTOTAL			

CONTINUES

Destination Wedding Worksheets

	Budget	Actual	Notes
STATIONERY 2–4%			
Save-the-dates			
Invitations			
Programs			
Menus/place cards/escort cards			
Calligraphy			
SUBTOTAL			
CEREMONY 2–5%			
Location fee			
Officiant fee/donation			
Officiant transportation			
Officiant lodging			
Accessories (ring pillow, candles)			
SUBTOTAL			
GIFTS 3%			
Wedding favors			
Welcome bags/baskets			
Attendants' gifts			
Parents' gifts			
Other gifts			
SUBTOTAL			
TOTAL			

Wedding planners usually charge a percentage of the wedding budget, typically 5 to 10 percent. See page 52.

your guest activities budget

	Budget	Actual	Notes
BRIDESMAIDS' BRUNCH			
Site and catering			
Beverages			
Flowers and decor			
Favors			
Music			
Tips			
SUBTOTAL			
ATTENDANTS' OUTINGS (SPA, GOLF, ETC.)			
Activity expense			
Site and catering			
Beverages			
Transportation			
Special attire (T-shirt, etc.)			
Tips			
SUBTOTAL			
WELCOME PARTY			
Site and catering			
Bar and beverages			
Flowers and decor			
Music			
Tips			
SUBTOTAL			

CONTINUES

	Budget	Actual	Notes
REHEARSAL DINNER			
Site			
Catering			
Bar			
Flowers and decor			
Music			
AV rental (for couples' slide show)			
Tips			
SUBTOTAL			
RECEPTION/AFTER-PARTY			
DJ/entertainment			
Bar			
Snacks and service			
Special activities (cigar roller, etc.)			
Extras (glow sticks, maracas, etc.)			
SUBTOTAL			
MORNING-AFTER BREAKFAST/BRUNCH			
Site			
Catering			
Beverages			
Flowers and decor			
Music			
Tips			
SUBTOTAL			
TOTAL			

your honeymoon budget

	Budget	Actual	Notes
Plane tickets			
Accommodations (room rate x # of nights)			
Excursions			
Meals (daily allowance x # days)			
Big nights out (plan on 2 or 3)			
Souvenirs			
TOTAL			

your "party back home" budget

	Budget	Actual	Notes
Invitations			
Site and catering			
Bar			
Flowers and decor			
Music			
Photographer			
Favors			
Tips			
TOTAL			

your vendors

On-site Planner

Contact name:

Phone:

Address:

E-mail:

Website:

Planner

Contact name:

Phone:

Address:

E-mail:

Website:

Reception Site/Venue

Contact name:

Phone:

Address:

E-mail:

Website:

Caterer

Contact name:

Phone:

Address:

E-mail:

Website:

Cake

Contact name:

Phone:

Address:

E-mail:

Website:

Florist

Contact name:

Phone:

Address:

E-mail:

Website:

Photographer

Contact name:

Phone:

Address:

E-mail:

Website:

Videographer

Contact name:

Phone:

Address:

E-mail:

Website:

Ceremony Musicians

Contact name:

Phone:

Address:

E-mail:

Website:

DJ/Band

Contact name:

Phone:

Address:

E-mail:

Website:

Officiant

Contact name:

Phone:

Address:

E-mail:

Website:

Ceremony Site

Contact name:

Phone:

Address:

E-mail:

Website:

Travel Agent

Contact name:

Phone:

Address:

E-mail:

Website:

Gown Shop

Contact name:

Phone:

Address:

E-mail:

Website:

Formal Wear

Contact name:

Phone:

Address:

E-mail:

Website:

Invitations/Printer

Contact name:

Phone:

Address:

E-mail:

Website:

Hair

Contact name:

Phone:

Address:

E-mail:

Website:

Makeup

Contact name:

Phone:

Address:

E-mail:

Website:

Transportation

Contact name:

Phone:

Address:

E-mail:

Website:

Rehearsal Dinner Site

Contact name:

Phone:

Address:

E-mail:

Website:

Other

Contact name:

Phone:

Address:

E-mail:

Website:

floral and decor checklist

CEREMONY

O Bridal bouquet

O Tossing bouquet

O Bridesmaids' bouquets: total needed _____

O Flower girl's flowers and petals for tossing

O Corsages for moms and grandmothers: total
needed _____

O Groom's boutonniere

O Boutonnieres for the groomsmen and
ushers: total needed _____

O Boutonnieres for dads and grandfathers:
total needed _____

O Aisle arrangements

O Aisle runner

O Petals for tossing

O Doorway decorations

RECEPTION

O Entry room

O Additional greenery, plants, space fillers

O Cocktail hour floral arrangements

O Bar decorations and flowers

O Fabric for draping room

O Lighting

O Lounge furniture

O Dining tables and chairs

O Chair covers

O Decorative element for bride's and groom's
chairs

O Table centerpieces: total needed _____

O Buffet table flowers

O Other tables: gifts, favors, guest book, cake

O Linens

O Escort cards

O Place cards

O Cake table flowers

O Cake pedestal and topper

O Guest book and pen

reception schedule

On the day of your wedding, make sure all vendors have updated copies of your intended schedule. Writing down cues (for example, "as guests arrive from the ceremony" or "immediately after the first toast") lets you, the vendors, and the staff all know who's in charge at each stage so there are no awkward "What do we do now?" moments. Your planner or a day-of coordinator will make sure everything keeps moving during the actual reception.

MOMENTS	START TIME	CUE
Cocktail hour		
Receiving line		
Entry into reception		
Bridal party intro		
First dance		
Dinner service		
Host toasts		
Dancing begins		
Special dances		
Couple's toast		
Cake cutting		
Bouquet toss		
Last dance		
Getaway		

essential documents

Don't depart for your destination wedding without triple-checking that you have all of these documents in hand—and carry them on you at all times:

O Passports and/or driver's licenses

O Visas for your destination country (if required)

O Certified copies of your birth certificates

O Plane tickets

O Copies of all vendor contracts

O Contact info for all of your vendors

O List of all of your guests' travel info, arrival times, and hotels where they'll be staying at the destination

O Copies of your wedding insurance policy

O If you've been married before: certified copies of your divorce decree or the death certificate of your former spouse

O Any other legal documents that your destination requires for marriage, and any that your officiant requires for a religious ceremony

TIP: If you're traveling outside the country for your wedding or honeymoon, make sure your passport is valid. Do it six months before the wedding, just in case there are any problems or delays. All foreign countries, even Canada, Mexico, and the Caribbean islands, now require a valid passport.

Destination Wedding Worksheets

your packing list

to carry on

○ Essential documents (and copies); see Tip, opposite

○ Credit cards and ATM cards (take only those you'll need)

○ Hotel reservation confirmations

○ Photocopies of medical and/or trip insurance coverage

○ Phone numbers for your doctor, house/pet sitter, and credit
   card companies (in case your cards are lost or stolen)

○ Prescription medicine (in the original bottle)

○ Contraception (unless you want a honeymoon baby!)

○ Jewelry, including wedding rings

○ Change of clothes (just in case)

○ Your vows, if you've written them

○ Wedding dress

○ Veil

○ Tiara/headpiece

○ Groom's suit or tux

○ Cell phone

○ Laptop (if a lot of your planning has been done online)

Notes

how to pack your gown

Place it into a hanging garment bag, then put it into the dress box, if you have one. As soon as you arrive at your destination, hang your outfits in an area where there's lots of room, to get out as many wrinkles as possible.

Bring an emergency kit of clothing care supplies: steamer, needle and thread, spot remover, and lots of safety pins and bobby pins. Make sure your hotel can arrange to have an iron and an ironing board in each of your rooms.

Finally, it's a smart idea to line up a local seamstress at your destination, so you'll have someone to call if anyone in the wedding party has a last-minute crisis.

checked bag 1

Clothes and essentials for the wedding:

O Wedding night sleepwear

O Makeup

O Perfume

O Nail polish

O Thong/underwear

O Bustier/bra

O Shoes

O Change of shoes for dancing

O Panty hose (plus spare)

O Garter

O Purse

O Wrap

O Crinoline/petticoat/slip

O Groom's accessories

O Sweatshirt or white button-down for makeup application

O Robe for dressing

O Something old

O Something new

O Something borrowed

O Something blue

O Her rehearsal dinner dress

O Her good-bye brunch outift

checked bag 2

Clothes and essential accessories for all other events (and your honeymoon):

For warm destinations:

- O Skirts, pants, and shorts
- O T-shirts, tank tops, and blouses
- O Bathing suits
- O Beach wrap
- O Sandals
- O Dresses and sundresses
- O Wraps and sweaters
- O Exercise clothes and shoes

For cool destinations:

- O Skirts, pants, and shirts
- O Sweaters, including turtlenecks
- O Thermals
- O Hiking boots
- O Parka
- O Scarf, hat, and gloves

For all destinations:

- O Camera/film and extra batteries
- O Sunscreen
- O Sunglasses
- O Sun hat or baseball cap
- O After-sun care or aloe vera
- O Electrical converter/adapter (if necessary)
- O Insect repellent

Toiletries:

- O Travel-size toothpaste and toothbrushes
- O Deodorant
- O Cosmetics and makeup remover
- O Cotton balls and swabs
- O Comb/brush and hair accessories
- O Hair gel/spray
- O Nail file/clippers
- O Shaving cream and razors
- O Contact lens and rewetting solution, case
- O Tampons/pads
- O Favorite nail polish

TIP: Pack an extra piece of luggage to send home with your parents items you no longer need, such as your wedding dress or accessories, as well as any gifts guests may have brought to the wedding.

your beauty emergency kit

You'll need to have a few beauty tools handy at all times on your wedding day to do touch-ups and fix any beauty meltdowns. Stash all of the following in a makeup bag (along with anything else you deem necessary) and give it to one of your bridesmaids to carry throughout the event:

Tissues

Bobby pins

Mints

Pressed powder

Lipstick/gloss

Optional items (your hotel may provide these):

Shampoo and conditioner

Body lotion

Hair dryer

Alarm clock

bags 3 and 4

You, your parents, or your attendants can be responsible for these event-related accessories:

O Gifts for your attendants and parents

O Favors

O Welcome bags and contents (maps, snacks, itineraries, etc.)

O CDs/music

O Cake topper

O Special cake-cutting knife set

O Menus

O Programs

O Escort cards

O Signage

O Display photos

O Table decorations (disposable cameras, snapshots, etc.)

O Aisle runner

O Guest book and pens

O Ceremony accessories (unity candle, kiddush cup, etc.)

O Bathroom baskets

O Ring bearer pillow

O Flower girl basket

O Thank-you notes to vendors and envelopes for tips

O Fix-it kit: extras of all materials used to make favors, welcome bags, and escort cards—glue gun, double-sided tape, card stock, ribbon in your wedding colors, etc.

O Your wedding-planning folder with your guest list and all the details of your arrangements

O Extra site decorations

to leave behind

Give copies to friends or coworkers:

O Your itinerary and hotel phone numbers

O Photocopies of your passport and credit cards

O A sealed copy of your wills, life insurance policy
   numbers, and pertinent financial info

TIP: Many airlines have per-bag weight limits on
your luggage: fifty pounds for domestic and seventy pounds for international. It may be better to
divide your luggage into more bags and take
advantage of the two-checked-bags-per-person
quota than to go through the hassle of paying the
surcharge.

resources and credits

real weddings in our color insert

DIANA & JOHN
PHOTOGRAPHER: Shawn Connell/Christian Oth Photography, ChristianOth.com, New York
SITE: Seaside, Florida, SeasideFL.com

TRACY & BRAD
PHOTOGRAPHER: Francesco Mastalia Photography, FMPhotos.com, New York
SITE: Round Hill Hotel and Villas Resort, RoundHillJamaica.com, Jamaica
PLANNER: JoAnn Gregoli/Elegant Occasions, ElegantOccasions.com, New York

LINDSAY & TOM
PHOTOGRAPHER: Kristin Cioffi Duarte, KristinStudio.com, Rhode Island
SITE: Spring House Hotel, SpringHouseHotel.com, Block Island
PLANNER: Donna Kim/The Perfect Details, ThePerfectDetails.com, Boston

VANESSA & MATT
PHOTOGRAPHER: Julie Mikos, JulieMikos.com, San Francisco
SITE: Private residence in Sonoma

HEATHER & CHRISTOPHER
PHOTOGRAPHER: Suzy Clement, SuzyClement.com, San Francisco
SITE: Sant'Anna di Camprena, Tuscany

EILEEN & DEAN
PHOTOGRAPHER: Caroline Yang, CarolineYang.com, Minnesota
SITE: Sundance Resort, SundanceResort.com, Utah
PLANNER: Tonya Linky/Classic Beginnings (801) 910-2293

LAILA & ERIC
PHOTOGRAPHER: Angie Silvy, AngieSilvyPhotography.com, San Francisco
SITE: Private residence in Hawaii
PLANNER: Linda Santos/White Orchid Weddings, WhiteOrchidWedding.com

real weddings in our chapters

CHERI & JASON (pages 20, 21)
PHOTOGRAPHER: Raffaele Fazioli, RaffaeleFazioli.com
SITE: Hassler Hotel, HotelHasslerRoma.com, Rome
PLANNER: Brenda Babcock, Italia-Celebrations.com, Rome

EMILY & BRIAN (pages 46, 47)
PHOTOGRAPHER: Gary Oakley, OakleyPhotography.com, Colorado
SITE: The Lodge at Vail, LodgeAtVail.RockResorts.com, Colorado
PLANNER: Gala Events, GalaEvents.com, Maryland

SANDRA & KEVIN (pages 76, 77)
PHOTOGRAPHER: Karina Marie Diaz, KarinaMarieDiaz.com, San Francisco
SITE: The Princeville Resort, Princeville.com, Kauai, Hawaii

AMY & MARK (pages 98, 99)
PHOTOGRAPHER: Brian Wedge Photography, BrianWedge.com, Maine
SITE: One and Only Palmilla, OneandOnly.com, Los Cabos

STEPHANIE & MATT (page 113)
PHOTOGRAPHER: Laura Moss, LauraMoss.com, New York
SITE: Half Moon Resort, HalfMoon.com, Montego Bay, Jamaica

KATHRYN & CHAD (pages 128, 129)
PHOTOGRAPHER: Karen Zieff Photography, ZieffPhoto.com, New York
SITE: Westcliff Estate, Nantucket

TERESA & PRESTON (pages 148, 149)
PHOTOGRAPHER: Jessica Claire Photography, JCSPhoto.com, Los Angeles
SITE: Marquis Los Cabos, Marquis-los-Cabos.com, Mexico
PLANNER: Mary Jones/MJ Weddings, mjWeds.com, Atlanta

additional photo credits

Francesco Mastalia Photography, FMPhoto.com (pages v, vii, 212)

Kathi Littwin Photography, KathiLittwin.com (pages xix, 91, details in insert)

Stewart Pinsky Photography, MauiWeddingGallery.com (details in insert)

Allen King Wedding Photography, Allen-King.com (page 147, details in insert)

Chrissy Lambert Photography, ChrissyLambert.com (page 188, details in insert)

Angie Silvy, AngieSilvyPhotography.com (page 150)

Brian Wedge Photography, BrianWedge.com (details in insert)

David Wolfe Photography, DavidWolfePhotography.com (details in insert)

Kristin Cioffi Duarte, KristinStudio.com (details in insert)

Karen Wise Photography, KarenWise.com (page 218)

FOR UP-TO-DATE LISTINGS AND MORE RESOURCES, VISIT: THEKNOT.COM/DESTINATIONWEDDINGS

acknowledgments

Carley says thank you . . .

To Rosie Armodio and The Knot team, Kathleen Murray, Anja Winikka, Meredith Gray, Amy Keith, Liz Zack, Kristen Hawley, Linda DiProperzio, and Rebecca Crumley. You were instrumental in developing, researching, and editing this book. A special thanks to Celeste Perron, who put it all into well-crafted paragraphs.

To JoAnn Gregoli, my coauthor and long-standing friend of The Knot: Your insights and in-the-trenches experience were vital in making this book as rich as it should be.

To the contributing photographers and event designers: Your work is inspiring—I so appreciate you sharing it with our brides.

To Christine Tomasino, our brilliant agent and recent destination bride: Your vision for The Knot publishing program over the years has been remarkable. I am thrilled to have you on our team.

To Pam Krauss, our steadfast editor at Clarkson Potter: Your guidance in crafting this book was invaluable. . . . May there be many fabulous welcome baskets in your future! In addition, your team is top-notch and I look forward to our upcoming projects.

To my husband (and The Knot cofounder), David; our kids, Havana and Cairo; and our parents: Having such a marvelous, fun, supportive family makes it all worthwhile.

And, finally, to The Knot community of brides, grooms, moms, event planners, photographers, musicians, and more: Your interest, enthusiasm, and support over the years have helped make The Knot what we are today. Thank you.

JoAnn says thank you . . .

To my wonderful, dedicated husband, Frank, for your continued support in my career and for giving me six incredible children.

To my children: Melissa, Jessica, Cassie, Joshua, Jason, and Jordan, for your unconditional love despite my crazy hours and many trips.

To my parents, for always being there whenever I need you.

To Carley, for your constant support and true friendship.

To my amazing vendors, who are my backbone, for helping make the magic happen for my brides.

And to my mentors, for keeping my dream alive.

index

A

absent guests, honoring of, 126
accessories:
    for bride, 19
    for bridesmaids, 82
activities, *see* guest activities
adventure weddings, 10
after-party, 13, 108, 134, 198
all-inclusive venues, 27, 38
Amalfi Coast, Italy, 182
Anguilla, 17, 27, 154–55, 163
announcements, 92
Antigua, 27, 155, 163
arrivals of guests, 14, 102
Aruba, 163
Aspen, CO, 27, 107, 127, 168
attire:
    costs of, 13, 195
    dress codes for guests and, 88, 89
    formality of venue and, 35
    for wedding party, 81, 82, 83, 84,
      85–86
    see also wedding dress
Australia, 27, 29, 186

B

babysitters, 59
Bahamas, 17, 26, 27, 140, 156, 163
Baja Peninsula, Mexico, 178
Barbados, 163
Barbuda, 163
bar offerings, printed cards for, 138
beach formal (dress code), 89
beach weddings, 27, 76–77, 98–99,
    113, 148–49
    attire for, 18, 83, 84
    ceremony design for, 124
    flowers and decor for, 137, 138
    microphone and sound system for,
      122
    programs for, 127
    public vs. private beaches and, 40
    save-the-dates for, 87
    see also island weddings; *specific*
      destinations
beauty emergency kit, 208
beauty tips, 73–75

Bermuda, 27, 29, 157
    local wedding traditions in, 124
    musical traditions in, 145
    passports for, 155
Big Island, HI, 166
black tie optional (dress code), 89
Bonaire, 163
bouquet toss, 134
breakfast or brunch:
    morning-after, 14, 15, 16, 109, 110,
      198
    with parents on wedding day, 111
bridal party, *see* bridesmaids;
    groomsmen; wedding party
bride:
    beauty tips for, 71, 73–75
    style sheet for, 19
    see also wedding dress
bridesmaids, 80–86
    attire for, 81, 82, 84, 85–86
    see also wedding party
brunch, *see* breakfast or brunch
budgets, 13–17, 58
    adjusting, 17
    for guest activities, 13–15, 197–98
    for honeymoon, 15, 199
    for postwedding party (at home), 15,
      199
    research and, 17
    savings tips for, 16
    for wedding, 13, 194–96
    wedding planners and, 52
    worksheets for, 13, 194–99

C

Cabo San Lucas, Mexico, 27, 148–49
cake, *see* wedding cake
cake-cutting fees, 61
California, 27, 28, 140, 174
Canada, 27, 204
Cape Cod, 173
Caribbean, 17, 38, 107, 120, 125,
    154–64, 204
    best times to go to, 26, 29
    musical traditions in, 145
    passports for, 155, 204
castles, weddings at, 124

caterers, 57–62
    in-house, 57
    tastings and, 59
Catholic ceremony, 118, 120
Cayman Islands, 163
Central America, 178–80
    passports for, 155
    see also Mexico
ceremony, 115–27
    civil, 119
    costs of, 13, 16, 196
    finding officiant for, 39, 120–22
    flowers for, 202
    interfaith, 118
    legal issues and, 25–26, 30, 36,
      116–17
    local traditions and, 123–24
    music, 125, 126
    outline of, 121
    programs for, 90, 125–27
    religious, 85, 117–18, 120
    stateside, before or after destination
      wedding, 30, 116, 117
    timeline for, 190–91
    working with officiant on, 122–23
champagne toast, 61
children, 27, 35, 59
china, 16, 136
city chic weddings, 6, 176–77
civil ceremony, 119
    stateside, before or after destination
      wedding, 30, 116, 117
climate, *see* weather
cocktail hour, 132
Colorado, 27, 46–47, 107, 127, 168
corking fees, 61
Costa Rica, 180
country weddings, 18, 83, 124, 127
cruise weddings, 10, 27, 36, 38
Curaçao, 163

D

dancing, 132, 133, 134
    music selection and, 144–45
date of wedding:
    save-the-dates and, 59, 87–88, 90,
      97

scheduling conflicts and, 12
decor, 40
  checklist for, 202
  costs of, 13, 16, 195
  reception mood and, 134–38
deposits, 34
  wedding insurance and, 56
destination, deciding on, 23, 25–29
dinner service, 133
DIY savings, 16
documents, essential, 121, 204
Dominica, 163
Dominican Republic, 163
dress codes, 88, 89
dresses:
  for bridesmaids, 81, 82, 84, 85
  see also wedding dress

E

elderly guests, 7
e-mail, 16, 94
England, 137, 184–85
escort cards, 16, 90, 138, 142
Europe, 181–85
  old-world, 8, 18, 21, 127
exchange rates, 17

F

fall foliage, best destinations for, 27
favors, 16, 90, 138, 143
Fiji, 186
first dance, 132
flip-flops required (dress code), 89
Florida, 27, 28, 140, 145, 169–70
florists, 66–67, 136
flower girls, 84, 125
flowers, 66–67
  checklist for, 202
  containers for, 137
  costs of, 13, 16, 195
  creating mood for reception with,
    134, 135–36, 137, 138
  for wedding cake, 64
food and drink:
  for reception, 13, 16, 61, 138–41,
    194
  for welcome bags, 103
France, 25–26, 27, 107, 141, 183
French Polynesia, 26

G

garter toss, 134
getaway, 134

gifts:
  for bridesmaids and groomsmen, 85,
    105
  budget for, 196
  favors, 16, 90, 138, 143
  postwedding parties and, 96
  registering for, 95
  sending home after wedding, 207
  welcome bags, 15, 38, 90, 102–4,
    106
golf, 27, 87
Greece, 29, 137
Grenada, 163
Grenadines, 164
groom, fashion tips for, 83
groomsmen, 80–86
  attire for, 82, 83, 84, 85–86
  see also wedding party
Guadeloupe, 163
guest activities, 101–12
  after-party, 13, 108, 134, 198
  costs of, 13–15, 16, 112, 197–98
  destination-specific, 110–11
  dos and don'ts for, 111–12
  local transportation and, 102, 106
  morning-after breakfast or brunch,
    14, 15, 16, 109, 110, 198
  outings with attendants, 13–15, 104,
    197
  questions to ask venue about, 34,
    39
  rehearsal dinner, 14, 16, 105, 198
  wedding party's duties at, 80
  welcome bags and, 102–4
  welcome party, 13, 14, 15, 107, 197
guest list, 2, 7, 11, 17, 86–87
  size of wedding and, 11–12
  timeline for, 97
  tracking information on, 97
guests, 79–97
  absent, honoring of, 126
  arrivals of, 14, 102
  dress codes for, 88, 89
  expenses paid by, 14, 15, 25, 35, 36
  favors for, 16, 90, 138, 143
  invitations and other
    communications for, 87–93
  subsidizing, 14, 15
  travel of, see transportation
  welcome bags for, 15, 38, 90, 102–4,
    106
  see also wedding party
guidebooks, 30

H

hairstylists, 71, 74–75
Hawaii, 26, 27, 76–77, 125, 165–67
  best times to go to, 26, 28
  classic dishes from, 140
  floral arrangements for, 137
  local wedding traditions in, 123
high season, 16, 26
honeymoon, 110
  budget for, 15, 199
  origin of word, 184
  planning, 44–45, 57
  saving money on, 16, 38
hotel rooms, 26, 34, 40, 88
  expenses for, 14, 15, 35, 194

I

India, 145
Indonesia, 186–87
inner circle weddings, 11, 86
insurance, 56
interfaith ceremony, 118
Internet research, 30
invitations, 59, 93
  dress codes specified on, 88,
    89
  guest list and, 86–87
  save-the-dates and, 59, 87–88, 90,
    97
  saving money on, 16
  stationery order for, 90
  timeline for, 97
Ireland, 26, 124, 145
island weddings, 7–8, 17, 18, 26, 27
Italy, 20–21, 26, 27, 63, 107, 120, 125,
  181–82
  best times to go to, 26, 29
  classic dishes from, 141
  floral arrangements for, 137
  musical traditions in, 145

J

Jamaica, 17, 26, 27, 113, 158, 163
  classic dishes from, 141
  local wedding traditions in, 124
  musical traditions in, 145
Japan, 124
Jewish ceremony, 120
junior bridesmaids, 84

K

Kauai, HI, 27, 76–77, 167
Kenya, 26

L

labels:
  for favors, 90
  for tables at reception, 135
Lanai, HI, 167
landscape of locale, as inspiration for
    reception, 134
last dance, 134
Las Vegas, NV, 26, 27, 28, 171
Latin America, 178–80
  passports for, 155
  see also Mexico
legal issues, 116–17
  residency requirements, 25–26, 30,
    36
liability issues, 56
Liberia, 36
lighting, 135
linens, 16, 60, 136
liquor, corking or pouring fees for, 61
lodging, *see* hotel rooms
Loire Valley, France, 183
Los Cabos, Mexico, 98–99
luggage:
  packing lists for, 205–8
  per-bag weight limits on, 209

M

maid of honor, 84
  see also bridesmaids; wedding party
Maine, 172
makeup artists, 71, 74–75
marriage licenses, 8, 36
Martinique, 163
Massachusetts, 128–29, 173
Maui, HI, 166
menu cards, 90, 138
Mexico, 27, 38, 98–99, 107, 148–49,
    178–79
  best times to go to, 29
  classic dishes from, 140
  local wedding traditions in, 124
  musical traditions in, 125, 145
  passports for, 155, 204
Miami, FL, 27, 140, 145
Montego Bay, Jamaica, 113
Montserrat, 163
morning-after breakfast or brunch, 14,
    15, 16, 109, 110, 198
mother of the bride, attire for, 84
mountain weddings, 46–47, 124, 127
  ski destinations and, 7, 18, 27
  see also specific destinations

music:
  costs of, 13, 195
  hiring musicians for, 68–69
  for reception, 144–45
  setting ceremony to, 125, 126

N

Nantucket, MA, 128–29
Napa Valley, CA, 27, 140, 174
napkin rings, 137
native culture of locale, 135
negotiating tips, 58
Nevis, 159, 163
New England, 9, 28, 128–29, 140,
    172–73, 175
Newport, RI, 175
newsletters, 94
New York City, 27, 28, 107, 176–77
New Zealand, 29, 187
nightlife, best destinations for, 27
Northern Ireland, 185

O

Oahu, HI, 165
officiants, 15, 39
  finding, 120–22
  inviting to rehearsal dinner and
    wedding reception, 119
  working with, 122–23
one-trip plan, 31
on-site planners or coordinators, 33,
    36, 37, 39, 52, 53

P

Pacific Rim, 186–87
package deals, 32, 33, 36
packing lists, 205–9
paper products, *see* stationery
parents:
  destination choice and, 24
  mother of the bride, attire for, 84
  seating of, at reception, 142
  spending time with, 111
  travel and lodging costs for, 15
Paris, 27, 183
passports, 155, 204
photo/video:
  costs of, 13, 15, 16, 194
  hiring vendors for, 70–72
  imported vs. local photographers
    and, 70
  as parting mementos, 109
  for postwedding party, 96

place cards, 90, 138
place settings, 16, 60, 136
postwedding party (at home), 11, 15,
    96–97
pouring fees, 61
Princess Cruises, 36
programs, for ceremony, 90, 125–27
Puerto Rico, 27, 28, 123, 160, 163

R

receiving line, 132, 146
reception, 14, 131–46
  bride and groom's enjoyment of,
    146
  budget for, 13, 194
  creating mood for, 134–38
  dancing at, 132, 133, 134, 144–45
  defining moments of, 132–34
  floral and decor checklist for, 202
  food and drink for, 13, 16, 61, 138–41,
    194
  kid-free, 59
  music for, 68–69, 144–45
  paper products for, 136, 138
  saving money on, 16, 38
  schedule for, 203
  seating at, 92, 142
  timeline for, 191–92
references, 33
registering for gifts, 95
rehearsal dinner, 14, 16, 105, 198
religious ceremony, 85, 117–18, 120
reputation of locale, as inspiration for
    reception, 134–35
residency requirements, 25–26, 30,
    36
ring bearers, 84
rings, 194
Rocky Mountains, 28, 168

S

Saba, 163
St. Barthelemy, 163
St. Croix, 163
St. Eustatius, 163
St. John, 27, 161, 163
St. Kitts, 163
St. Lucia, 27, 164
St. Maarten, 26, 164
St. Martin, 164
St. Thomas, 161, 164
St. Vincent, 164
Saturday night, 16, 34

save-the-dates, 59, 87–88, 90, 97
scents, at reception, 137
scheduling conflicts, 12
Scotland, 27, 185
scuba, best destinations for, 27
seating, at reception, 92, 142
ship's captains, 10
shopping, best destinations for, 27
shoulder season, 33
site visits, 15, 31, 37
size of wedding, 11–12
ski weddings, 7, 18, 27
snorkeling, best destinations for, 27
sound systems, 122
South Pacific, 29
Southwest, 127, 177
Spain, 27, 137
spas, best, 27
stationery:
    costs of, 16, 196
    invitations, 90, 93
    paper products for reception, 136,
        138
    save-the-dates, 87–88
    total run-down of, 90
    wedding announcements, 92
subsidizing guests, 14, 15
sunset ceremony, 123

T
Tahiti, 27, 187
tastings, 59, 63
Thailand, 26, 187
thank-you cards and envelopes, 90
thank-yous, to attendees, 126
three-trip plan, 31
timeline, for wedding day, 190–92
toasts, 133
    champagne for, 61
to-do lists, vi–xviii
Tortola, 27, 164
tourist boards, 30
transportation, on-site, 35, 103, 106
    between airport and hotel, 14, 25,
        102, 106
    costs of, 13, 14, 16, 194
    wedding party's duties and, 80
travel agents, 11, 16, 54
travel search engines, 25
travel to and from destination, 88, 109
    costs of, 13, 14, 15, 16, 194
    deciding on a destination and, 25, 26
    of wedding party, 14, 85

Trinidad and Tobago, 164
Tucson, AZ, 177
Turks and Caicos, 27, 162, 164
tuxedos, 83, 84
two-trip plan, 31

U
United Kingdom, 29, 184–85
United States mainland, destination
    guide to, 168–77

V
Vail, CO, 46–47
Vatican City, 20–21
vendors, 40, 49–75
    bakers, 63–64
    caterers, 57–62
    florists, 66–67
    hairstylists and makeup artists, 71,
        74–75
    importing, 15, 16, 62
    interviewing, 50–51
    managing from afar, 16, 65
    musicians, 68–69
    negotiating with, 58
    photographers and videographers,
        70–72
    worksheet for, 200–201
    see also wedding planners
venues, 25, 30–43
    all-inclusive, 27, 38
    contracts with, 42–43
    cost considerations and, 17
    deciding on, 41
    discounts or other perks from, 41
    questions to ask about, 32–35,
        39–40, 42
    site visits to, 15, 31, 37
Virgin Gorda, 27, 164

W
water activities, best destinations for,
    27
weather, 26
    attendants' attire and, 85
    beauty strategy and, 73
    flower selection and, 136
    wedding cake and, 139
    wedding dress and, 18
website, wedding, 16, 59, 88, 89,
    93–94
wedding announcements, 92
wedding budget, 13, 194–96

wedding cake, 63–64, 139
    cutting, 133–34
    cutting fee for, 61
wedding coordinators, on-site, 33, 36,
    37, 39, 52, 53
wedding day, timeline for, 190–92
wedding dress, 18–19
    carry-on arrangements for, 19
    packing, 18, 206
    sending home after wedding, 207
wedding insurance, 56
wedding party, 80–86
    being good leader for, 81–85
    duties of, 80–81
    expenses of, 14, 82
    gifts for, 85, 105
    introduction of, at reception, 132
    outings with, 104, 197
    see also bridesmaids; groomsmen
wedding planners, 11, 26, 33, 39, 50,
    52–57
    determining need for, 52
    interviewing, 55–57
    types of, 53–54
    see also wedding coordinators, on-
        site
welcome bags, 15, 38, 90, 102–4, 106
welcome letter, 102
welcome party, 13, 14, 15, 107, 197
wine, 61
wine country weddings, 9
winter destinations, 87
    ski weddings and, 7, 18, 27
worksheets, 189–209
    essential documents, 204
    floral and decor checklist, 202
    guest activities budget, 197–98
    honeymoon budget, 199
    for legal aspects of wedding, 117
    packing lists, 205–9
    "party back home" budget, 199
    reception schedule, 203
    vendors, 200–201
    wedding budget, 194–96
    wedding day timeline, 190–92

Y
Yucatán Peninsula, Mexico, 179